THE LAST FALL

WRITTEN BY **TOM WALTZ**
ART BY **CASEY MALONEY**
COLORS BY **DUSTY YEE**
LETTERS BY **SHAWN LEE** AND
ROBBIE ROBBINS
SERIES EDITS BY **CHRIS RYALL**

COVER BY **CASEY MALONEY**
COVER COLORS BY **DUSTY YEE**
COLLECTION EDITS BY **JUSTIN EISINGER** AND
ALONZO SIMON
PUBLISHED BY **TED ADAMS**
COLLECTION DESIGN BY **RON ESTEVEZ**

Very special thanks to Kristy Miller, Brian Miller, and
Eric White of Hi-Fi Colour Design for their invaluable
assistance in the creation of this comic book.

ISBN: 978-1-63140-222-7

19 18 17 16   1 2 3 4

IDW®

www.IDWPUBLISHING.com
IDW founded by Ted Adams, Alex Garner, Kris Oprisko, and Robbie Robbins

Ted Adams, C EO & Publisher
Greg Goldstein, President & COO
Robbie Robbins, EVP/Sr. Graphic Artist
Chris Ryall, Chief Creative Officer/Editor-in-Chief
Matthew Ruzicka, CPA, Chief Financial Officer
Dirk Wood, VP of Marketing
Lorelei Bunjes, VP of Digital Services
Jeff Webber, VP of Licensing, Digital and Subsidiary Rights
Jerry Bennington, VP of New Product Development

Facebook: **facebook.com/idwpublishing**
Twitter: **@idwpublishing**
YouTube: **youtube.com/idwpublishing**
Tumblr: **tumblr.idwpublishing.com**
Instagram: **instagram.com/idwpublishing**

"THIS WAS NO TASK FOR MEN OF CLASHING

METAL, IT WAS A DEED SUITED TO SQUEAMISH-

STOMACHED COURTIERS; BUT, LACKING

BACKBONE, THEY HAVE EVER NEEDED

OTHERS TO DO THEIR DIRTY WORK SPAWNED

THROUGH INTRIGUE AND CONSPIRACY. LORD,

HASTEN THE DAY WHEN REAL MEN ARE NO

LONGER MANIPULATED BY HALF MEN!"

—*THE KOLBRIN BIBLE*

THE LAST FALL

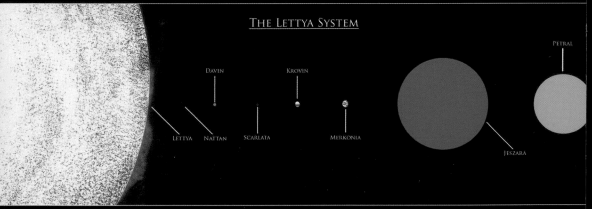

The Lettya System

PETRAL

DAVIN

KROVIN

LETTYA   NATTAN   SCARLATA   MERKONIA

JESZARA

A Short History...

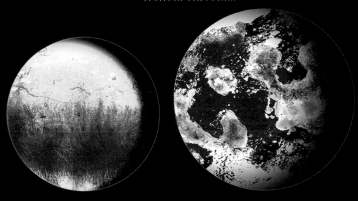

KROVIN

MERKONIA

The Lettya system is comprised of seven orbiting planets, of which only two are habitable–Krovin and Merkonia.

Krovin is a primarily desert planet rich in natural subterranean resources, originally occupied by primitive, pantheistic, tribe-based natives. Merkonia is lush and environmentally diverse, occupied by a highly sophisticated citizenry and ruled by a theocracy.

Long ago, Krovin was colonized and mined by Merkonia for its abundant geological resources, including a powerful natural energy source found only on Krovin. The Merkonians utilized the primitive inhabitants of Krovin–called Krovinites–as slave labor for their mining purposes. In time, the Merkonian exploitation of Krovin came (seemingly) to an end, and the Merkonians all but abandoned the desert planet, leaving behind much of their technology, which the Krovinites ultimately adapted to their own evolving social and political needs.

However, when Merkonian scientists discovered that Lettya was entering its red giant phase, they quickly realized time was running out for their own planet and that they would need to develop an escape plan to ensure the continuation of their people. Any plan hinged on once again mining the abundant fuel source found on Krovin, thus prompting the Merkonians to return in the guise of a religious war.

Now, however, the Krovinites–far more technologically advanced and militarily stronger– would not hand over their home world without a fight. After years of fierce and bloody warfare, and numerous failed peace talks, tens of thousands have died on both sides–and continue to do so– with only ultimate doom waiting for both planets as their shared sun burns hotter and hotter.

Sergeant Marcus Fall, a Merkonian soldier fighting in this futile war, has experienced his fair share of tragedy, both on the battlefield and on the home front. This is his story...

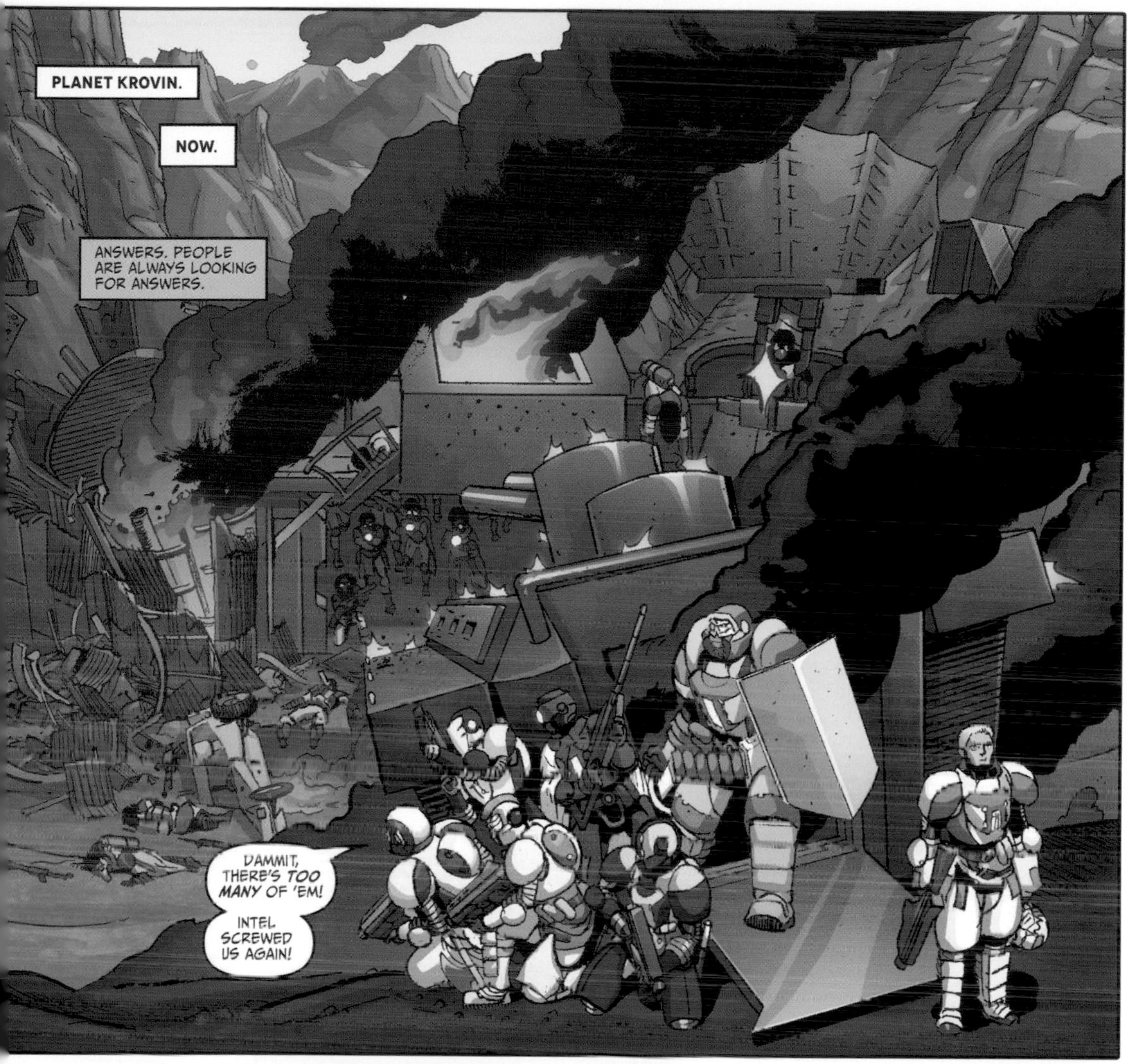
PLANET KROVIN.
NOW.
ANSWERS. PEOPLE ARE ALWAYS LOOKING FOR ANSWERS.
DAMMIT, THERE'S TOO MANY OF 'EM!
INTEL SCREWED US AGAIN!

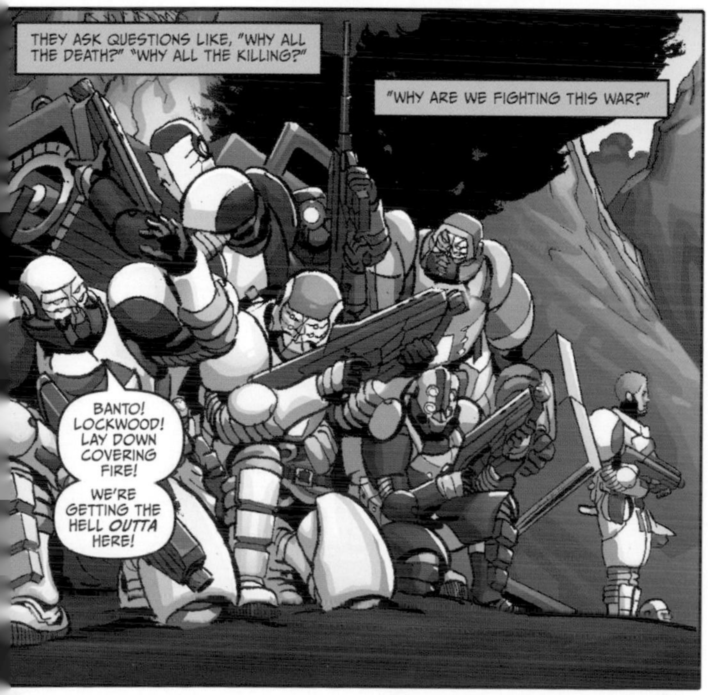
THEY ASK QUESTIONS LIKE, "WHY ALL THE DEATH?" "WHY ALL THE KILLING?"
"WHY ARE WE FIGHTING THIS WAR?"
BANTO! LOCKWOOD! LAY DOWN COVERING FIRE!
WE'RE GETTING THE HELL OUTTA HERE!

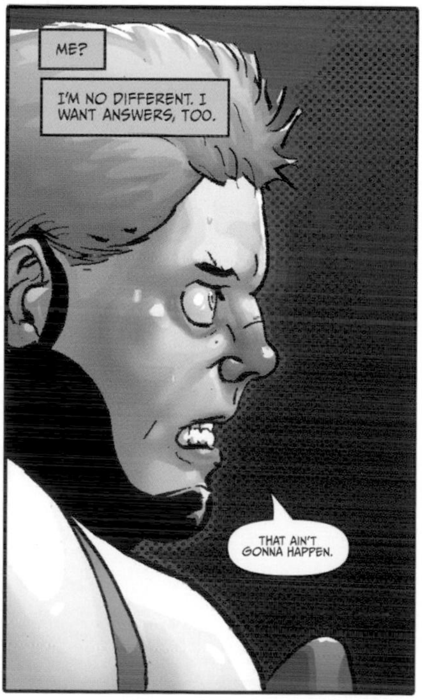
ME?
I'M NO DIFFERENT. I WANT ANSWERS, TOO.
THAT AIN'T GONNA HAPPEN.

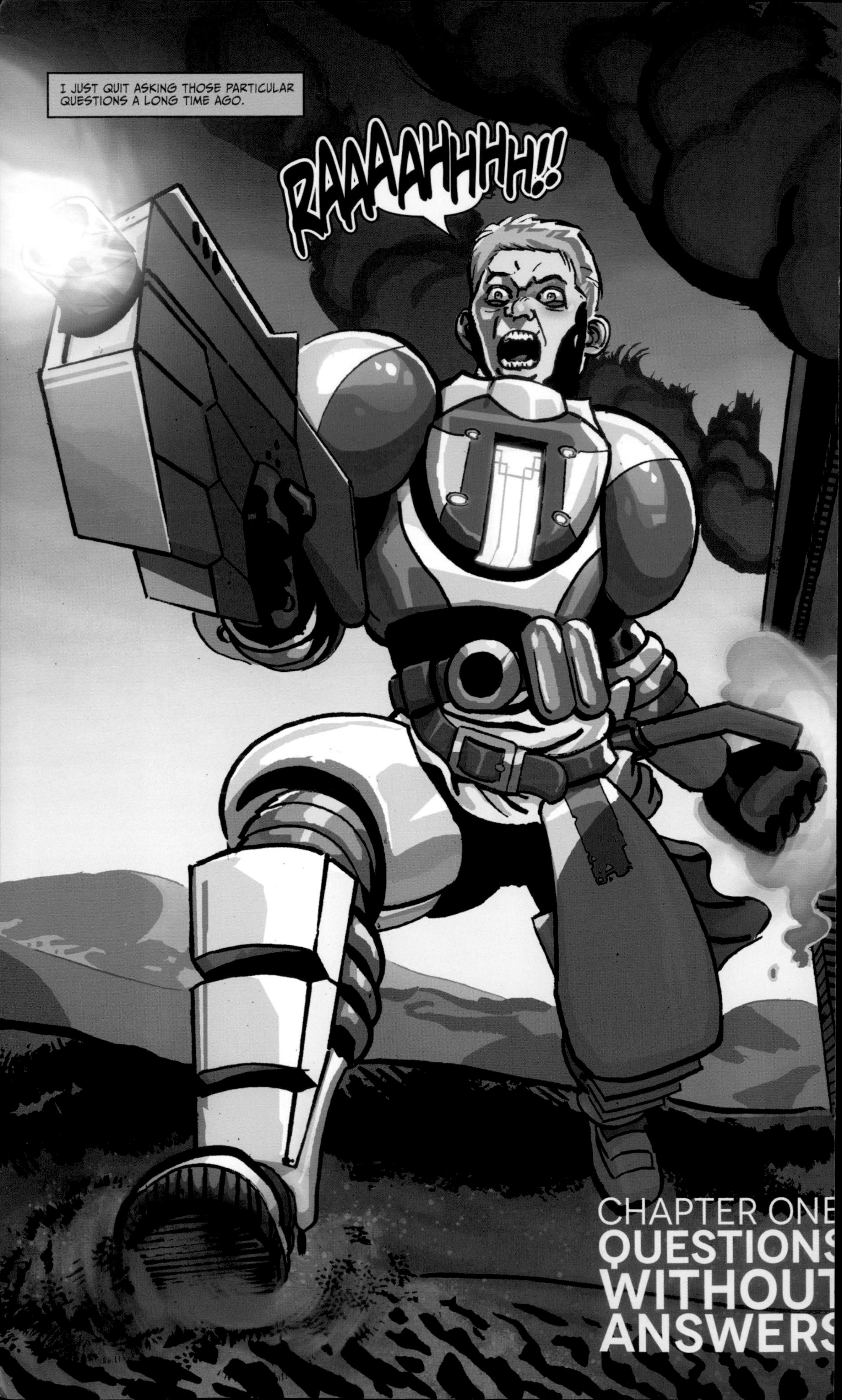
I JUST QUIT ASKING THOSE PARTICULAR QUESTIONS A LONG TIME AGO.
RAAAAHHHH!!
CHAPTER ONE
QUESTIONS WITHOUT ANSWERS

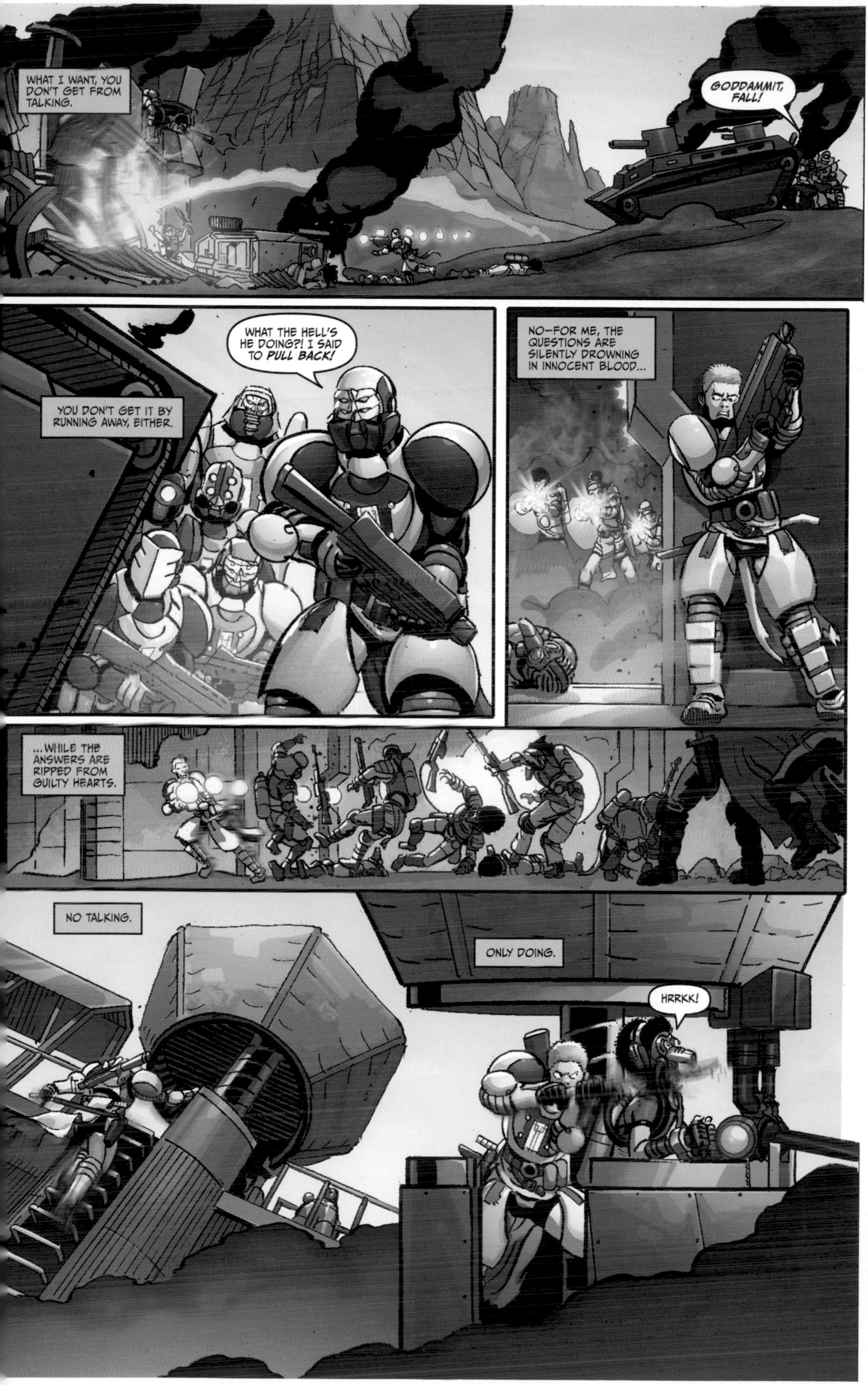
WHAT I WANT, YOU DON'T GET FROM TALKING.
GODDAMMIT, FALL!
WHAT THE HELL'S HE DOING?! I SAID TO PULL BACK!
YOU DON'T GET IT BY RUNNING AWAY, EITHER.
NO—FOR ME, THE QUESTIONS ARE SILENTLY DROWNING IN INNOCENT BLOOD...
...WHILE THE ANSWERS ARE RIPPED FROM GUILTY HEARTS.
NO TALKING.
ONLY DOING.
HRRKK!

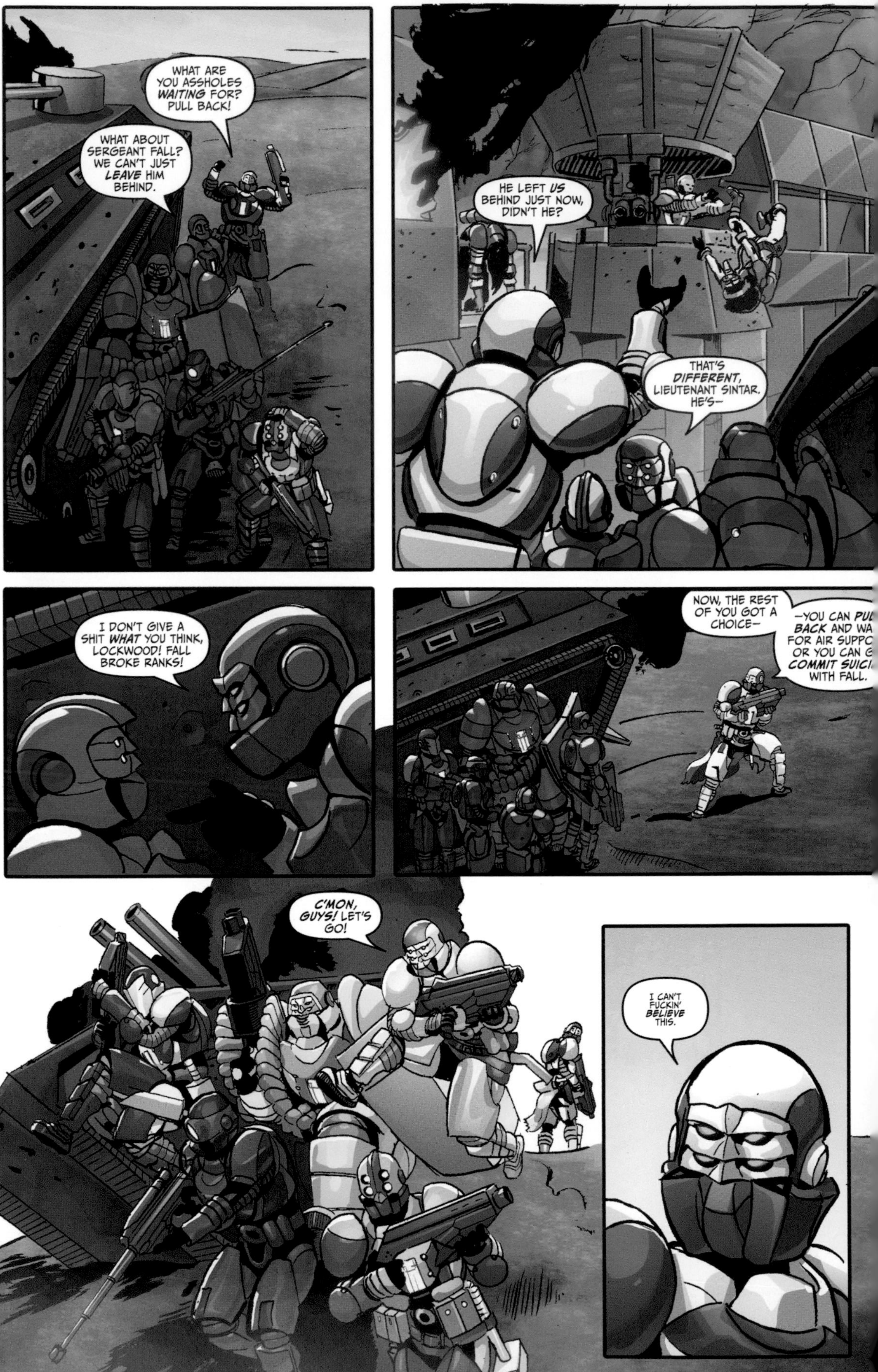

WHAT ARE YOU ASSHOLES *WAITING* FOR? PULL BACK!
WHAT ABOUT SERGEANT FALL? WE CAN'T JUST *LEAVE* HIM BEHIND.
HE LEFT *US* BEHIND JUST NOW, DIDN'T HE?
THAT'S *DIFFERENT*, LIEUTENANT SINTAR. HE'S—
I DON'T GIVE A SHIT *WHAT* YOU THINK, LOCKWOOD! FALL BROKE RANKS!
NOW, THE REST OF YOU GOT A CHOICE—
—YOU CAN *PU* *BACK* AND WA FOR AIR SUPPO OR YOU CAN G *COMMIT SUICI* WITH FALL.
C'MON, GUYS! LET'S GO!
I CAN'T FUCKIN' *BELIEVE* THIS.

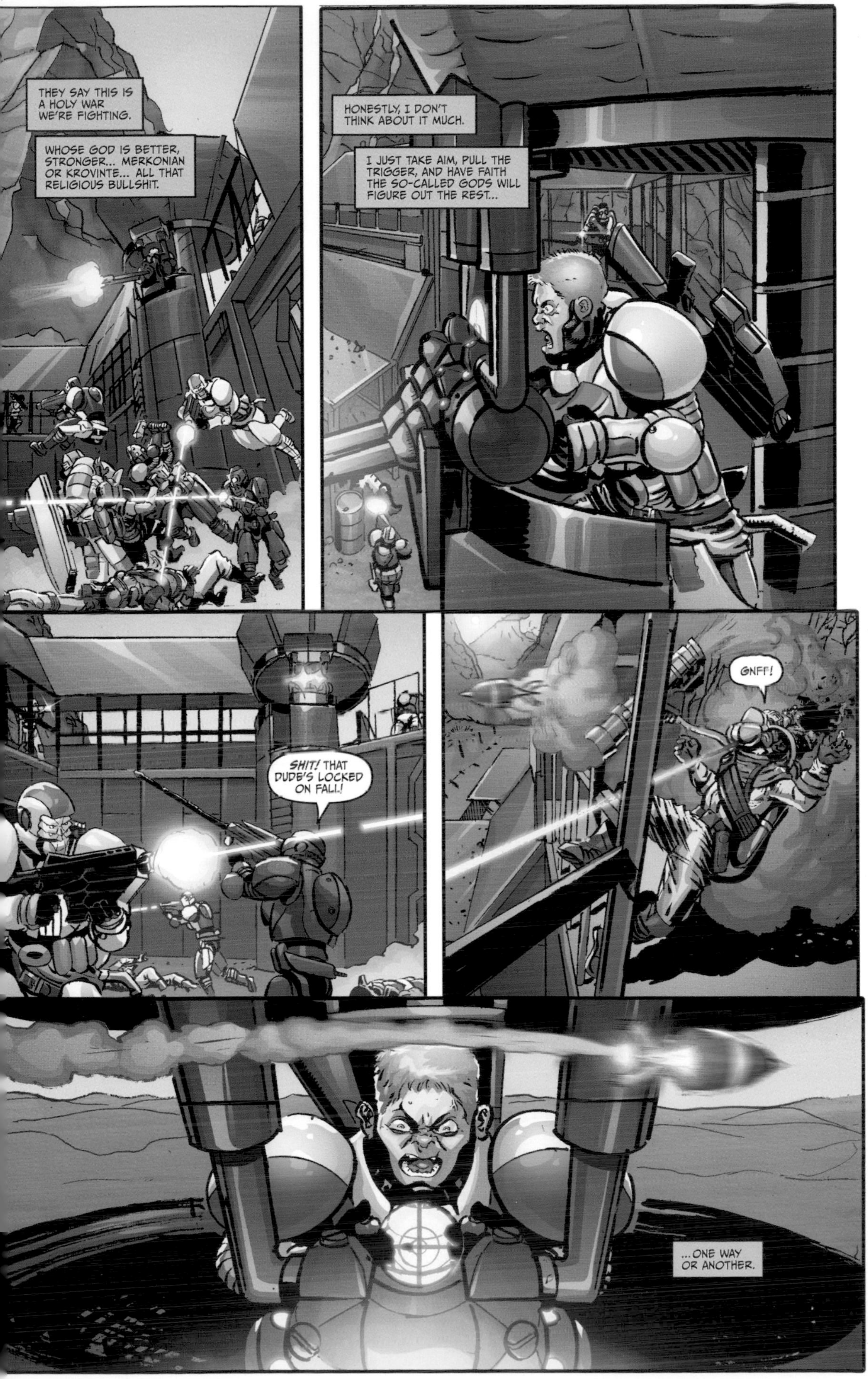
THEY SAY THIS IS A HOLY WAR WE'RE FIGHTING.
WHOSE GOD IS BETTER, STRONGER... MERKONIAN OR KROVINTE... ALL THAT RELIGIOUS BULLSHIT.
HONESTLY, I DON'T THINK ABOUT IT MUCH.
I JUST TAKE AIM, PULL THE TRIGGER, AND HAVE FAITH THE SO-CALLED GODS WILL FIGURE OUT THE REST...
SHIT! THAT DUDE'S LOCKED ON FALI!
GNFF!
...ONE WAY OR ANOTHER.

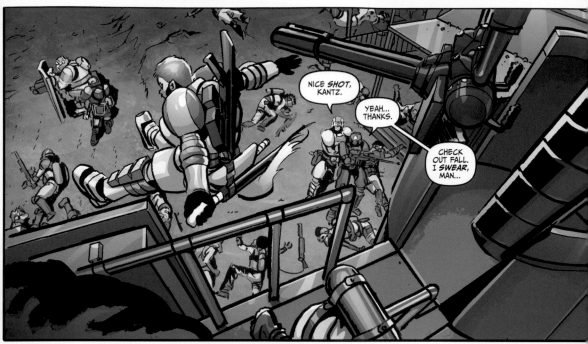

NICE *SHOT*, KANTZ.

YEAH... THANKS.

CHECK OUT FALL. I *SWEAR*, MAN...

"...THAT IS ONE *CRAZY* MOTHER."

WHAT THE *FUCK* ARE YOU TWO DOIN'?! GET YOUR ASSES BACK INTO THE GODDAMN FIGHT!

AND AS FOR *YOU*, ASSHOLE...

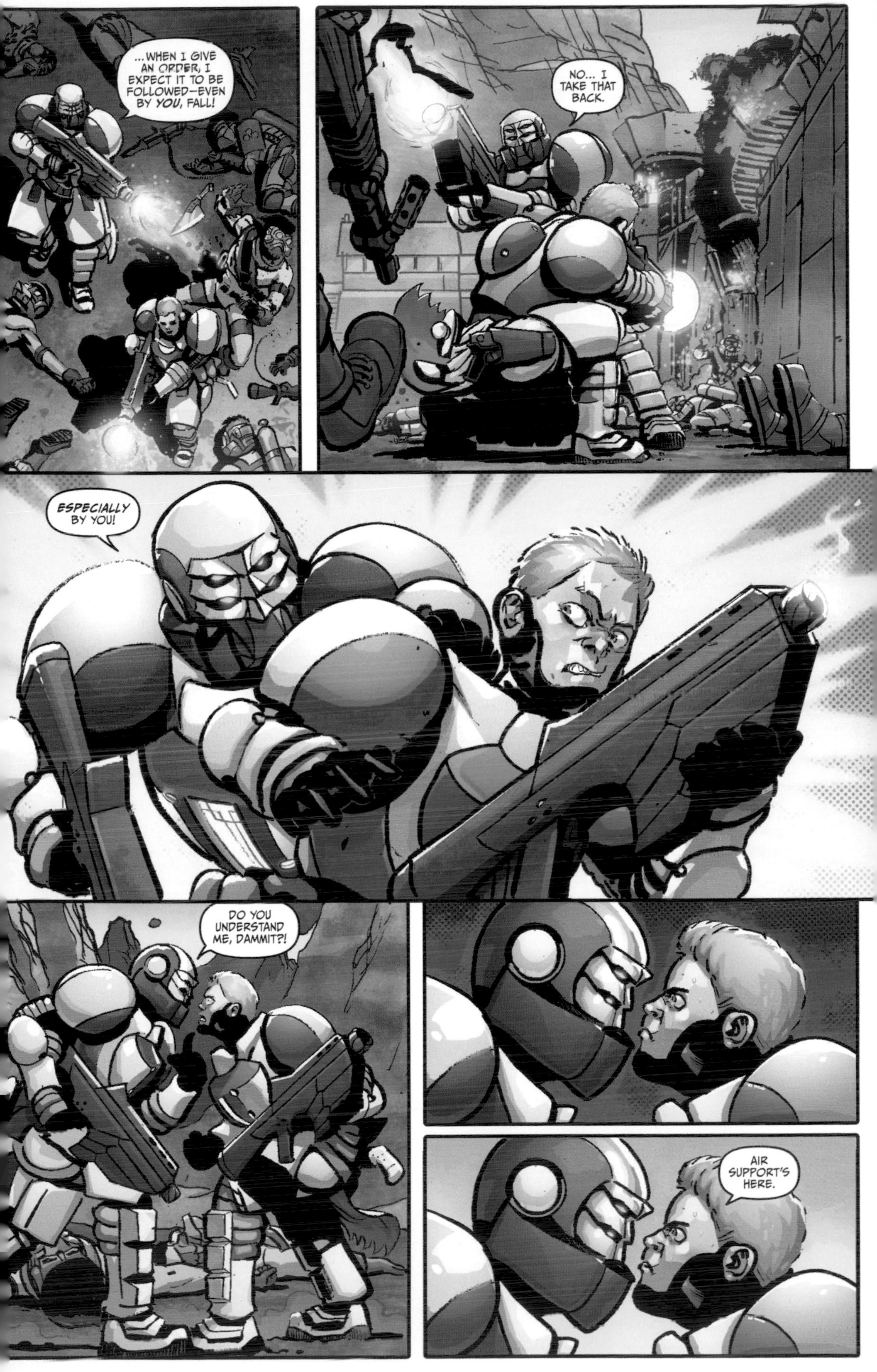
...WHEN I GIVE AN ORDER, I EXPECT IT TO BE FOLLOWED—EVEN BY *YOU*, FALL!
NO... I TAKE THAT BACK.
ESPECIALLY BY YOU!
DO YOU UNDERSTAND ME, DAMMIT?!
AIR SUPPORT'S HERE.

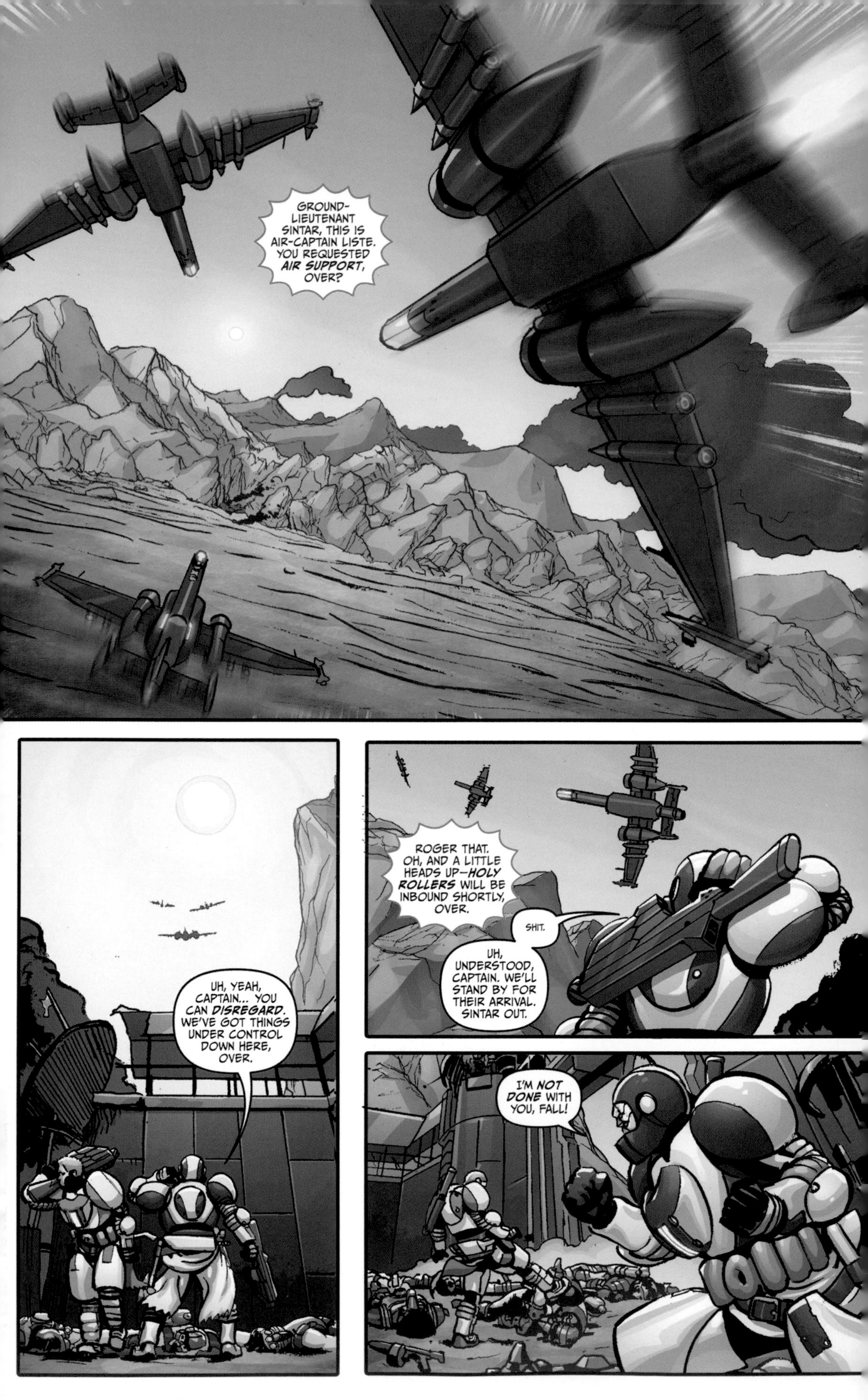
GROUND-LIEUTENANT SINTAR, THIS IS AIR-CAPTAIN LISTE. YOU REQUESTED AIR SUPPORT, OVER?
UH, YEAH, CAPTAIN... YOU CAN DISREGARD. WE'VE GOT THINGS UNDER CONTROL DOWN HERE, OVER.
ROGER THAT. OH, AND A LITTLE HEADS UP—HOLY ROLLERS WILL BE INBOUND SHORTLY, OVER.
SHIT.
UH, UNDERSTOOD, CAPTAIN. WE'LL STAND BY FOR THEIR ARRIVAL. SINTAR OUT.
I'M NOT DONE WITH YOU, FALL!

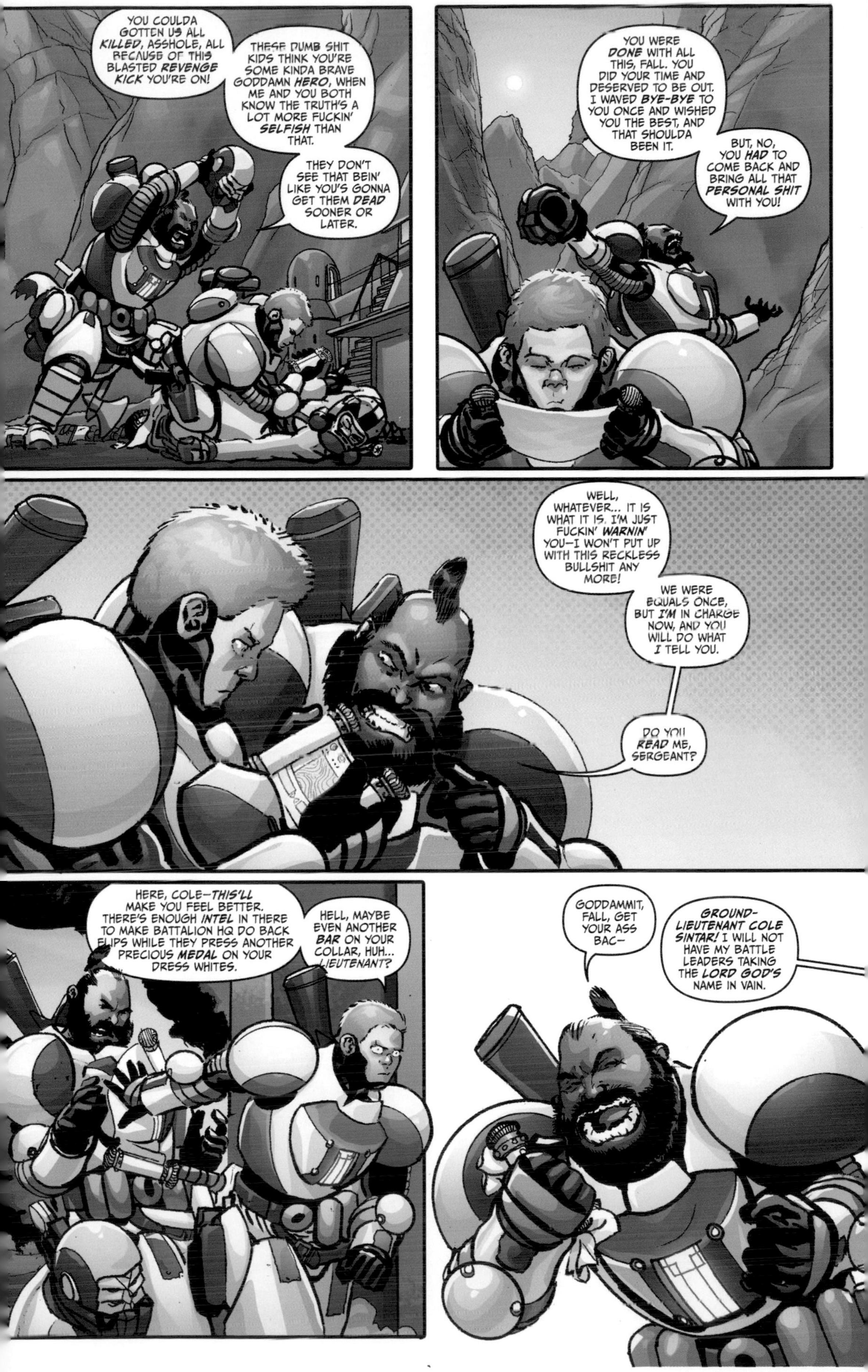
YOU COULDA GOTTEN US ALL KILLED, ASSHOLE, ALL BECAUSE OF THIS BLASTED REVENGE KICK YOU'RE ON!
THESE DUMB SHIT KIDS THINK YOU'RE SOME KINDA BRAVE GODDAMN HERO, WHEN ME AND YOU BOTH KNOW THE TRUTH'S A LOT MORE FUCKIN' SELFISH THAN THAT.
THEY DON'T SEE THAT BEIN' LIKE YOU'S GONNA GET THEM DEAD SOONER OR LATER.
YOU WERE DONE WITH ALL THIS, FALL. YOU DID YOUR TIME AND DESERVED TO BE OUT. I WAVED BYE-BYE TO YOU ONCE AND WISHED YOU THE BEST, AND THAT SHOULDA BEEN IT.
BUT, NO, YOU HAD TO COME BACK AND BRING ALL THAT PERSONAL SHIT WITH YOU!
WELL, WHATEVER... IT IS WHAT IT IS. I'M JUST FUCKIN' WARNIN' YOU—I WON'T PUT UP WITH THIS RECKLESS BULLSHIT ANY MORE!
WE WERE EQUALS ONCE, BUT I'M IN CHARGE NOW, AND YOU WILL DO WHAT I TELL YOU.
DO YOU READ ME, SERGEANT?
HERE, COLE—THIS'LL MAKE YOU FEEL BETTER. THERE'S ENOUGH INTEL IN THERE TO MAKE BATTALION HQ DO BACK FLIPS WHILE THEY PRESS ANOTHER PRECIOUS MEDAL ON YOUR DRESS WHITES.
HELL, MAYBE EVEN ANOTHER BAR ON YOUR COLLAR, HUH... LIEUTENANT?
GODDAMMIT, FALL, GET YOUR ASS BAC—
GROUND-LIEUTENANT COLE SINTAR! I WILL NOT HAVE MY BATTLE LEADERS TAKING THE LORD GOD'S NAME IN VAIN.

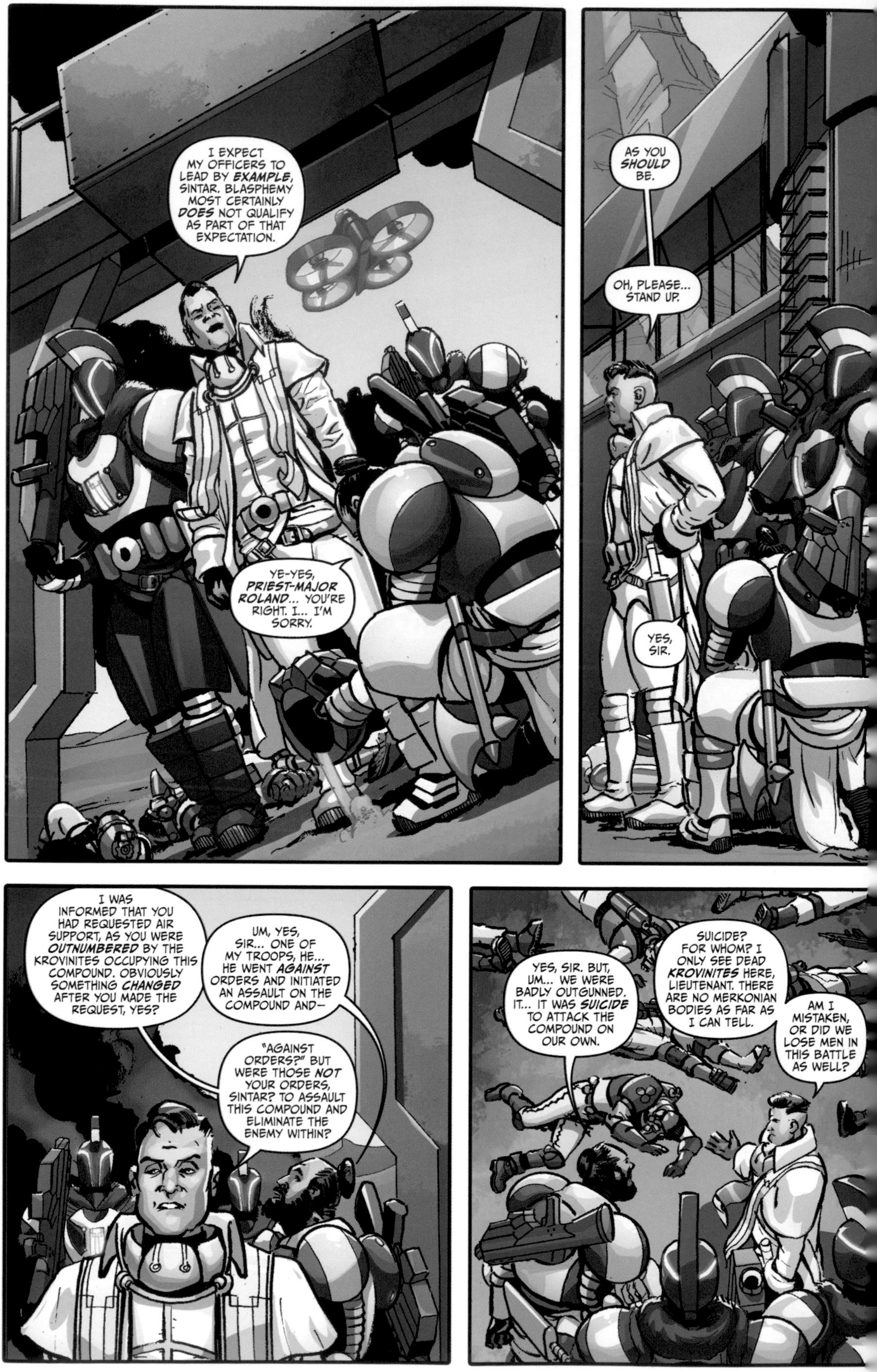
I EXPECT MY OFFICERS TO LEAD BY EXAMPLE, SINTAR. BLASPHEMY MOST CERTAINLY DOES NOT QUALIFY AS PART OF THAT EXPECTATION.
YE-YES, PRIEST-MAJOR ROLAND... YOU'RE RIGHT. I... I'M SORRY.
AS YOU SHOULD BE.
OH, PLEASE... STAND UP.
YES, SIR.
I WAS INFORMED THAT YOU HAD REQUESTED AIR SUPPORT, AS YOU WERE OUTNUMBERED BY THE KROVINITES OCCUPYING THIS COMPOUND. OBVIOUSLY SOMETHING CHANGED AFTER YOU MADE THE REQUEST, YES?
UM, YES, SIR... ONE OF MY TROOPS, HE... HE WENT AGAINST ORDERS AND INITIATED AN ASSAULT ON THE COMPOUND AND–
"AGAINST ORDERS?" BUT WERE THOSE NOT YOUR ORDERS, SINTAR? TO ASSAULT THIS COMPOUND AND ELIMINATE THE ENEMY WITHIN?
YES, SIR. BUT, UM... WE WERE BADLY OUTGUNNED. IT... IT WAS SUICIDE TO ATTACK THE COMPOUND ON OUR OWN.
SUICIDE? FOR WHOM? I ONLY SEE DEAD KROVINITES HERE, LIEUTENANT. THERE ARE NO MERKONIAN BODIES AS FAR AS I CAN TELL.
AM I MISTAKEN, OR DID WE LOSE MEN IN THIS BATTLE AS WELL?

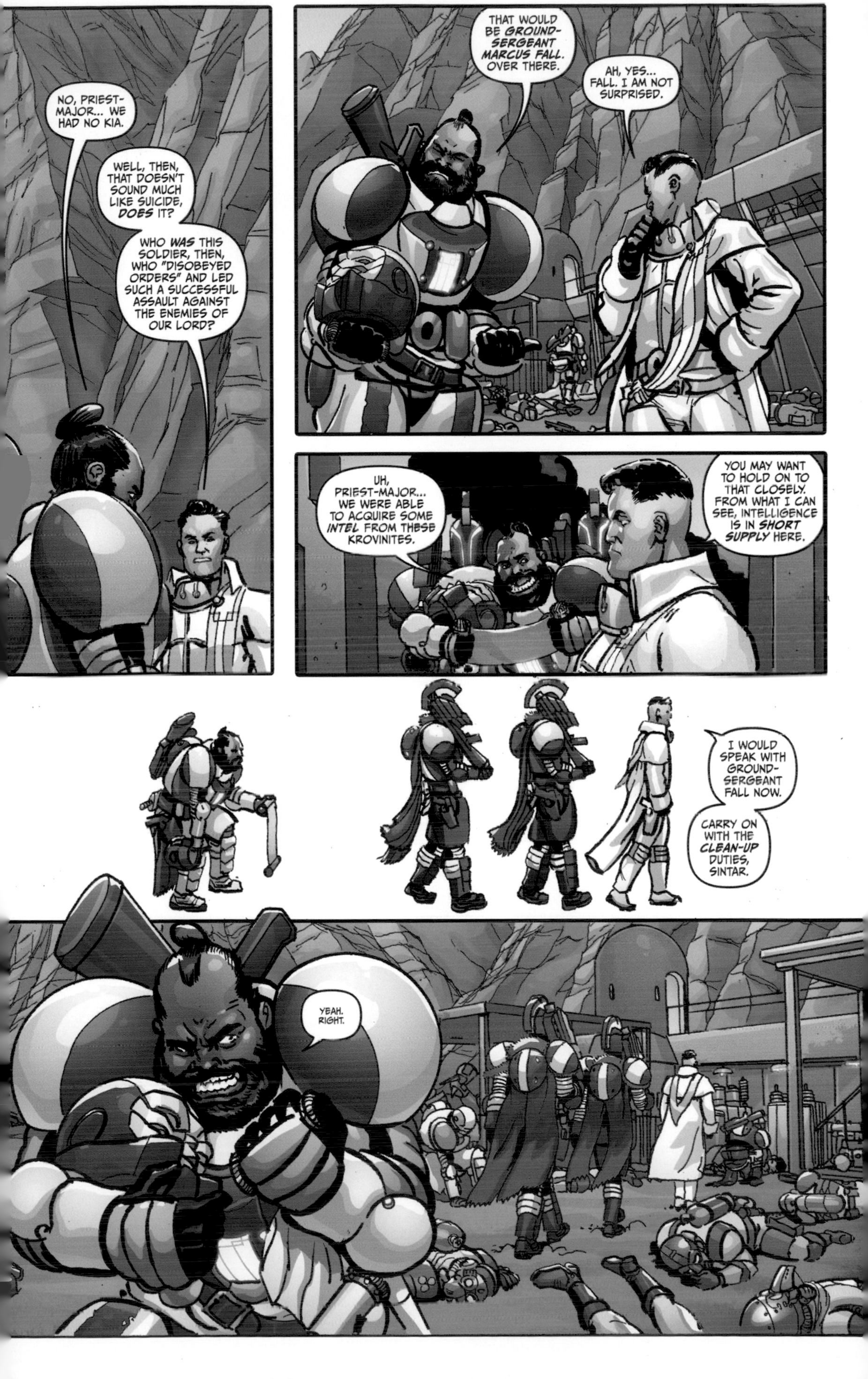

NO, PRIEST-MAJOR... WE HAD NO KIA.
WELL, THEN, THAT DOESN'T SOUND MUCH LIKE SUICIDE, DOES IT?
WHO WAS THIS SOLDIER, THEN, WHO "DISOBEYED ORDERS" AND LED SUCH A SUCCESSFUL ASSAULT AGAINST THE ENEMIES OF OUR LORD?
THAT WOULD BE GROUND-SERGEANT MARCUS FALL. OVER THERE.
AH, YES... FALL. I AM NOT SURPRISED.
UH, PRIEST-MAJOR... WE WERE ABLE TO ACQUIRE SOME INTEL FROM THESE KROVINITES.
YOU MAY WANT TO HOLD ON TO THAT CLOSELY. FROM WHAT I CAN SEE, INTELLIGENCE IS IN SHORT SUPPLY HERE.
I WOULD SPEAK WITH GROUND-SERGEANT FALL NOW.
CARRY ON WITH THE CLEAN-UP DUTIES, SINTAR.
YEAH. RIGHT.

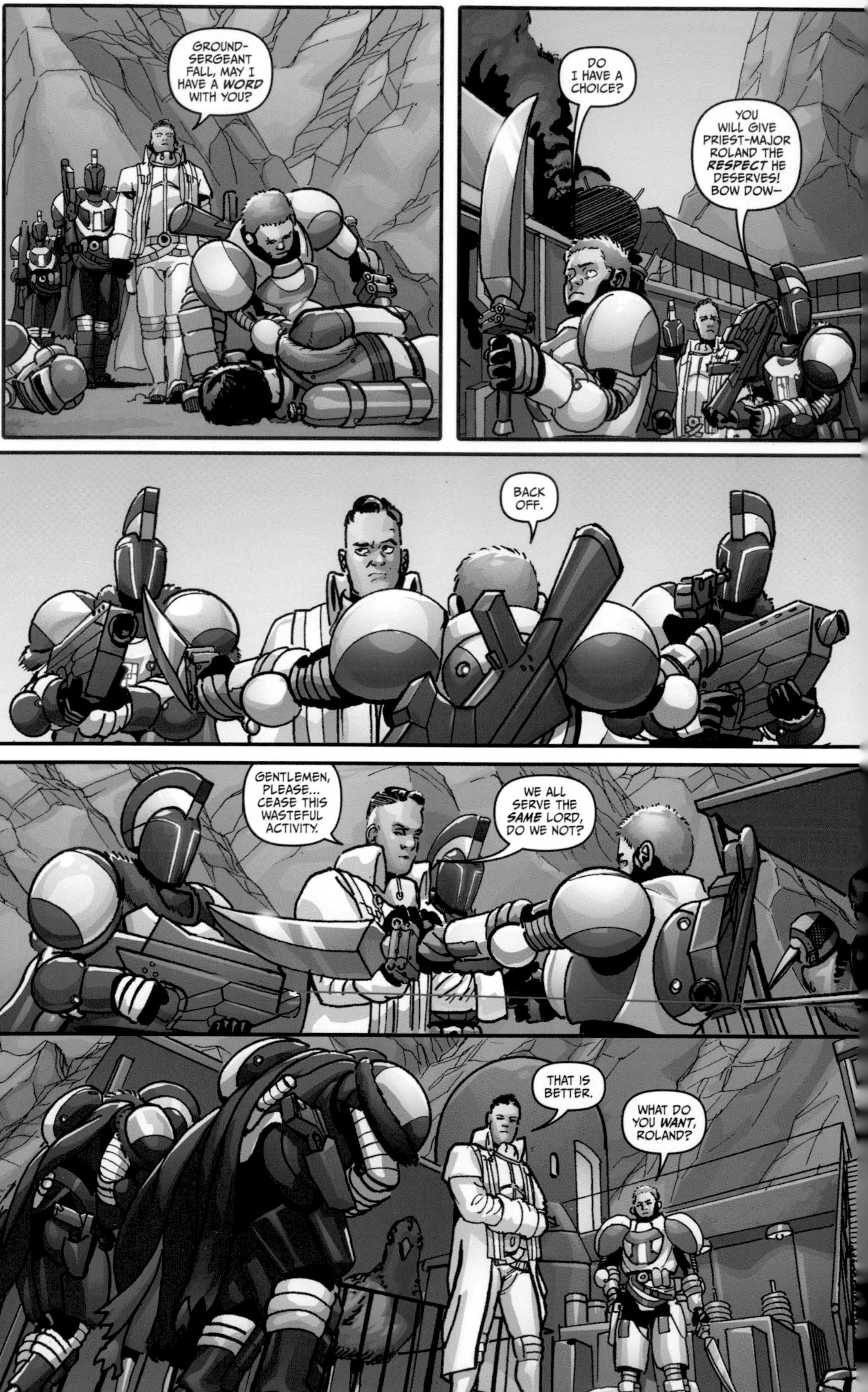
GROUND-SERGEANT FALL, MAY I HAVE A WORD WITH YOU?
DO I HAVE A CHOICE?
YOU WILL GIVE PRIEST-MAJOR ROLAND THE RESPECT HE DESERVES! BOW DOW—
BACK OFF.
GENTLEMEN, PLEASE... CEASE THIS WASTEFUL ACTIVITY.
WE ALL SERVE THE SAME LORD, DO WE NOT?
THAT IS BETTER.
WHAT DO YOU WANT, ROLAND?

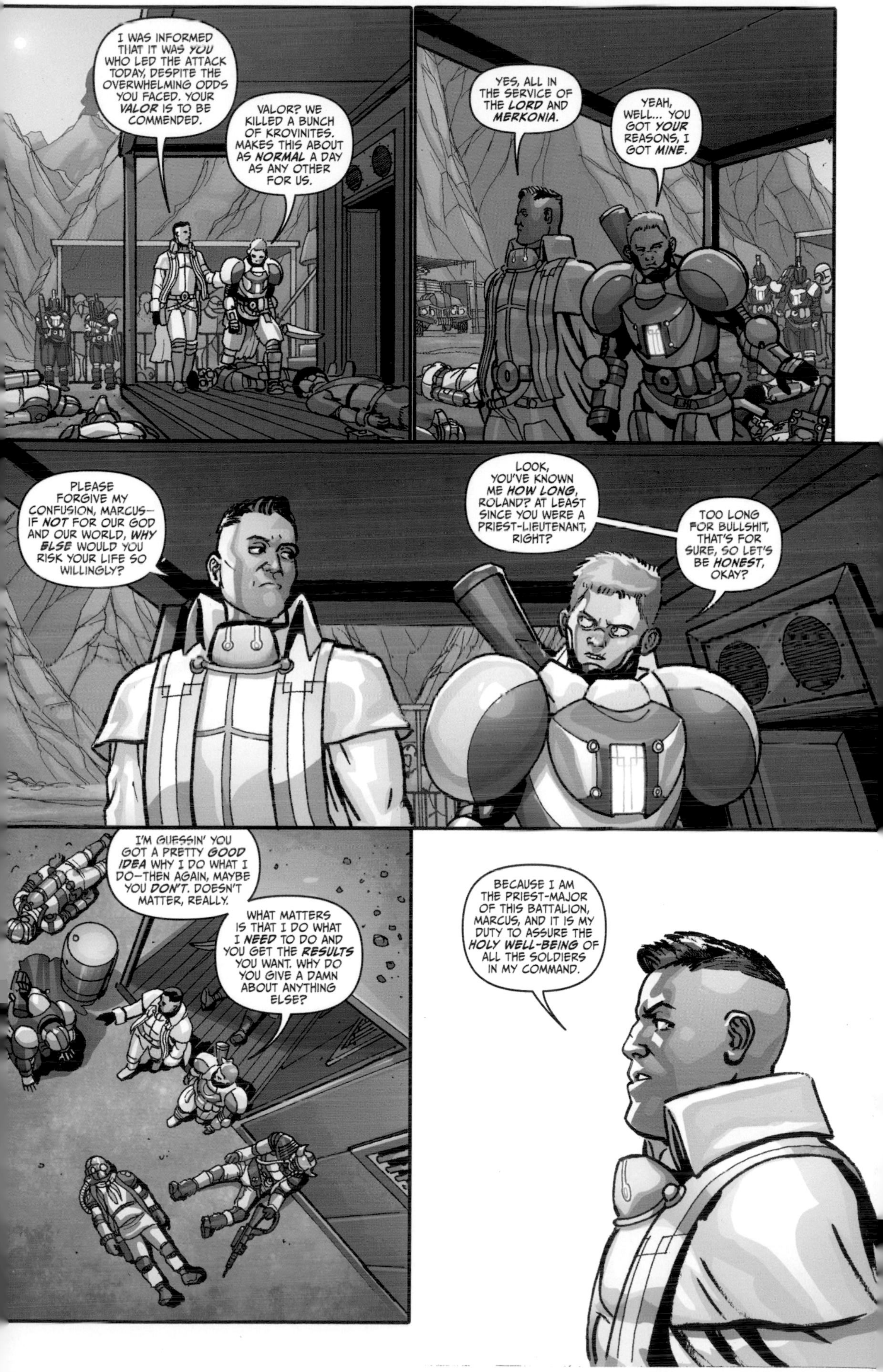
I WAS INFORMED THAT IT WAS *YOU* WHO LED THE ATTACK TODAY, DESPITE THE OVERWHELMING ODDS YOU FACED. YOUR *VALOR* IS TO BE COMMENDED.
VALOR? WE KILLED A BUNCH OF KROVINITES. MAKES THIS ABOUT AS *NORMAL* A DAY AS ANY OTHER FOR US.
YES, ALL IN THE SERVICE OF THE *LORD* AND *MERKONIA*.
YEAH, WELL... YOU GOT *YOUR* REASONS, I GOT *MINE*.
PLEASE FORGIVE MY CONFUSION, MARCUS— IF *NOT* FOR OUR GOD AND OUR WORLD, *WHY ELSE* WOULD YOU RISK YOUR LIFE SO WILLINGLY?
LOOK, YOU'VE KNOWN ME *HOW LONG*, ROLAND? AT LEAST SINCE YOU WERE A PRIEST-LIEUTENANT, RIGHT?
TOO LONG FOR BULLSHIT, THAT'S FOR SURE, SO LET'S BE *HONEST*, OKAY?
I'M GUESSIN' YOU GOT A PRETTY *GOOD IDEA* WHY I DO WHAT I DO—THEN AGAIN, MAYBE YOU *DON'T*. DOESN'T MATTER, REALLY.
WHAT MATTERS IS THAT I DO WHAT I *NEED* TO DO AND YOU GET THE *RESULTS* YOU WANT. WHY DO YOU GIVE A DAMN ABOUT ANYTHING ELSE?
BECAUSE I AM THE PRIEST-MAJOR OF THIS BATTALION, MARCUS, AND IT IS MY DUTY TO ASSURE THE *HOLY WELL-BEING* OF ALL THE SOLDIERS IN MY COMMAND.

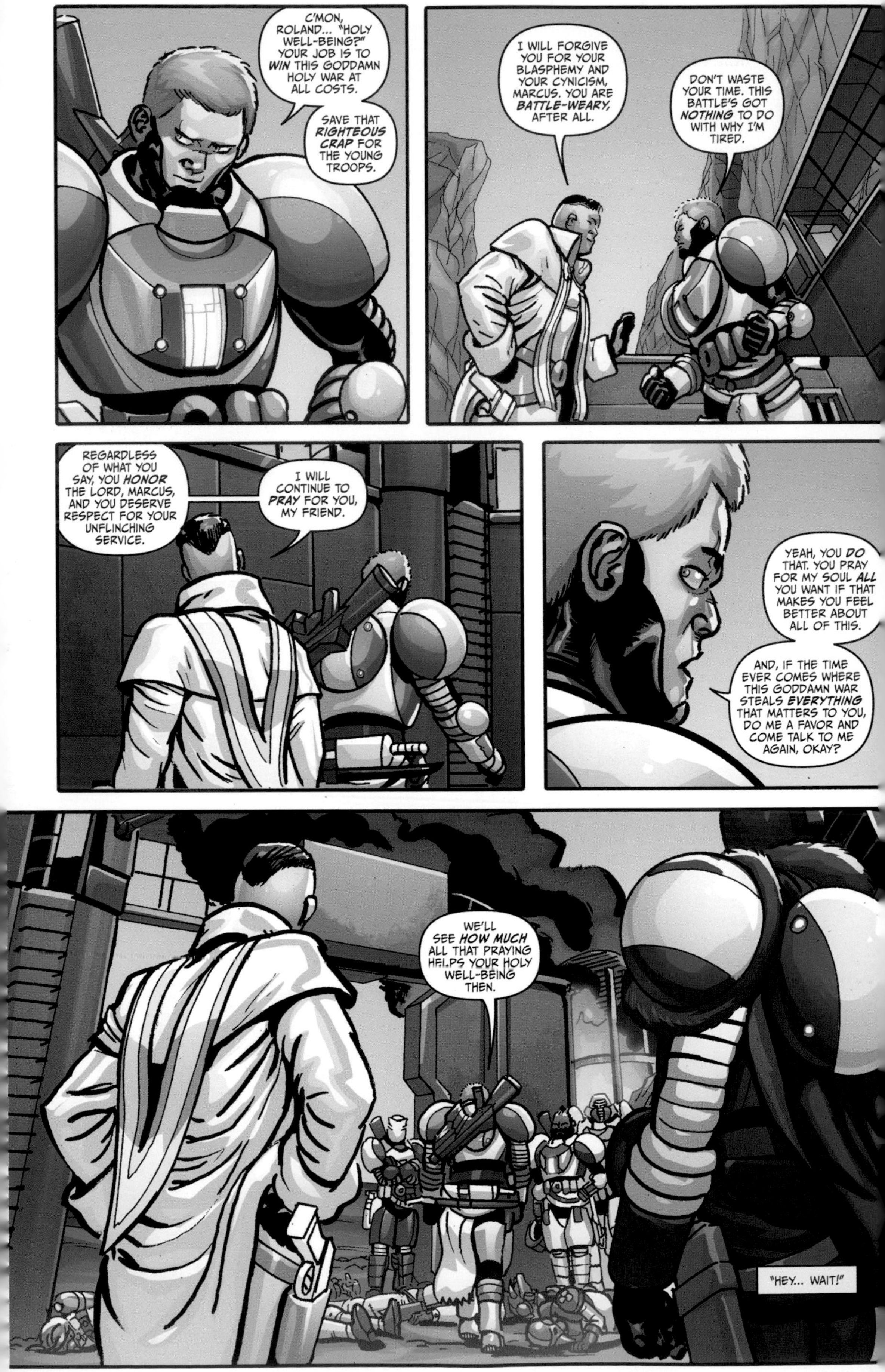
C'MON, ROLAND... "HOLY WELL-BEING?" YOUR JOB IS TO WIN THIS GODDAMN HOLY WAR AT ALL COSTS.
SAVE THAT RIGHTEOUS CRAP FOR THE YOUNG TROOPS.
I WILL FORGIVE YOU FOR YOUR BLASPHEMY AND YOUR CYNICISM, MARCUS. YOU ARE BATTLE-WEARY, AFTER ALL.
DON'T WASTE YOUR TIME. THIS BATTLE'S GOT NOTHING TO DO WITH WHY I'M TIRED.
REGARDLESS OF WHAT YOU SAY, YOU HONOR THE LORD, MARCUS, AND YOU DESERVE RESPECT FOR YOUR UNFLINCHING SERVICE.
I WILL CONTINUE TO PRAY FOR YOU, MY FRIEND.
YEAH, YOU DO THAT. YOU PRAY FOR MY SOUL ALL YOU WANT IF THAT MAKES YOU FEEL BETTER ABOUT ALL OF THIS.
AND, IF THE TIME EVER COMES WHERE THIS GODDAMN WAR STEALS EVERYTHING THAT MATTERS TO YOU, DO ME A FAVOR AND COME TALK TO ME AGAIN, OKAY?
WE'LL SEE HOW MUCH ALL THAT PRAYING HELPS YOUR HOLY WELL-BEING THEN.
"HEY... WAIT!"

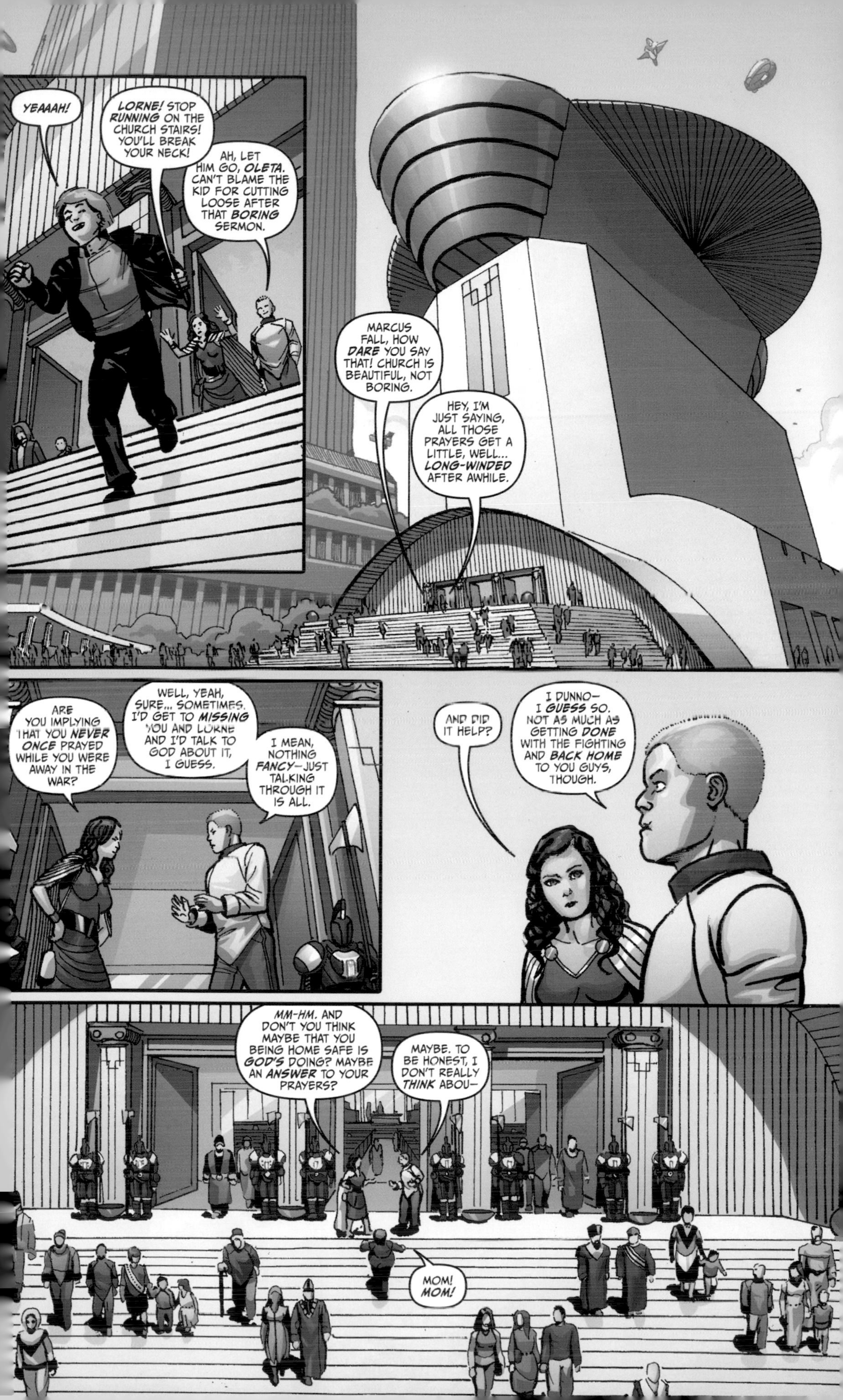
YEAAAH!
LORNE! STOP RUNNING ON THE CHURCH STAIRS! YOU'LL BREAK YOUR NECK!
AH, LET HIM GO, OLETA. CAN'T BLAME THE KID FOR CUTTING LOOSE AFTER THAT BORING SERMON.
MARCUS FALL, HOW DARE YOU SAY THAT! CHURCH IS BEAUTIFUL, NOT BORING.
HEY, I'M JUST SAYING, ALL THOSE PRAYERS GET A LITTLE, WELL... LONG-WINDED AFTER AWHILE.
ARE YOU IMPLYING THAT YOU NEVER ONCE PRAYED WHILE YOU WERE AWAY IN THE WAR?
WELL, YEAH, SURE... SOMETIMES. I'D GET TO MISSING YOU AND LORNE AND I'D TALK TO GOD ABOUT IT, I GUESS.
I MEAN, NOTHING FANCY—JUST TALKING THROUGH IT IS ALL.
AND DID IT HELP?
I DUNNO—I GUESS SO. NOT AS MUCH AS GETTING DONE WITH THE FIGHTING AND BACK HOME TO YOU GUYS, THOUGH.
MM-HM. AND DON'T YOU THINK MAYBE THAT YOU BEING HOME SAFE IS GOD'S DOING? MAYBE AN ANSWER TO YOUR PRAYERS?
MAYBE. TO BE HONEST, I DON'T REALLY THINK ABOU—
MOM! MOM!

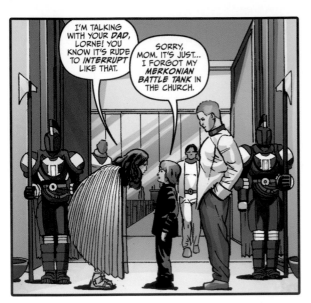

I'M TALKING WITH YOUR *DAD*, LORNE! YOU KNOW IT'S RUDE TO *INTERRUPT* LIKE THAT.

SORRY, MOM. IT'S JUST... I FORGOT MY *MERKONIAN BATTLE TANK* IN THE CHURCH.

LORNE MARCUS FALL, HOW MANY TIMES HAVE I TOLD YOU *NOT* TO BRING YOUR *WAR TOYS* TO CHURCH, HUH?

NO *BUTS*, YOUNG MAN. HOW MANY TIMES?

I KNOW, MOM. BUT—

C'MON, HO[N] WHAT'S THE [BIG] DEAL? THO[SE] TANKS ARE U[SED] TO *FIGHT WA[RS]* FOR THIS CH[URCH] ANYWAYS, RIGHT?

DON'T *HELP* HIM, MARCUS. HE'LL NEVER LEARN.

WELL, IT'S *TRUE*, ISN'T IT?

OH, YOU TWO!

COME ON, LORNE, LET'S GO GET YOUR TOY. THEN YOU AND I ARE GOING TO HAVE A *LONG TALK*... AWAY FROM YOUR FATHER.

AWW, MOM.

I'LL STAY RIGHT HERE. I'VE HAD *ENOUGH* WORSHIP FOR TODAY, THANK YOU VERY MUCH.

I CANNOT *BELIEVE* YOU BROUGHT THAT TANK TO CHURCH!

OLETA...?

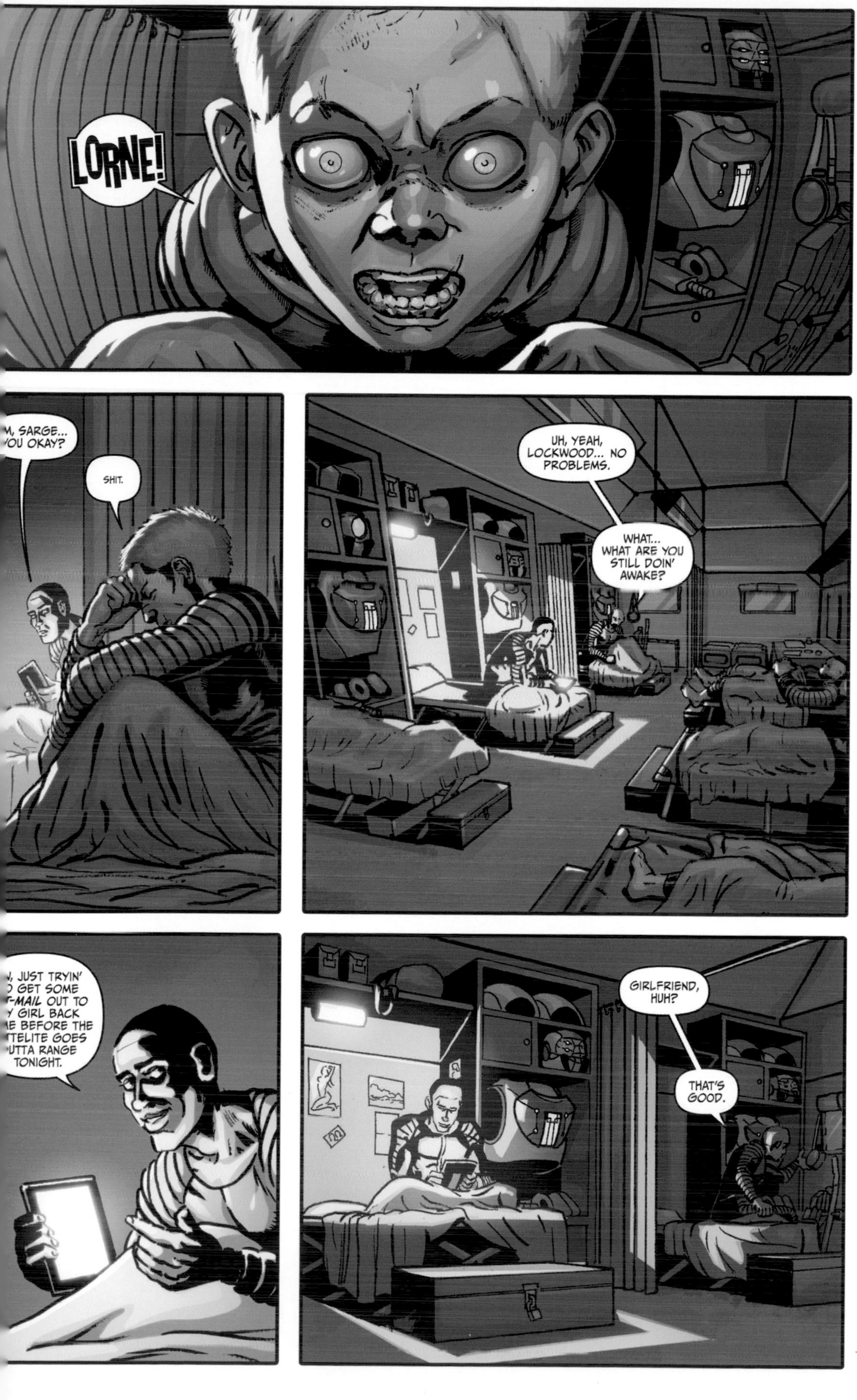

LORNE!
M, SARGE... OU OKAY?
SHIT.
UH, YEAH, LOCKWOOD... NO PROBLEMS.
WHAT... WHAT ARE YOU STILL DOIN' AWAKE?
, JUST TRYIN' O GET SOME -MAIL OUT TO Y GIRL BACK E BEFORE THE TELITE GOES UTTA RANGE TONIGHT.
GIRLFRIEND, HUH?
THAT'S GOOD.

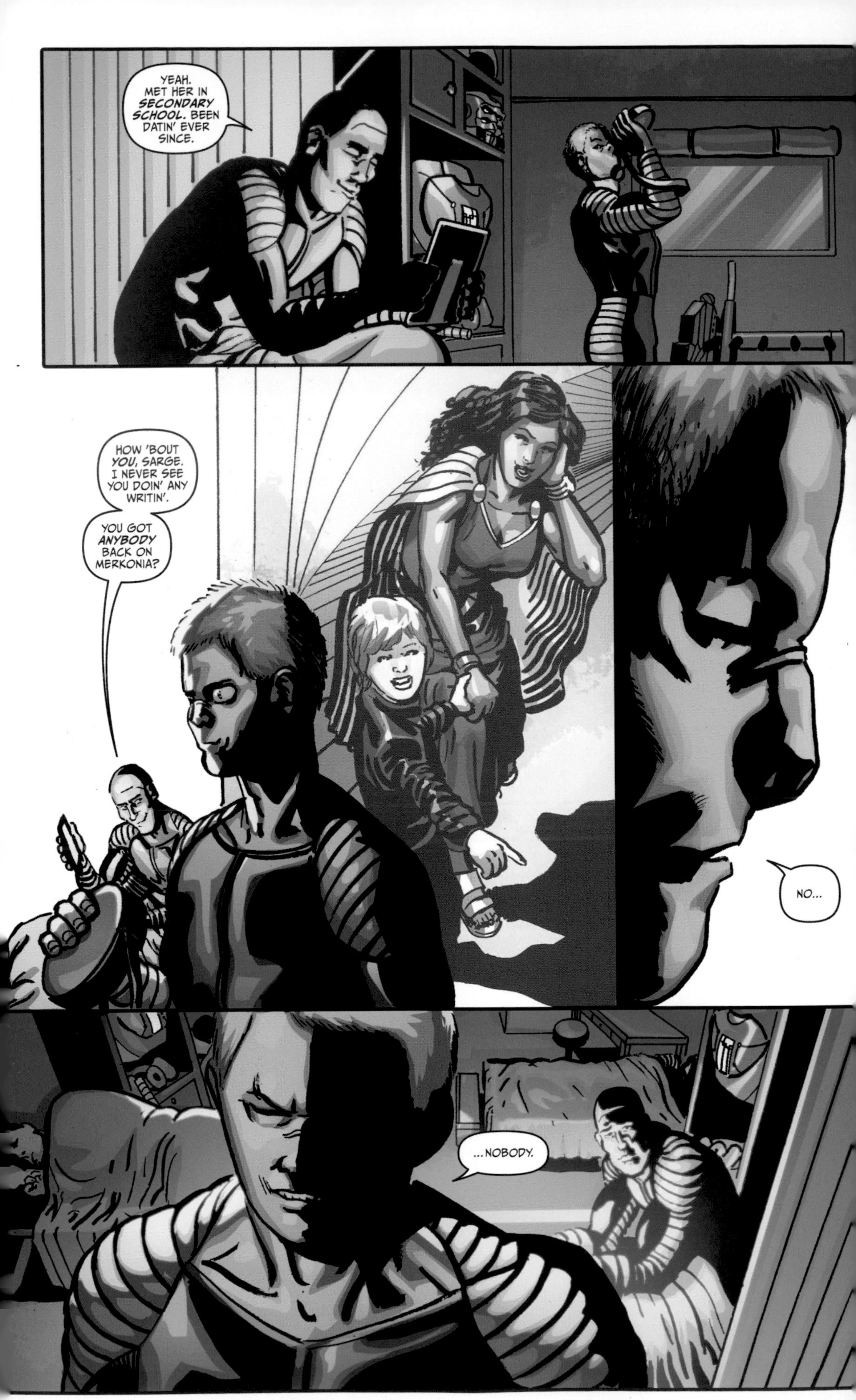
YEAH. MET HER IN SECONDARY SCHOOL. BEEN DATIN' EVER SINCE.
HOW 'BOUT YOU, SARGE. I NEVER SEE YOU DOIN' ANY WRITIN'.
YOU GOT ANYBODY BACK ON MERKONIA?
NO...
...NOBODY.

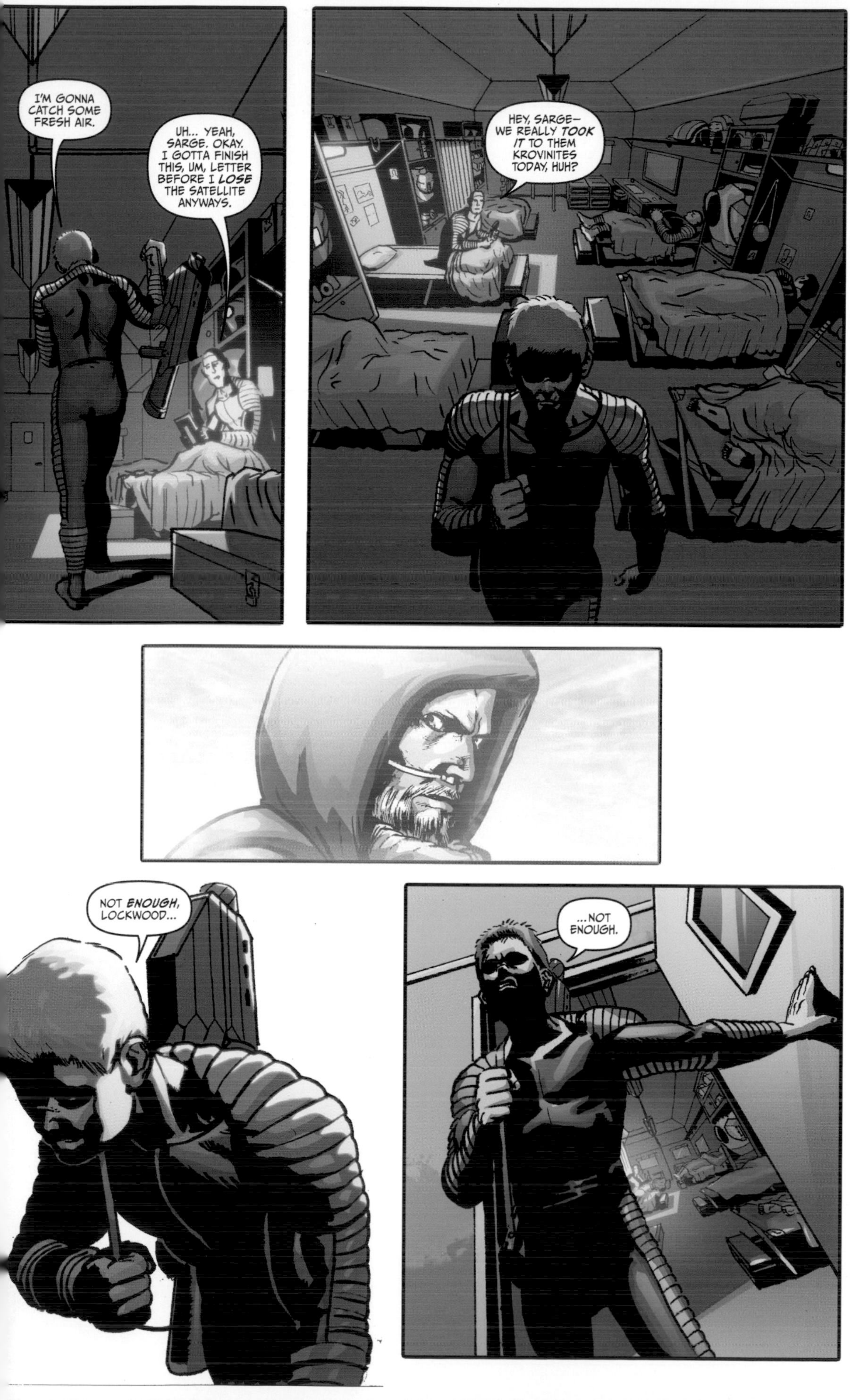
I'M GONNA CATCH SOME FRESH AIR.
UH... YEAH, SARGE. OKAY. I GOTTA FINISH THIS, UM, LETTER BEFORE I LOSE THE SATELLITE ANYWAYS.
HEY, SARGE— WE REALLY TOOK IT TO THEM KROVINITES TODAY, HUH?
NOT ENOUGH, LOCKWOOD...
...NOT ENOUGH.

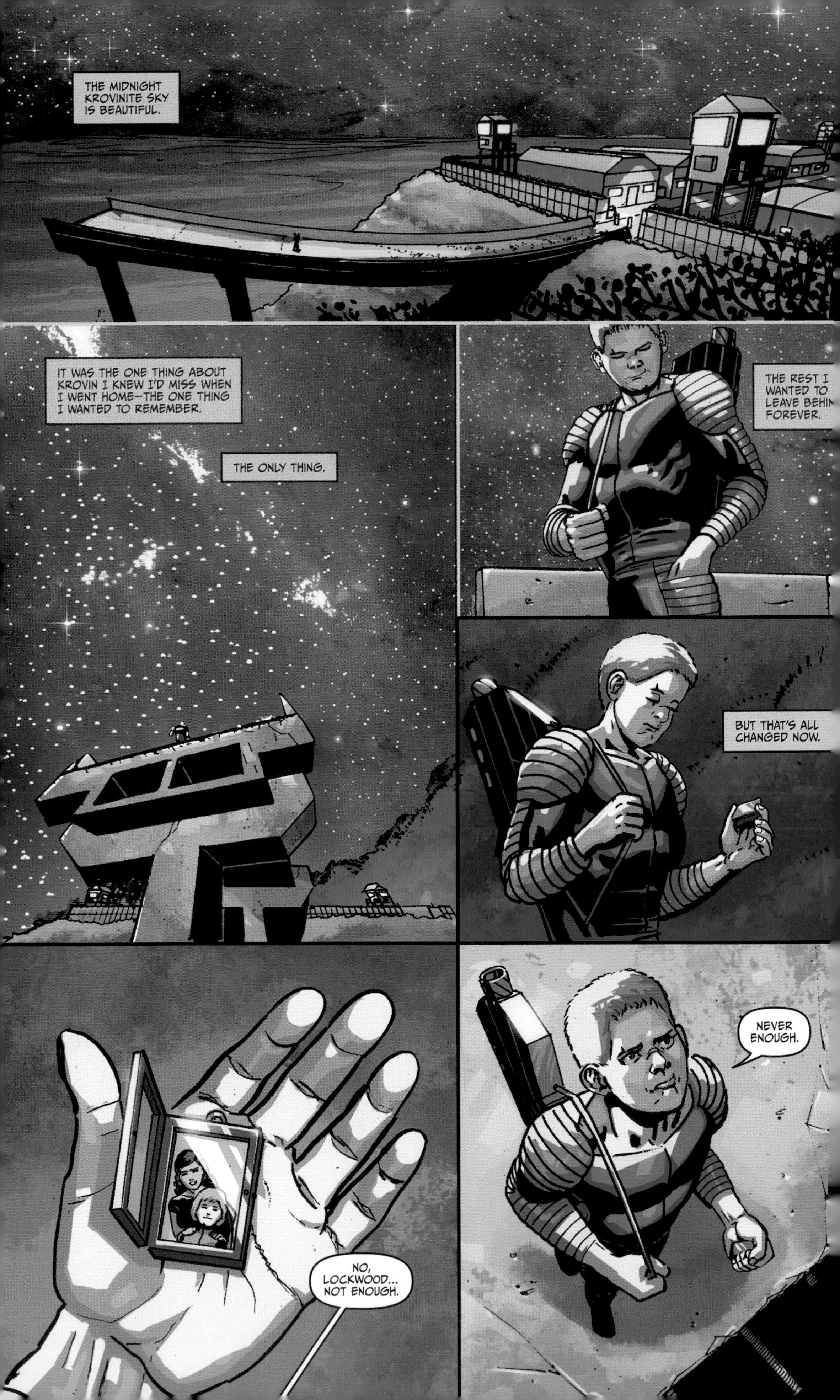
THE MIDNIGHT KROVINITE SKY IS BEAUTIFUL.
IT WAS THE ONE THING ABOUT KROVIN I KNEW I'D MISS WHEN I WENT HOME—THE ONE THING I WANTED TO REMEMBER.
THE ONLY THING.
THE REST I WANTED TO LEAVE BEHIN
FOREVER.
BUT THAT'S ALL CHANGED NOW.
NO, LOCKWOOD... NOT ENOUGH.
NEVER ENOUGH.

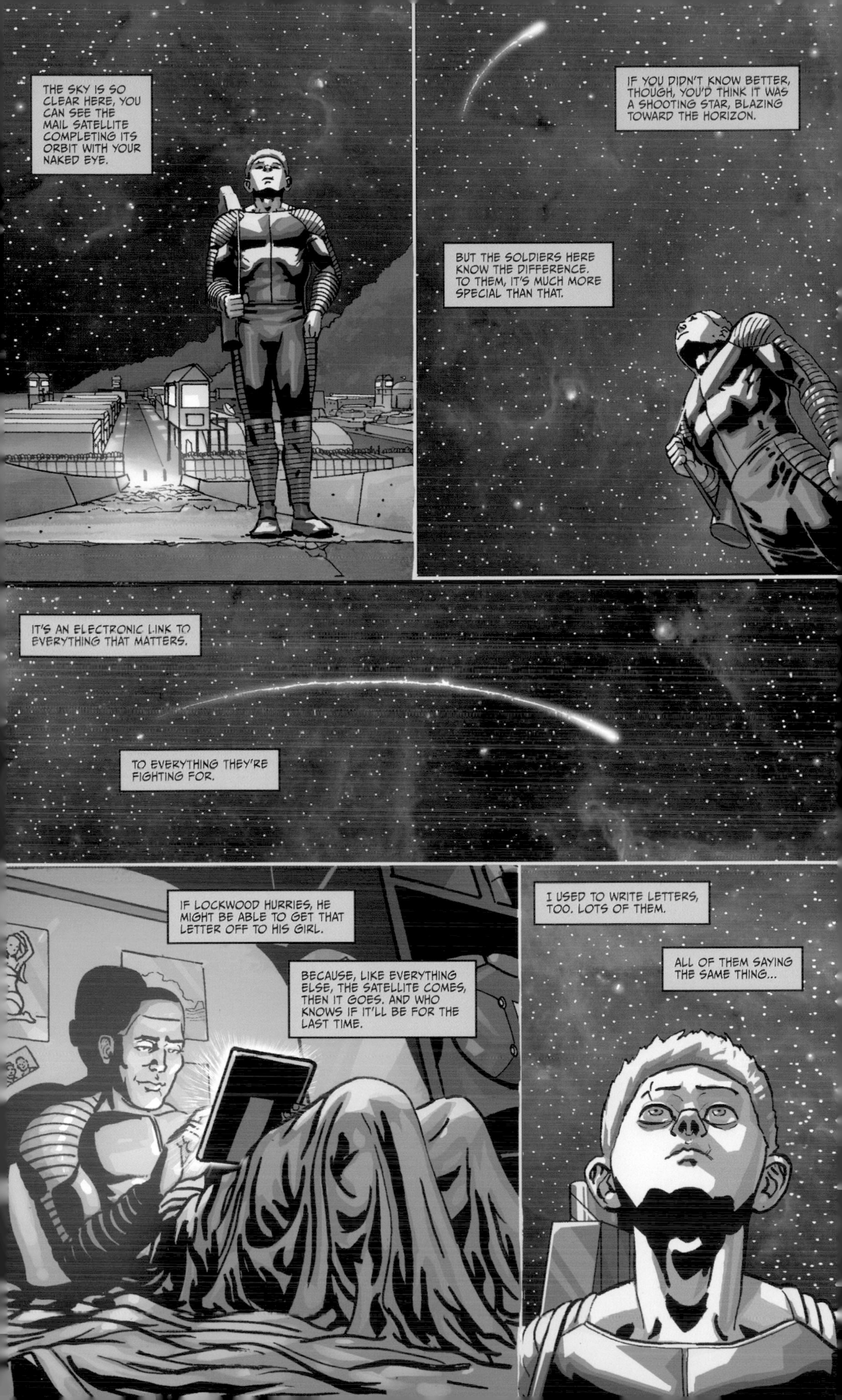
THE SKY IS SO CLEAR HERE, YOU CAN SEE THE MAIL SATELLITE COMPLETING ITS ORBIT WITH YOUR NAKED EYE.
IF YOU DIDN'T KNOW BETTER, THOUGH, YOU'D THINK IT WAS A SHOOTING STAR, BLAZING TOWARD THE HORIZON.
BUT THE SOLDIERS HERE KNOW THE DIFFERENCE. TO THEM, IT'S MUCH MORE SPECIAL THAN THAT.
IT'S AN ELECTRONIC LINK TO EVERYTHING THAT MATTERS.
TO EVERYTHING THEY'RE FIGHTING FOR.
IF LOCKWOOD HURRIES, HE MIGHT BE ABLE TO GET THAT LETTER OFF TO HIS GIRL.
BECAUSE, LIKE EVERYTHING ELSE, THE SATELLITE COMES, THEN IT GOES. AND WHO KNOWS IF IT'LL BE FOR THE LAST TIME.
I USED TO WRITE LETTERS, TOO. LOTS OF THEM.
ALL OF THEM SAYING THE SAME THING...

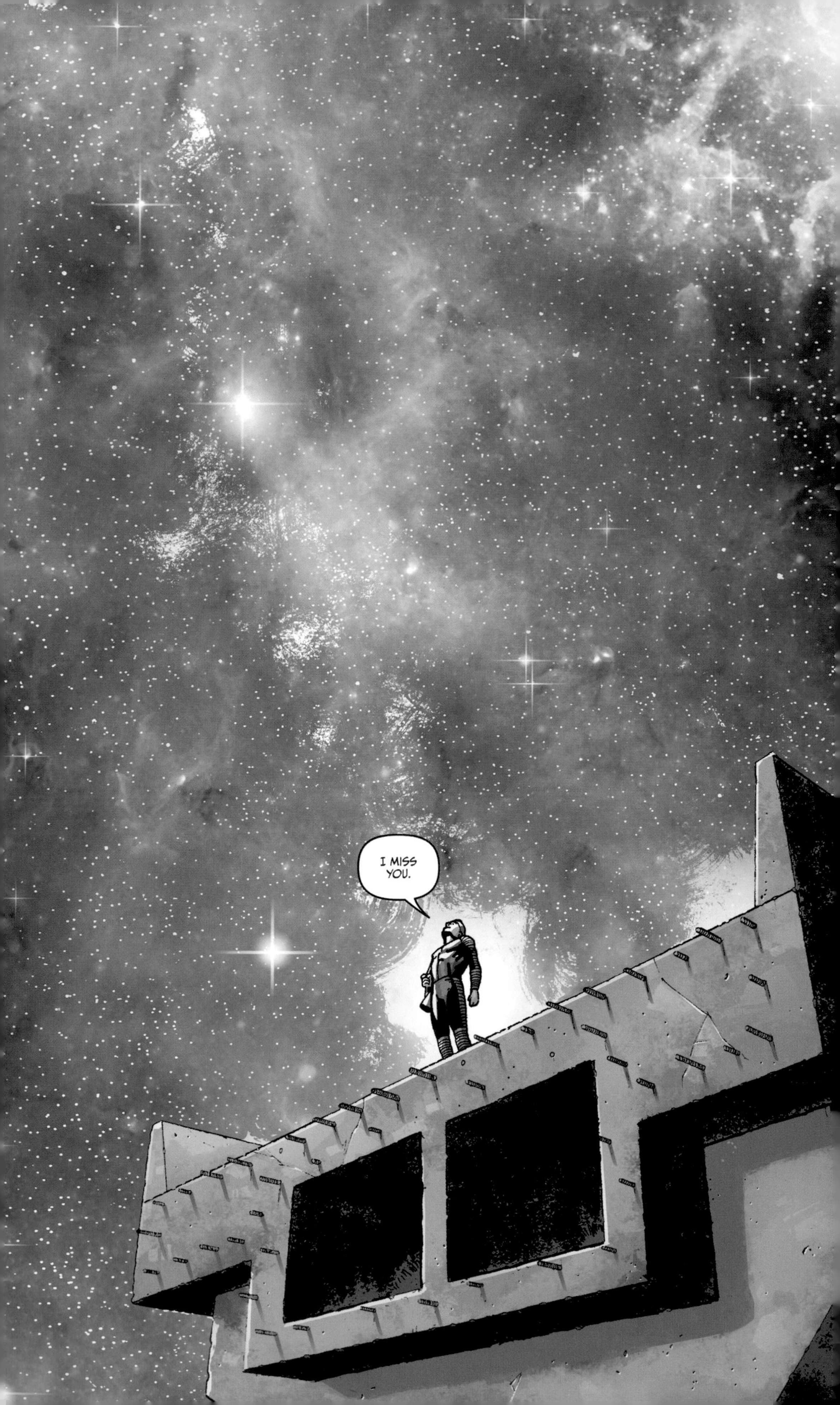
I MISS YOU.

"THE VERY WORD 'SECRECY' IS REPUGNANT

IN A FREE AND OPEN SOCIETY; AND WE ARE

AS A PEOPLE INHERENTLY AND HISTORICALLY

OPPOSED TO SECRET SOCIETIES, TO SECRET

OATHS AND TO SECRET PROCEEDINGS."

– PRESIDENT JOHN F. KENNEDY

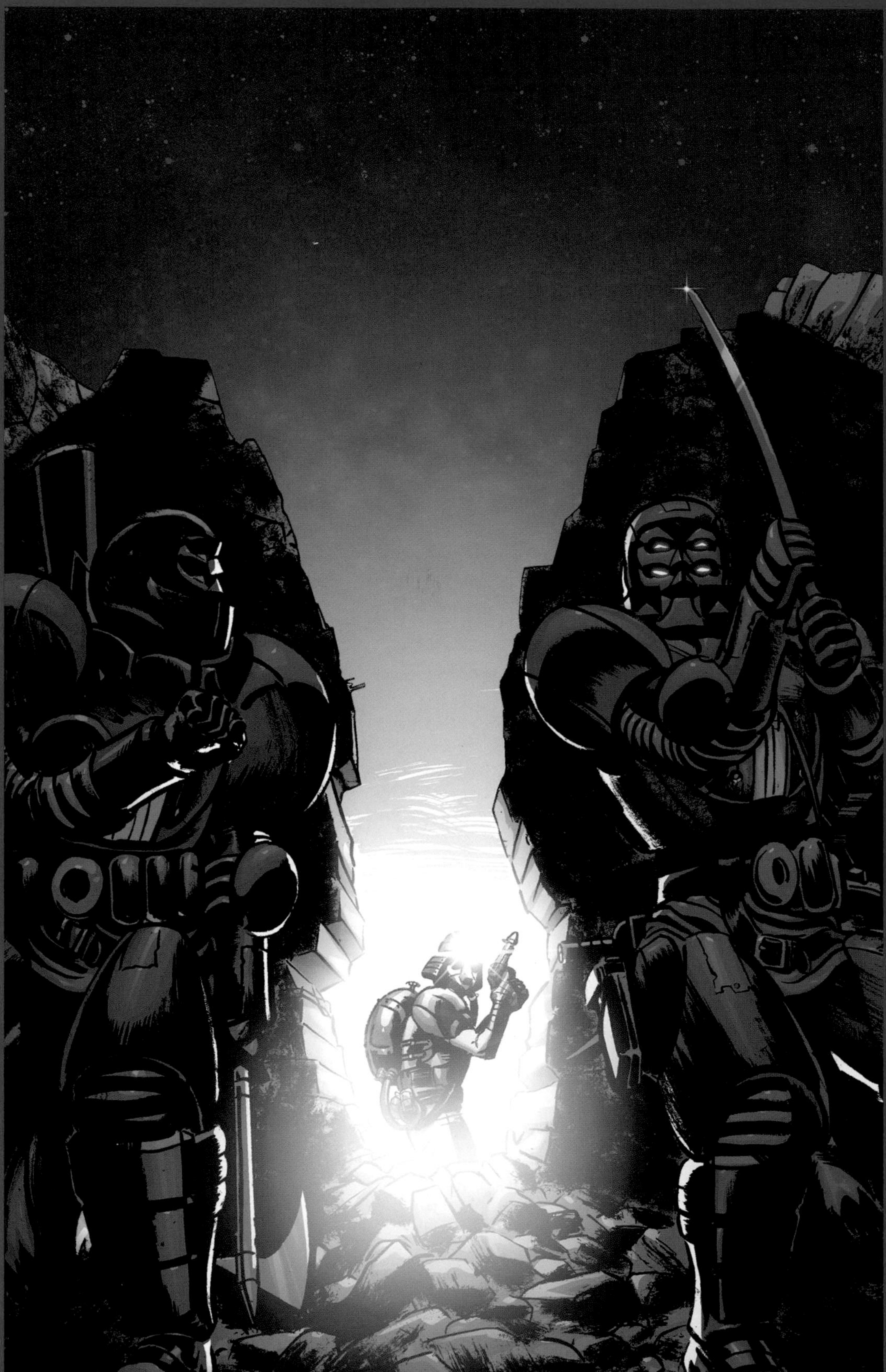

Art by Casey Maloney, Colors by Dusty Yee

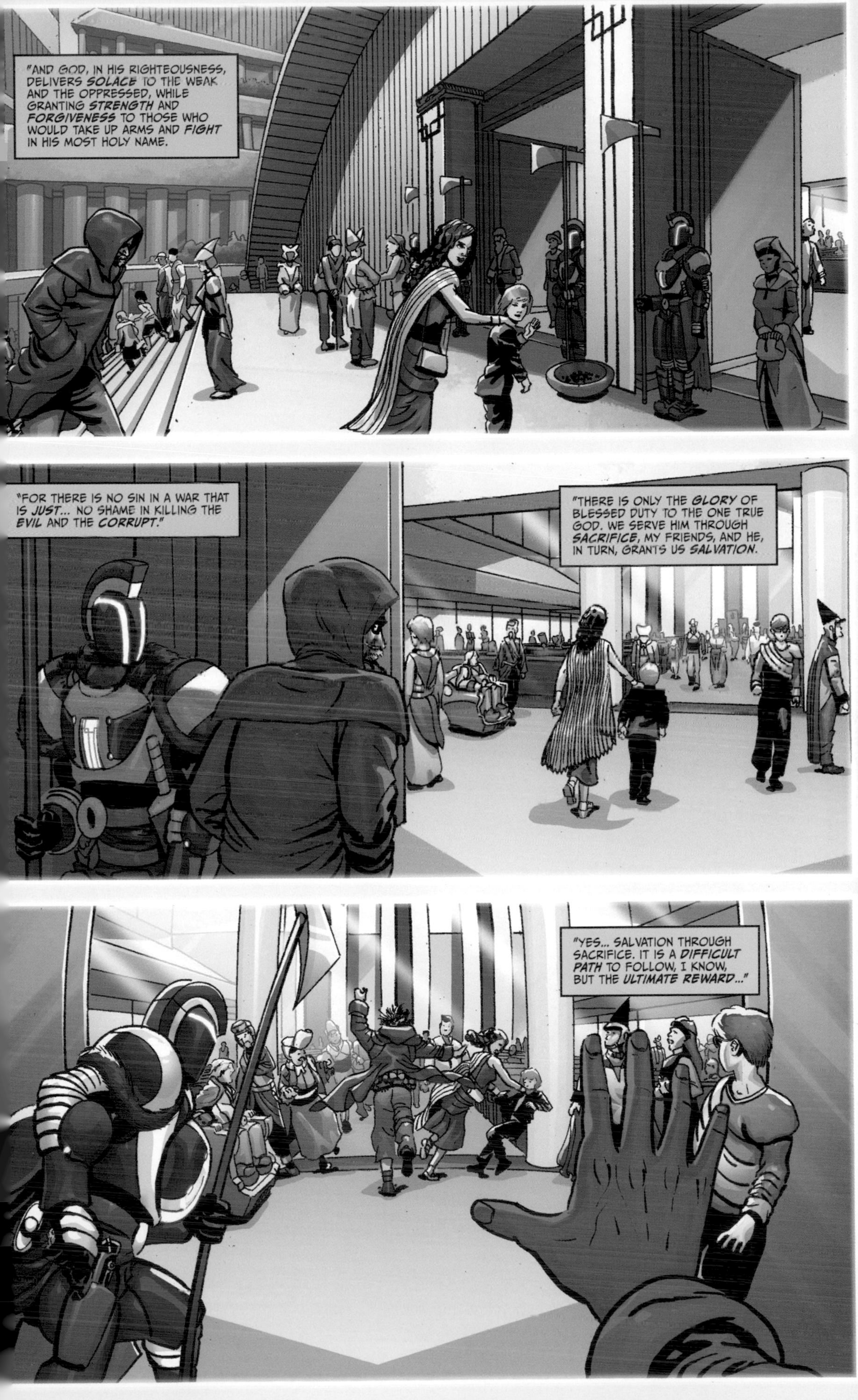
"AND GOD, IN HIS RIGHTEOUSNESS, DELIVERS SOLACE TO THE WEAK AND THE OPPRESSED, WHILE GRANTING STRENGTH AND FORGIVENESS TO THOSE WHO WOULD TAKE UP ARMS AND FIGHT IN HIS MOST HOLY NAME.
"FOR THERE IS NO SIN IN A WAR THAT IS JUST... NO SHAME IN KILLING THE EVIL AND THE CORRUPT."
"THERE IS ONLY THE GLORY OF BLESSED DUTY TO THE ONE TRUE GOD. WE SERVE HIM THROUGH SACRIFICE, MY FRIENDS, AND HE, IN TURN, GRANTS US SALVATION.
"YES... SALVATION THROUGH SACRIFICE. IT IS A DIFFICULT PATH TO FOLLOW, I KNOW, BUT THE ULTIMATE REWARD..."

CHAPTER TWO
SACRIFICE

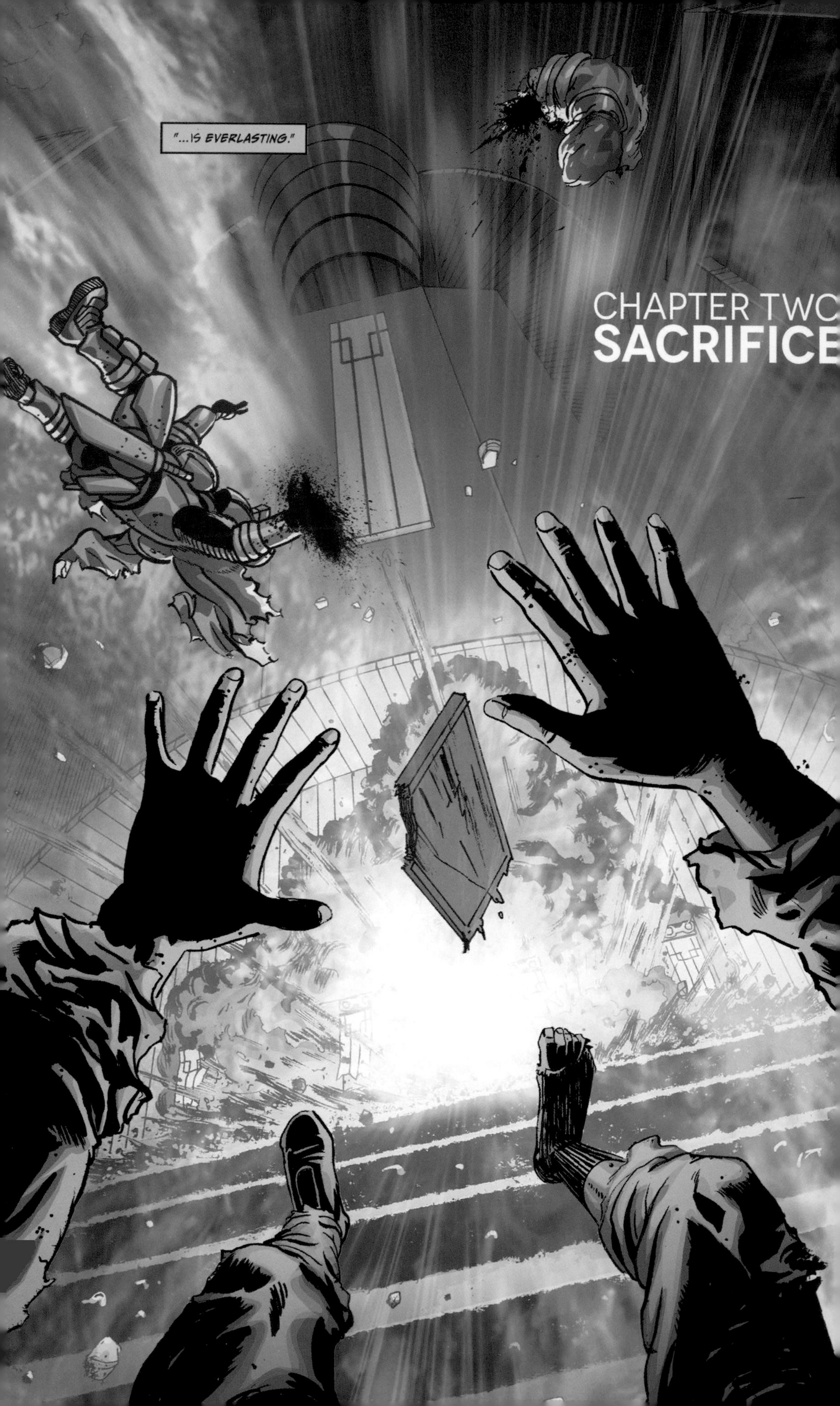
"...IS EVERLASTING."

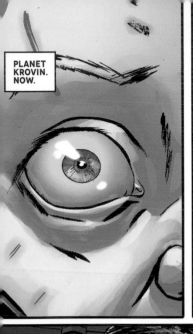

PLANET KROVIN. NOW.

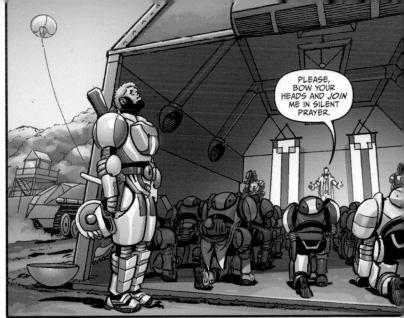

PLEASE, BOW YOUR HEADS AND *JOIN* ME IN SILENT PRAYER.

RISE NOW, SOLDIERS OF GOD.

RISE, AND GO...

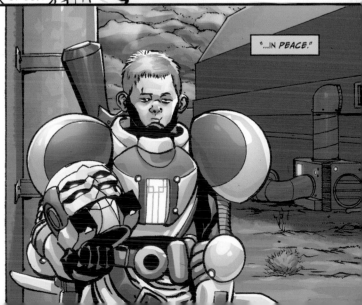

"...IN *PEACE.*"

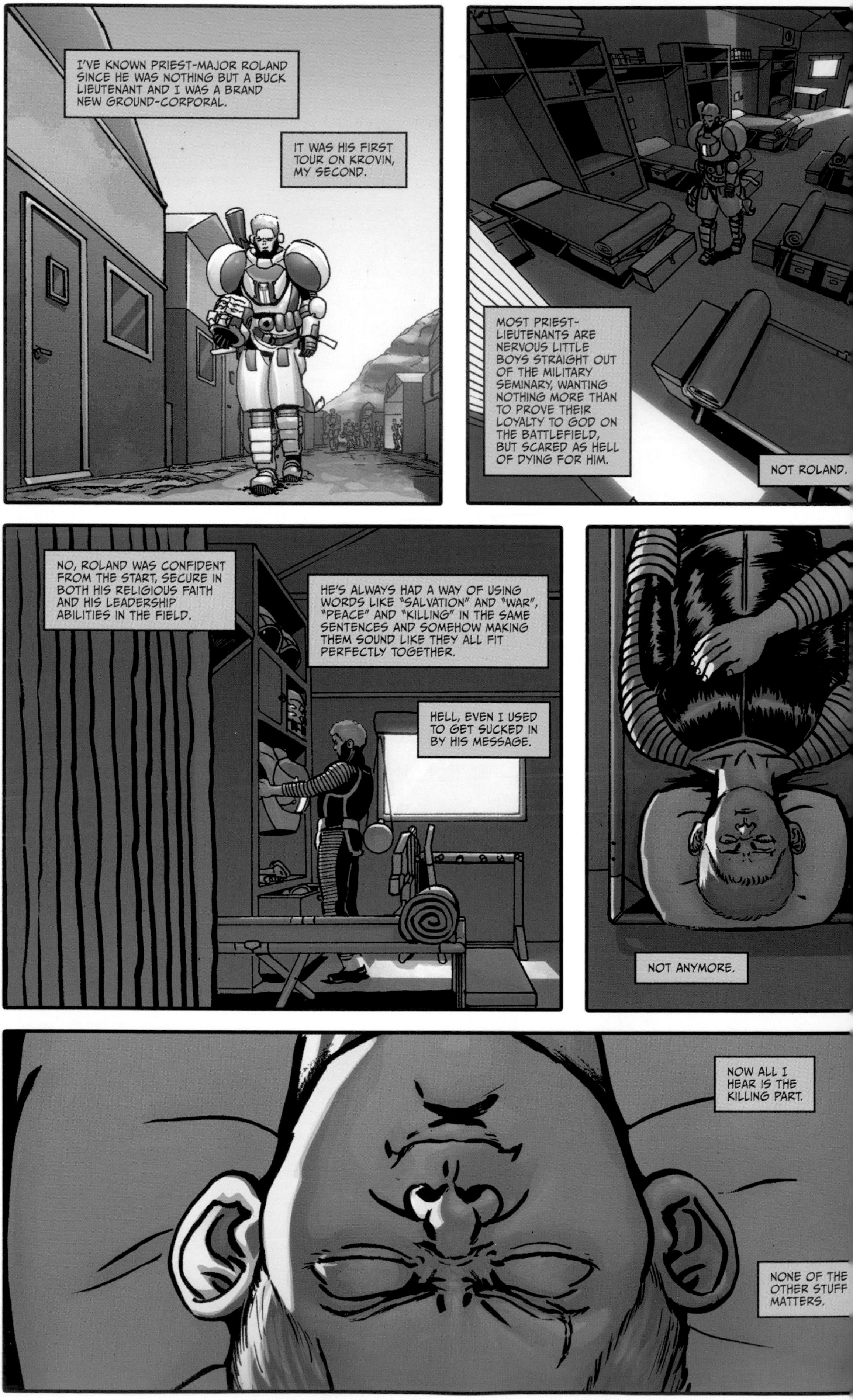
I'VE KNOWN PRIEST-MAJOR ROLAND SINCE HE WAS NOTHING BUT A BUCK LIEUTENANT AND I WAS A BRAND NEW GROUND-CORPORAL.
IT WAS HIS FIRST TOUR ON KROVIN, MY SECOND.
MOST PRIEST-LIEUTENANTS ARE NERVOUS LITTLE BOYS STRAIGHT OUT OF THE MILITARY SEMINARY, WANTING NOTHING MORE THAN TO PROVE THEIR LOYALTY TO GOD ON THE BATTLEFIELD, BUT SCARED AS HELL OF DYING FOR HIM.
NOT ROLAND.
NO, ROLAND WAS CONFIDENT FROM THE START, SECURE IN BOTH HIS RELIGIOUS FAITH AND HIS LEADERSHIP ABILITIES IN THE FIELD.
HE'S ALWAYS HAD A WAY OF USING WORDS LIKE "SALVATION" AND "WAR", "PEACE" AND "KILLING" IN THE SAME SENTENCES AND SOMEHOW MAKING THEM SOUND LIKE THEY ALL FIT PERFECTLY TOGETHER.
HELL, EVEN I USED TO GET SUCKED IN BY HIS MESSAGE.
NOT ANYMORE.
NOW ALL I HEAR IS THE KILLING PART.
NONE OF THE OTHER STUFF MATTERS.

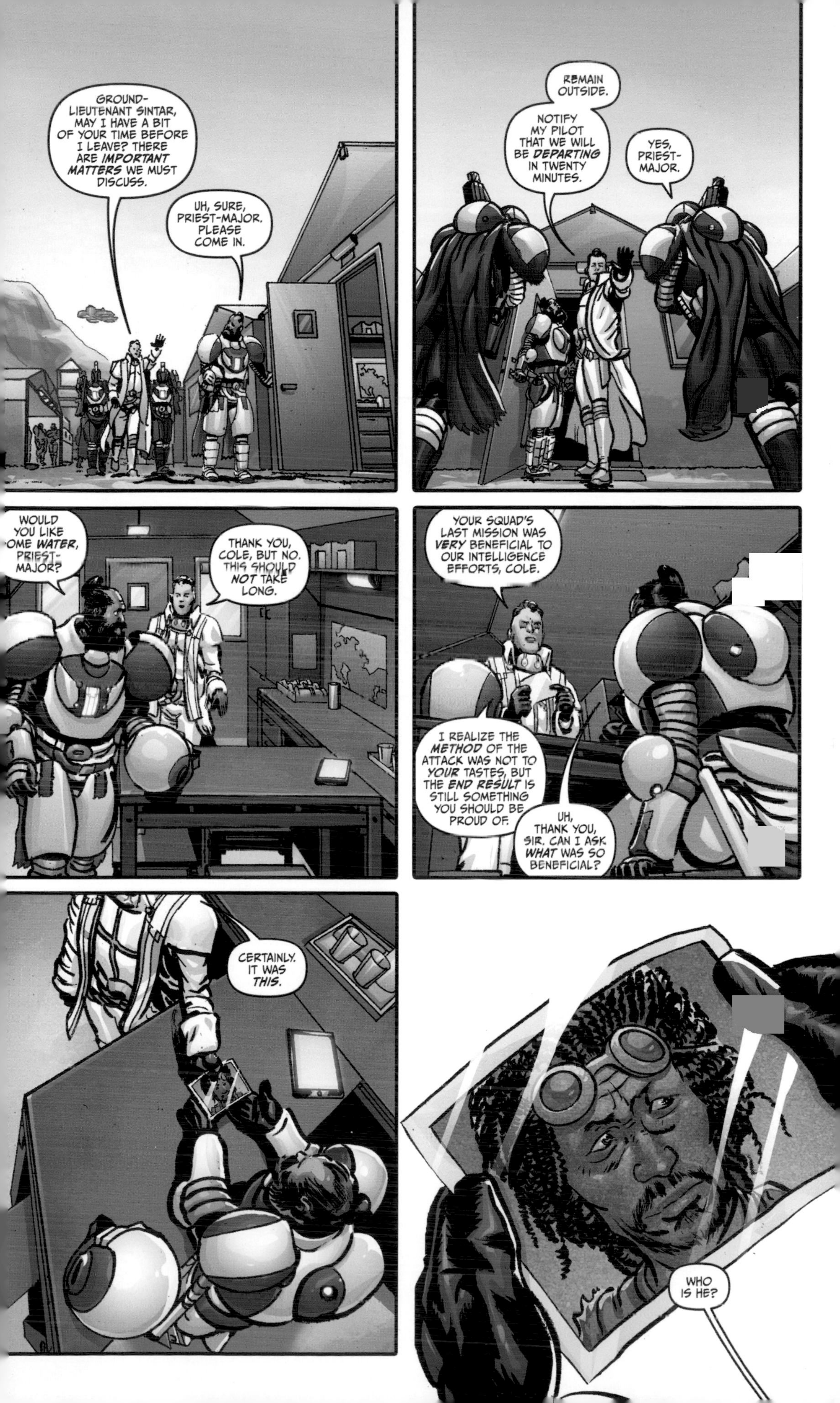
GROUND-LIEUTENANT SINTAR, MAY I HAVE A BIT OF YOUR TIME BEFORE I LEAVE? THERE ARE IMPORTANT MATTERS WE MUST DISCUSS.
UH, SURE, PRIEST-MAJOR. PLEASE COME IN.
REMAIN OUTSIDE.
NOTIFY MY PILOT THAT WE WILL BE DEPARTING IN TWENTY MINUTES.
YES, PRIEST-MAJOR.
WOULD YOU LIKE OME WATER, PRIEST-MAJOR?
THANK YOU, COLE, BUT NO. THIS SHOULD NOT TAKE LONG.
YOUR SQUAD'S LAST MISSION WAS VERY BENEFICIAL TO OUR INTELLIGENCE EFFORTS, COLE.
I REALIZE THE METHOD OF THE ATTACK WAS NOT TO YOUR TASTES, BUT THE END RESULT IS STILL SOMETHING YOU SHOULD BE PROUD OF.
UH, THANK YOU, SIR. CAN I ASK WHAT WAS SO BENEFICIAL?
CERTAINLY. IT WAS THIS.
WHO IS HE?

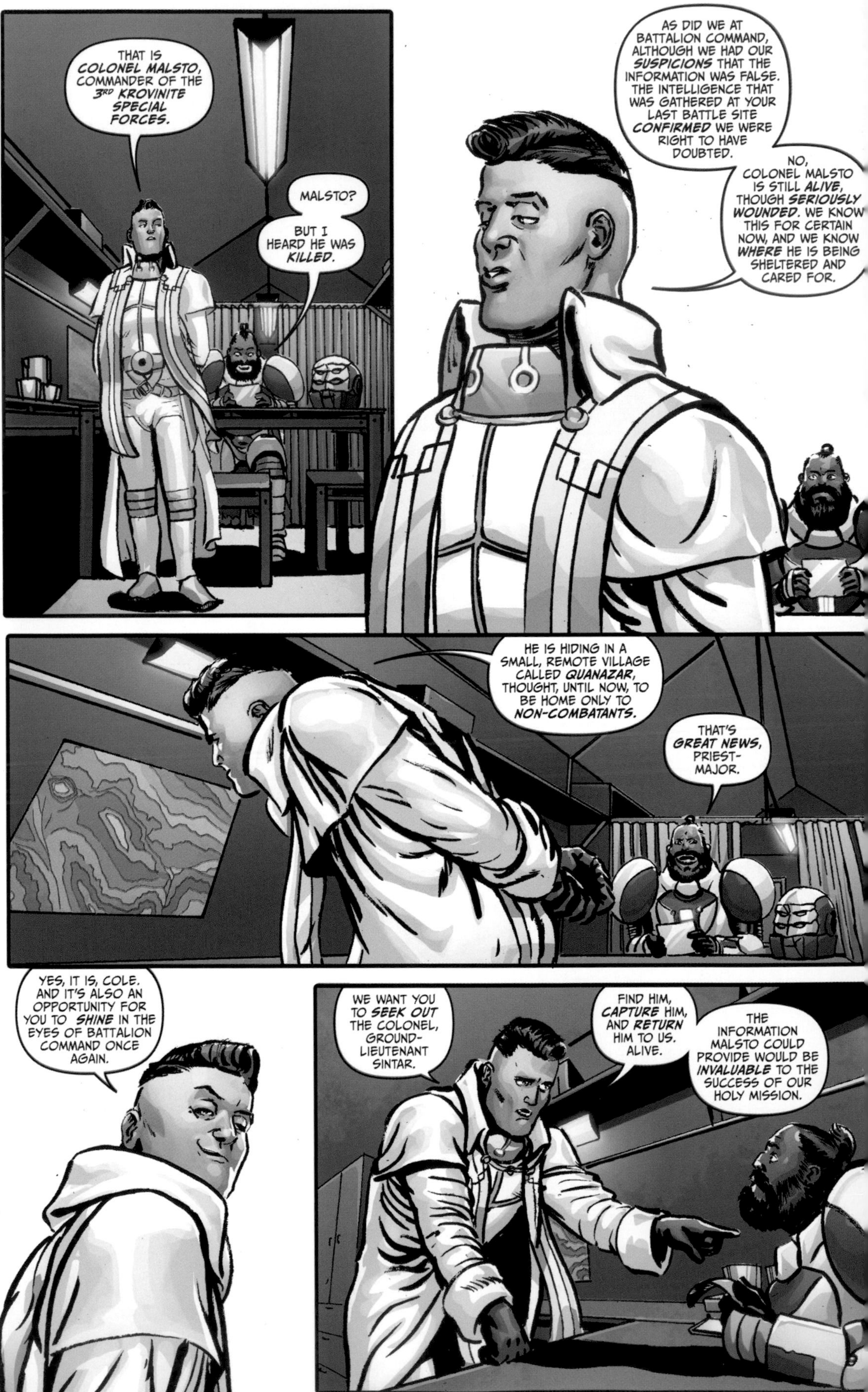

THAT IS COLONEL MALSTO, COMMANDER OF THE 3RD KROVINITE SPECIAL FORCES.
MALSTO?
BUT I HEARD HE WAS KILLED.
AS DID WE AT BATTALION COMMAND, ALTHOUGH WE HAD OUR SUSPICIONS THAT THE INFORMATION WAS FALSE. THE INTELLIGENCE THAT WAS GATHERED AT YOUR LAST BATTLE SITE CONFIRMED WE WERE RIGHT TO HAVE DOUBTED.
NO, COLONEL MALSTO IS STILL ALIVE, THOUGH SERIOUSLY WOUNDED. WE KNOW THIS FOR CERTAIN NOW, AND WE KNOW WHERE HE IS BEING SHELTERED AND CARED FOR.
HE IS HIDING IN A SMALL, REMOTE VILLAGE CALLED QUANAZAR, THOUGHT, UNTIL NOW, TO BE HOME ONLY TO NON-COMBATANTS.
THAT'S GREAT NEWS, PRIEST-MAJOR.
YES, IT IS, COLE. AND IT'S ALSO AN OPPORTUNITY FOR YOU TO SHINE IN THE EYES OF BATTALION COMMAND ONCE AGAIN.
WE WANT YOU TO SEEK OUT THE COLONEL, GROUND-LIEUTENANT SINTAR.
FIND HIM, CAPTURE HIM, AND RETURN HIM TO US. ALIVE.
THE INFORMATION MALSTO COULD PROVIDE WOULD BE INVALUABLE TO THE SUCCESS OF OUR HOLY MISSION.

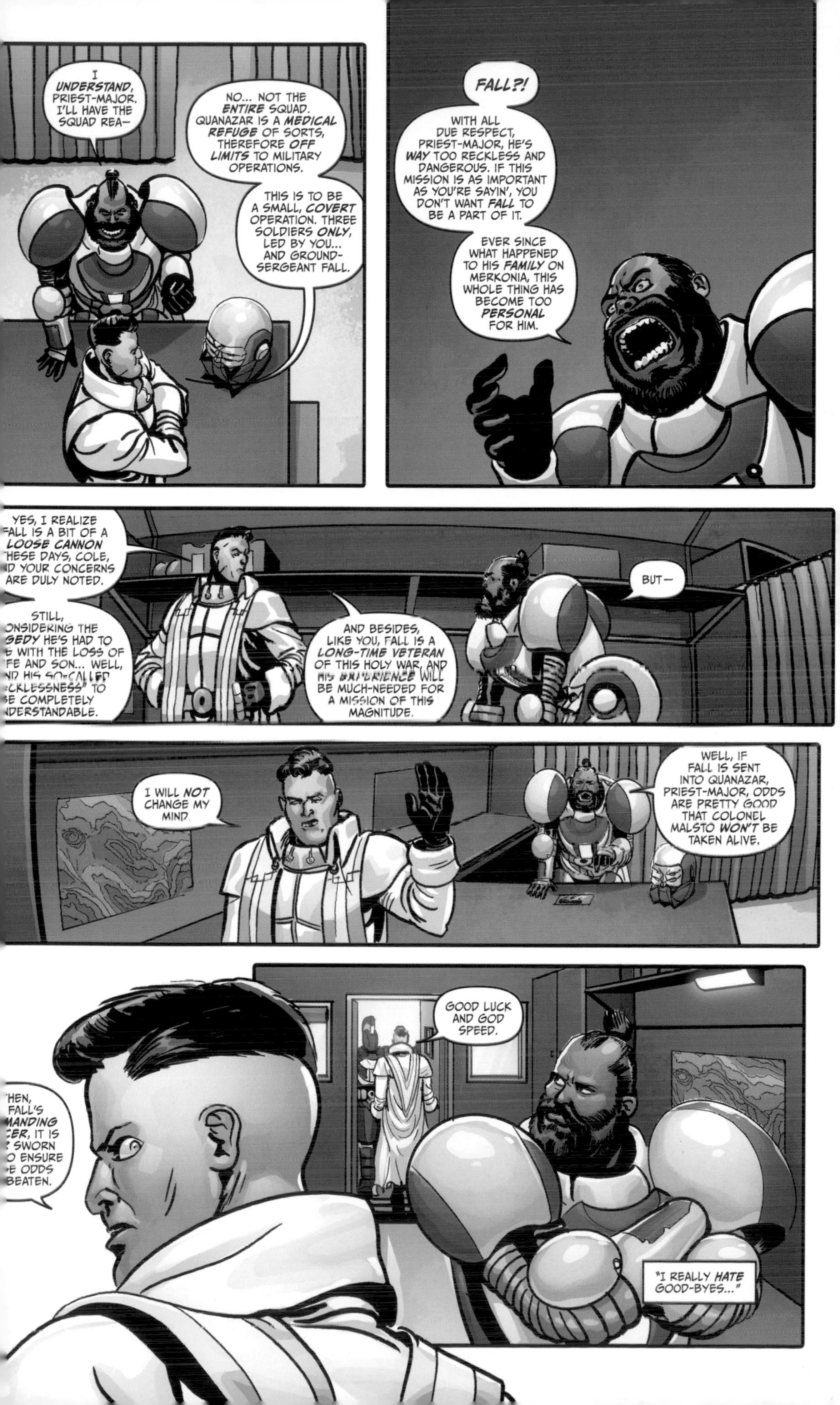

I UNDERSTAND, PRIEST-MAJOR. I'LL HAVE THE SQUAD REA—
NO... NOT THE ENTIRE SQUAD. QUANAZAR IS A MEDICAL REFUGE OF SORTS, THEREFORE OFF LIMITS TO MILITARY OPERATIONS.
THIS IS TO BE A SMALL, COVERT OPERATION. THREE SOLDIERS ONLY, LED BY YOU... AND GROUND-SERGEANT FALL.
FALL?!
WITH ALL DUE RESPECT, PRIEST-MAJOR, HE'S WAY TOO RECKLESS AND DANGEROUS. IF THIS MISSION IS AS IMPORTANT AS YOU'RE SAYIN', YOU DON'T WANT FALL TO BE A PART OF IT.
EVER SINCE WHAT HAPPENED TO HIS FAMILY ON MERKONIA, THIS WHOLE THING HAS BECOME TOO PERSONAL FOR HIM.
YES, I REALIZE FALL IS A BIT OF A LOOSE CANNON THESE DAYS, COLE, D YOUR CONCERNS ARE DULY NOTED.
STILL, ONSIDERING THE GEDY HE'S HAD TO WITH THE LOSS OF FE AND SON... WELL, ND HIS SO-CALLED CKLESSNESS" TO E COMPLETELY DERSTANDABLE.
AND BESIDES, LIKE YOU, FALL IS A LONG-TIME VETERAN OF THIS HOLY WAR, AND HIS EXPERIENCE WILL BE MUCH-NEEDED FOR A MISSION OF THIS MAGNITUDE.
BUT—
I WILL NOT CHANGE MY MIND.
WELL, IF FALL IS SENT INTO QUANAZAR, PRIEST-MAJOR, ODDS ARE PRETTY GOOD THAT COLONEL MALSTO WON'T BE TAKEN ALIVE.
HEN, FALL'S MANDING CER, IT IS SWORN O ENSURE E ODDS BEATEN.
GOOD LUCK AND GOD SPEED.
"I REALLY HATE GOOD-BYES..."

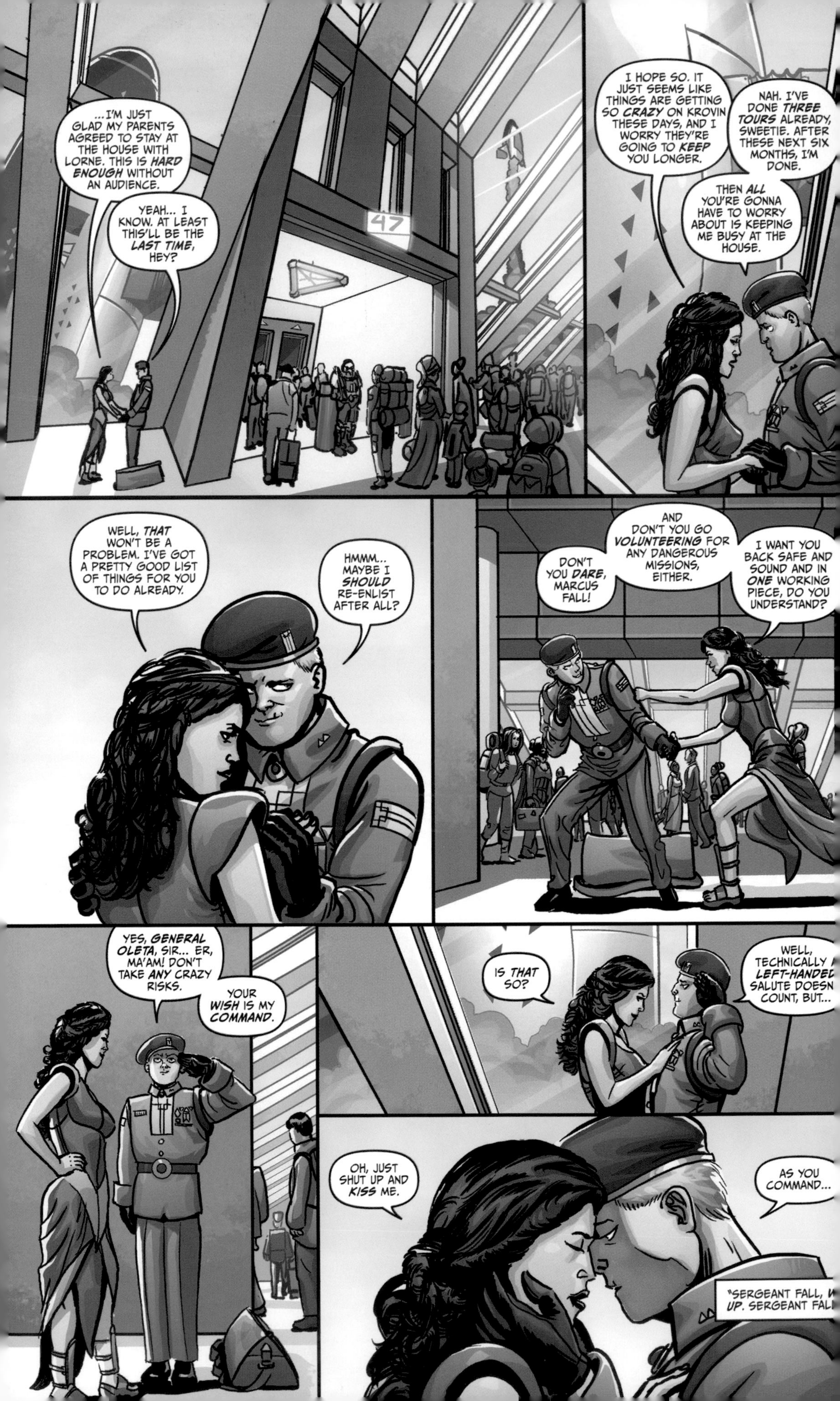

...I'M JUST GLAD MY PARENTS AGREED TO STAY AT THE HOUSE WITH LORNE. THIS IS HARD ENOUGH WITHOUT AN AUDIENCE.
YEAH... I KNOW. AT LEAST THIS'LL BE THE LAST TIME, HEY?
47
I HOPE SO. IT JUST SEEMS LIKE THINGS ARE GETTING SO CRAZY ON KROVIN THESE DAYS, AND I WORRY THEY'RE GOING TO KEEP YOU LONGER.
NAH. I'VE DONE THREE TOURS ALREADY, SWEETIE. AFTER THESE NEXT SIX MONTHS, I'M DONE.
THEN ALL YOU'RE GONNA HAVE TO WORRY ABOUT IS KEEPING ME BUSY AT THE HOUSE.
WELL, THAT WON'T BE A PROBLEM. I'VE GOT A PRETTY GOOD LIST OF THINGS FOR YOU TO DO ALREADY.
HMMM... MAYBE I SHOULD RE-ENLIST AFTER ALL?
DON'T YOU DARE, MARCUS FALL!
AND DON'T YOU GO VOLUNTEERING FOR ANY DANGEROUS MISSIONS, EITHER.
I WANT YOU BACK SAFE AND SOUND AND IN ONE WORKING PIECE, DO YOU UNDERSTAND?
YES, GENERAL OLETA, SIR... ER, MA'AM! DON'T TAKE ANY CRAZY RISKS.
YOUR WISH IS MY COMMAND.
IS THAT SO?
WELL, TECHNICALLY
LEFT-HANDED SALUTE DOESN
COUNT, BUT...
OH, JUST SHUT UP AND KISS ME.
AS YOU COMMAND...
"SERGEANT FALL,
UP. SERGEANT FAL

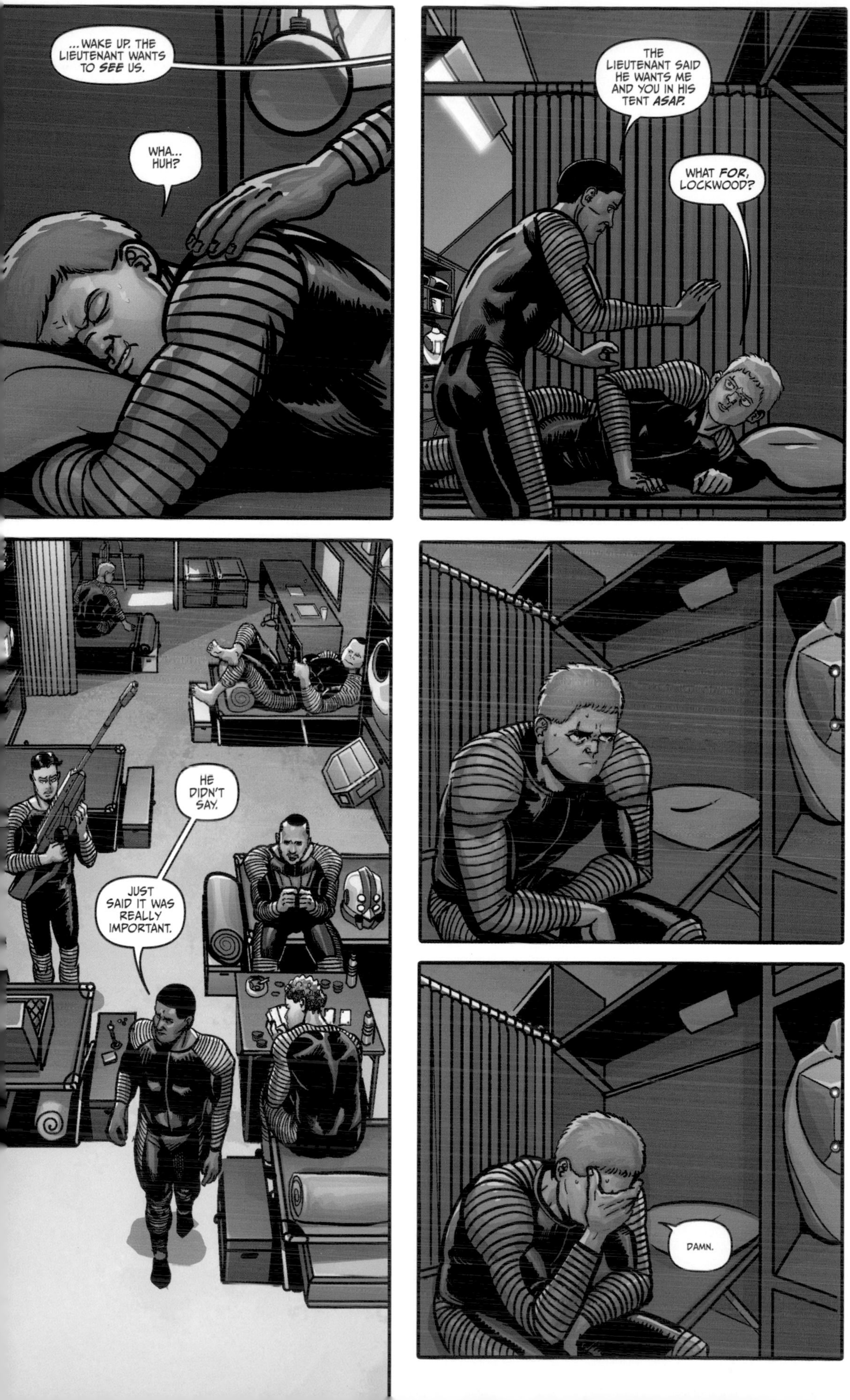
...WAKE UP. THE LIEUTENANT WANTS TO SEE US.
WHA... HUH?
THE LIEUTENANT SAID HE WANTS ME AND YOU IN HIS TENT ASAP.
WHAT FOR, LOCKWOOD?
HE DIDN'T SAY.
JUST SAID IT WAS REALLY IMPORTANT.
DAMN.

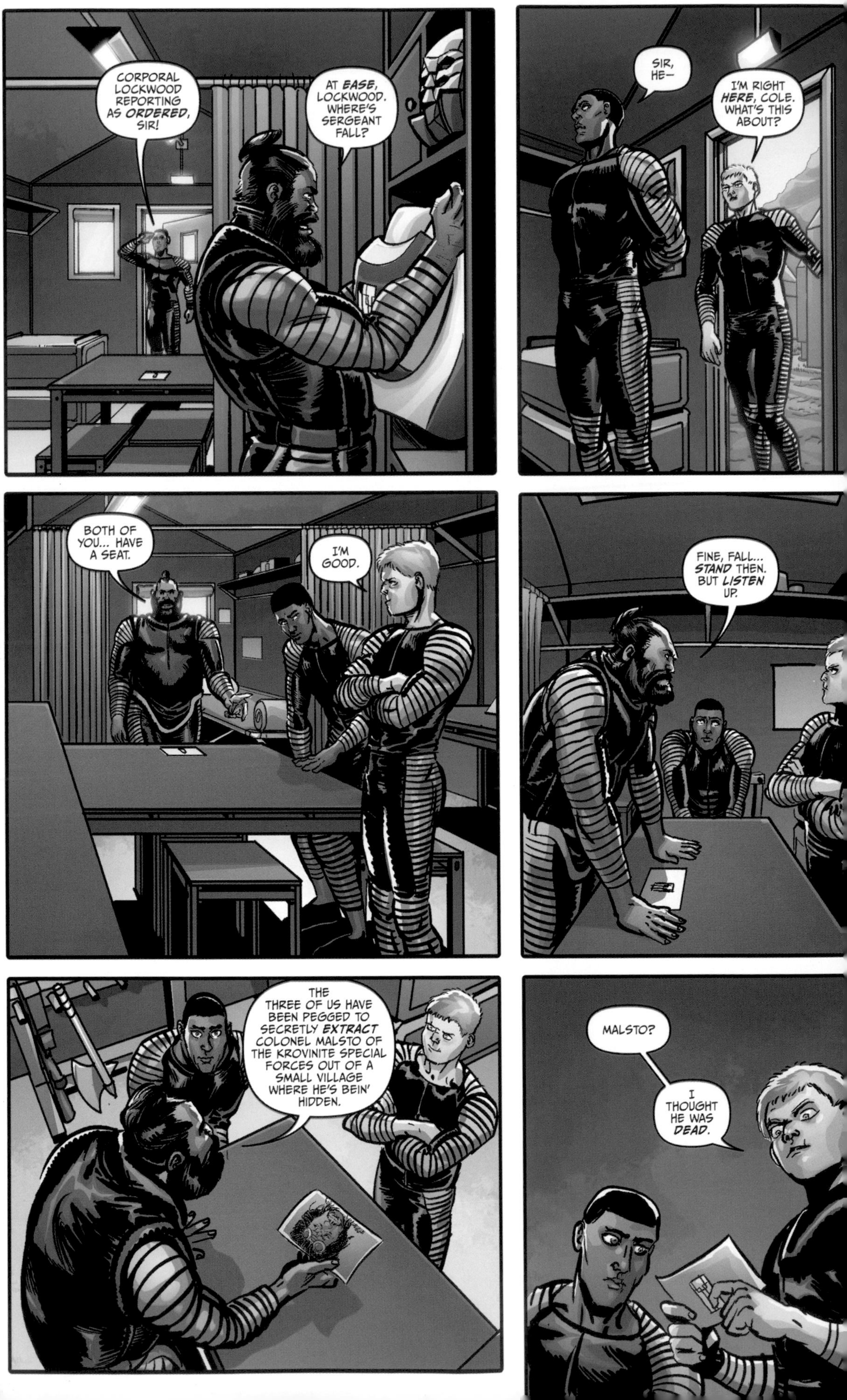
CORPORAL LOCKWOOD REPORTING AS ORDERED, SIR!
AT EASE, LOCKWOOD. WHERE'S SERGEANT FALL?
SIR, HE—
I'M RIGHT HERE, COLE. WHAT'S THIS ABOUT?
BOTH OF YOU... HAVE A SEAT.
I'M GOOD.
FINE, FALL... STAND THEN. BUT LISTEN UP.
THE THREE OF US HAVE BEEN PEGGED TO SECRETLY EXTRACT COLONEL MALSTO OF THE KROVINITE SPECIAL FORCES OUT OF A SMALL VILLAGE WHERE HE'S BEIN' HIDDEN.
MALSTO?
I THOUGHT HE WAS DEAD.

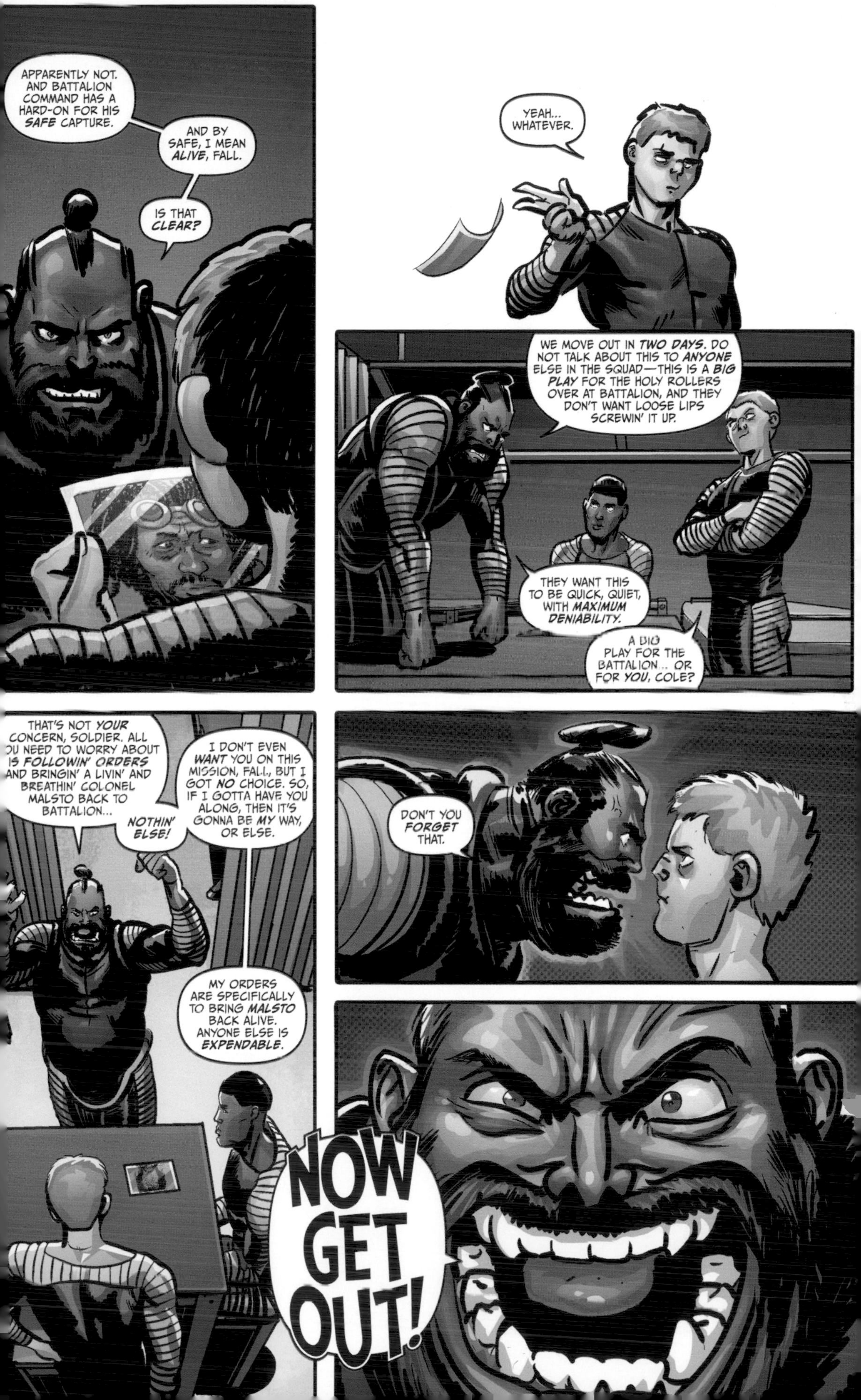
APPARENTLY NOT. AND BATTALION COMMAND HAS A HARD-ON FOR HIS SAFE CAPTURE.
AND BY SAFE, I MEAN ALIVE, FALL.
IS THAT CLEAR?
YEAH... WHATEVER.
WE MOVE OUT IN TWO DAYS. DO NOT TALK ABOUT THIS TO ANYONE ELSE IN THE SQUAD—THIS IS A BIG PLAY FOR THE HOLY ROLLERS OVER AT BATTALION, AND THEY DON'T WANT LOOSE LIPS SCREWIN' IT UP.
THEY WANT THIS TO BE QUICK, QUIET, WITH MAXIMUM DENIABILITY.
A BIG PLAY FOR THE BATTALION... OR FOR YOU, COLE?
THAT'S NOT YOUR CONCERN, SOLDIER. ALL YOU NEED TO WORRY ABOUT IS FOLLOWIN' ORDERS AND BRINGIN' A LIVIN' AND BREATHIN' COLONEL MALSTO BACK TO BATTALION...
NOTHIN' ELSE!
I DON'T EVEN WANT YOU ON THIS MISSION, FALL, BUT I GOT NO CHOICE. SO, IF I GOTTA HAVE YOU ALONG, THEN IT'S GONNA BE MY WAY, OR ELSE.
MY ORDERS ARE SPECIFICALLY TO BRING MALSTO BACK ALIVE. ANYONE ELSE IS EXPENDABLE.
DON'T YOU FORGET THAT.
NOW GET OUT!

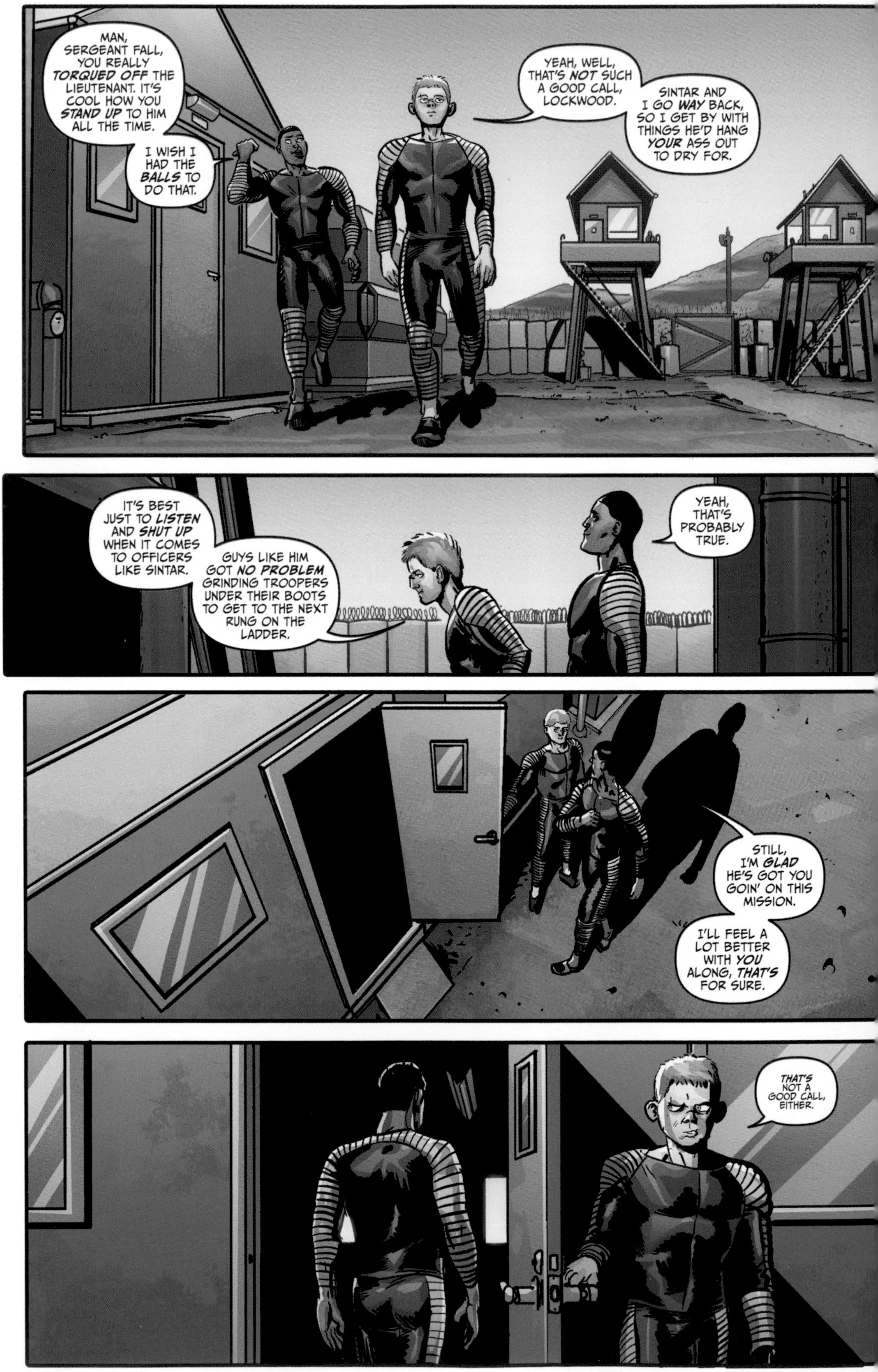
MAN, SERGEANT FALL, YOU REALLY TORQUED OFF THE LIEUTENANT. IT'S COOL HOW YOU STAND UP TO HIM ALL THE TIME.
I WISH I HAD THE BALLS TO DO THAT.
YEAH, WELL, THAT'S NOT SUCH A GOOD CALL, LOCKWOOD.
SINTAR AND I GO WAY BACK, SO I GET BY WITH THINGS HE'D HANG YOUR ASS OUT TO DRY FOR.
IT'S BEST JUST TO LISTEN AND SHUT UP WHEN IT COMES TO OFFICERS LIKE SINTAR.
GUYS LIKE HIM GOT NO PROBLEM GRINDING TROOPERS UNDER THEIR BOOTS TO GET TO THE NEXT RUNG ON THE LADDER.
YEAH, THAT'S PROBABLY TRUE.
STILL, I'M GLAD HE'S GOT YOU GOIN' ON THIS MISSION.
I'LL FEEL A LOT BETTER WITH YOU ALONG, THAT'S FOR SURE.
THAT'S NOT A GOOD CALL, EITHER.

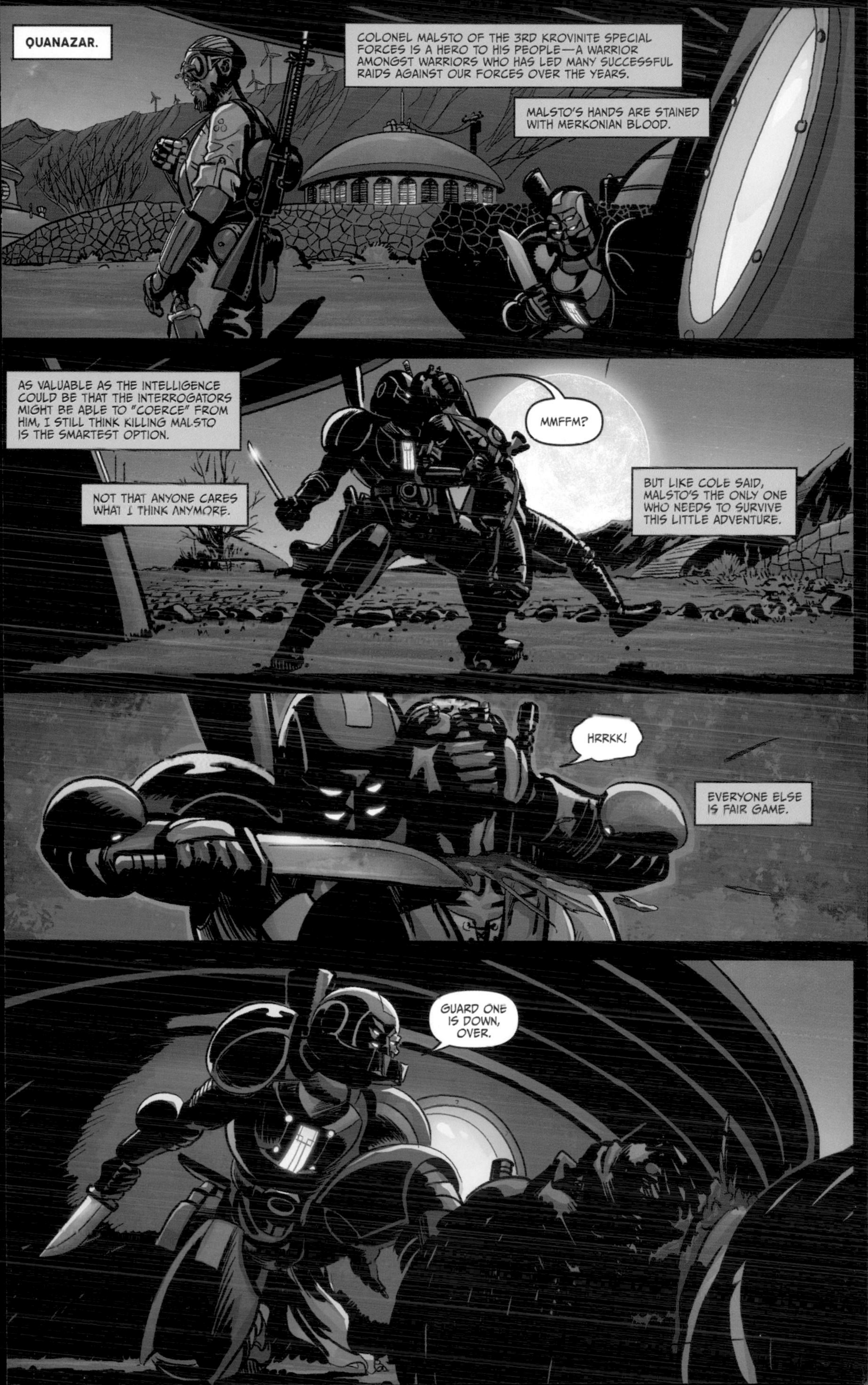
QUANAZAR.
COLONEL MALSTO OF THE 3RD KROVINITE SPECIAL FORCES IS A HERO TO HIS PEOPLE—A WARRIOR AMONGST WARRIORS WHO HAS LED MANY SUCCESSFUL RAIDS AGAINST OUR FORCES OVER THE YEARS.
MALSTO'S HANDS ARE STAINED WITH MERKONIAN BLOOD.
AS VALUABLE AS THE INTELLIGENCE COULD BE THAT THE INTERROGATORS MIGHT BE ABLE TO "COERCE" FROM HIM, I STILL THINK KILLING MALSTO IS THE SMARTEST OPTION.
MMFFM?
NOT THAT ANYONE CARES WHAT I THINK ANYMORE.
BUT LIKE COLE SAID, MALSTO'S THE ONLY ONE WHO NEEDS TO SURVIVE THIS LITTLE ADVENTURE.
HRRKK!
EVERYONE ELSE IS FAIR GAME.
GUARD ONE IS DOWN, OVER.

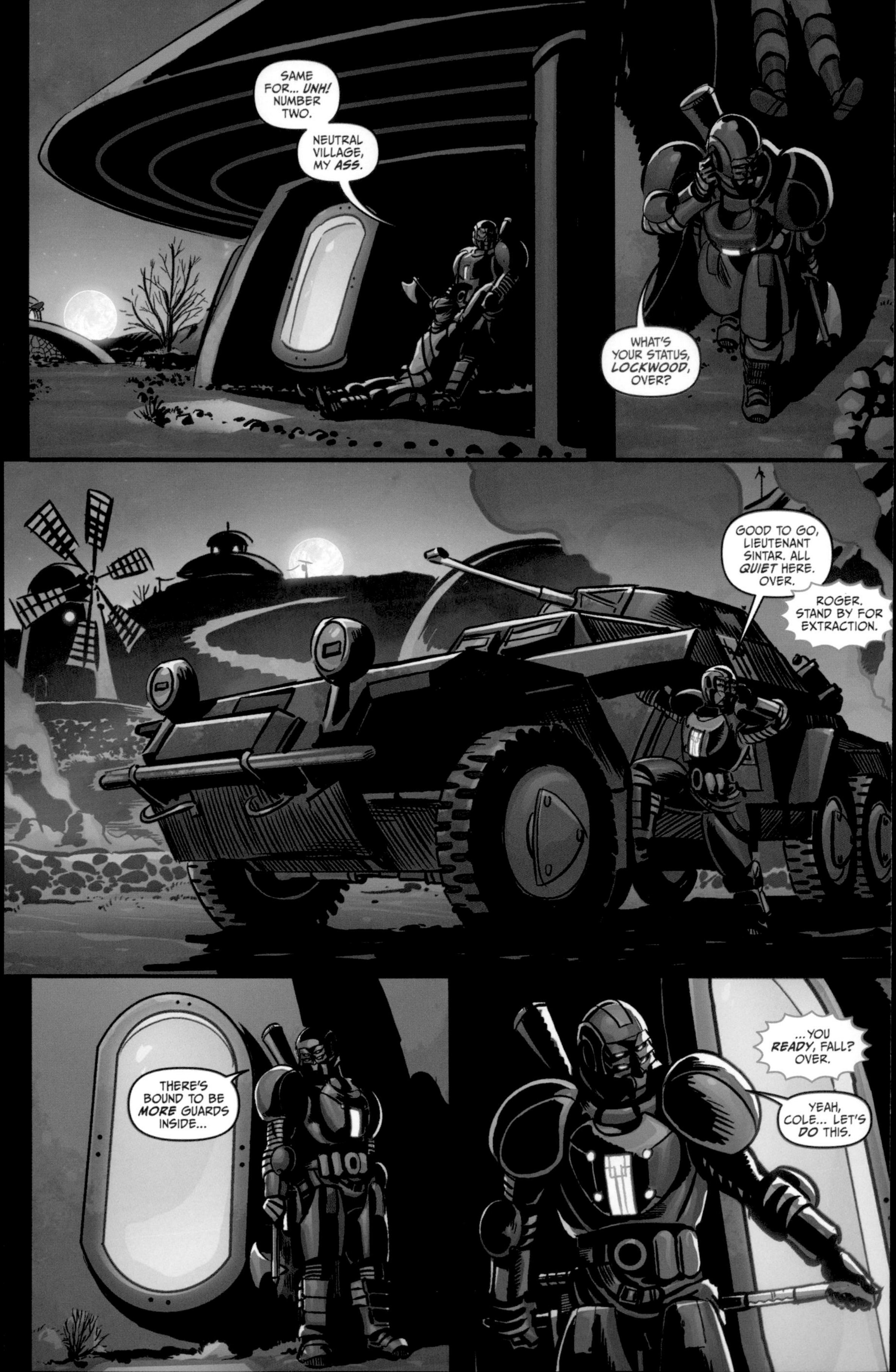
SAME FOR... UNH! NUMBER TWO.
NEUTRAL VILLAGE, MY ASS.
WHAT'S YOUR STATUS, LOCKWOOD, OVER?
GOOD TO GO, LIEUTENANT SINTAR. ALL QUIET HERE. OVER.
ROGER. STAND BY FOR EXTRACTION.
THERE'S BOUND TO BE MORE GUARDS INSIDE...
...YOU READY, FALL? OVER.
YEAH, COLE... LET'S DO THIS.

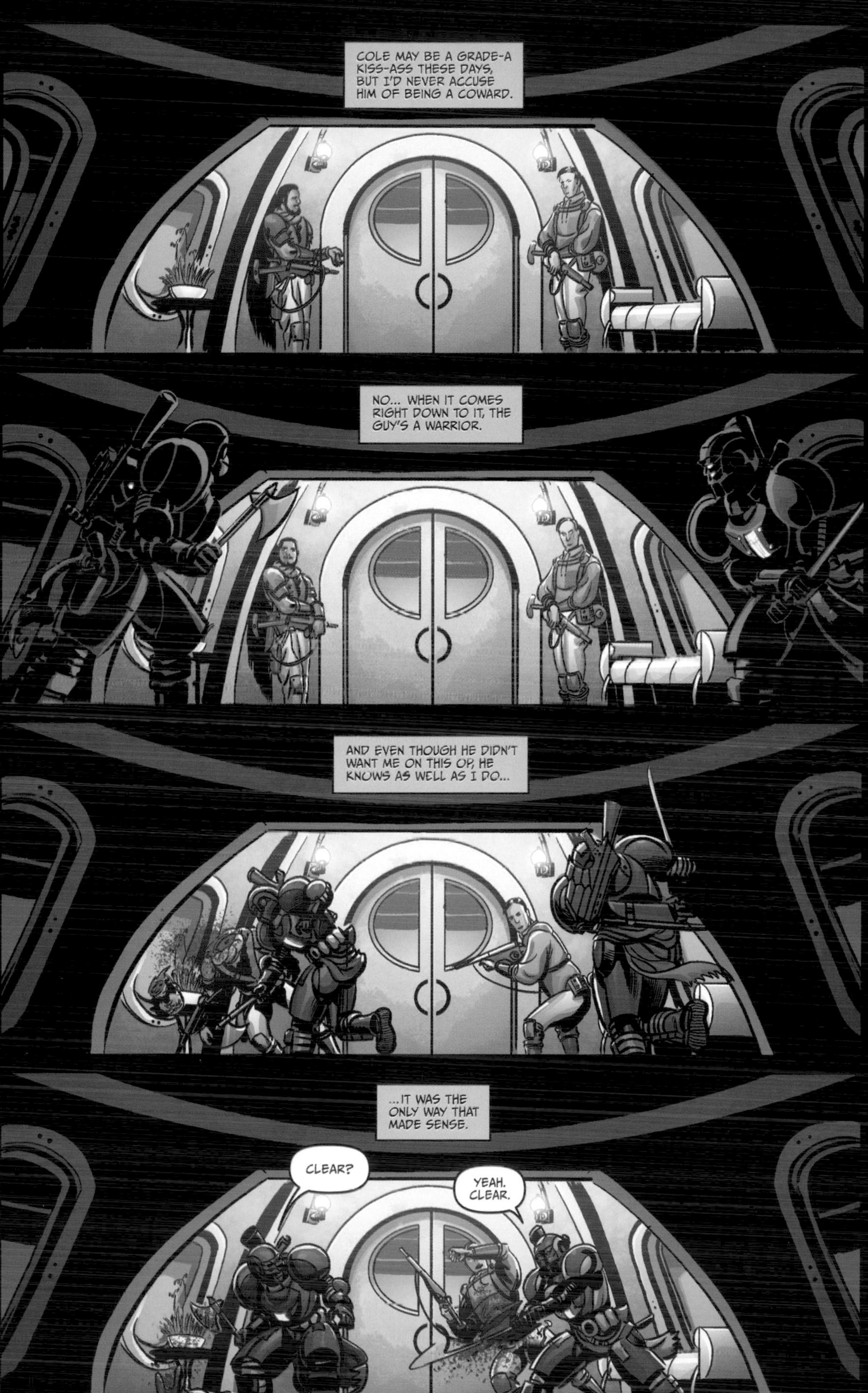
COLE MAY BE A GRADE-A KISS-ASS THESE DAYS, BUT I'D NEVER ACCUSE HIM OF BEING A COWARD.
NO... WHEN IT COMES RIGHT DOWN TO IT, THE GUY'S A WARRIOR.
AND EVEN THOUGH HE DIDN'T WANT ME ON THIS OP, HE KNOWS AS WELL AS I DO...
...IT WAS THE ONLY WAY THAT MADE SENSE.
CLEAR?
YEAH. CLEAR.

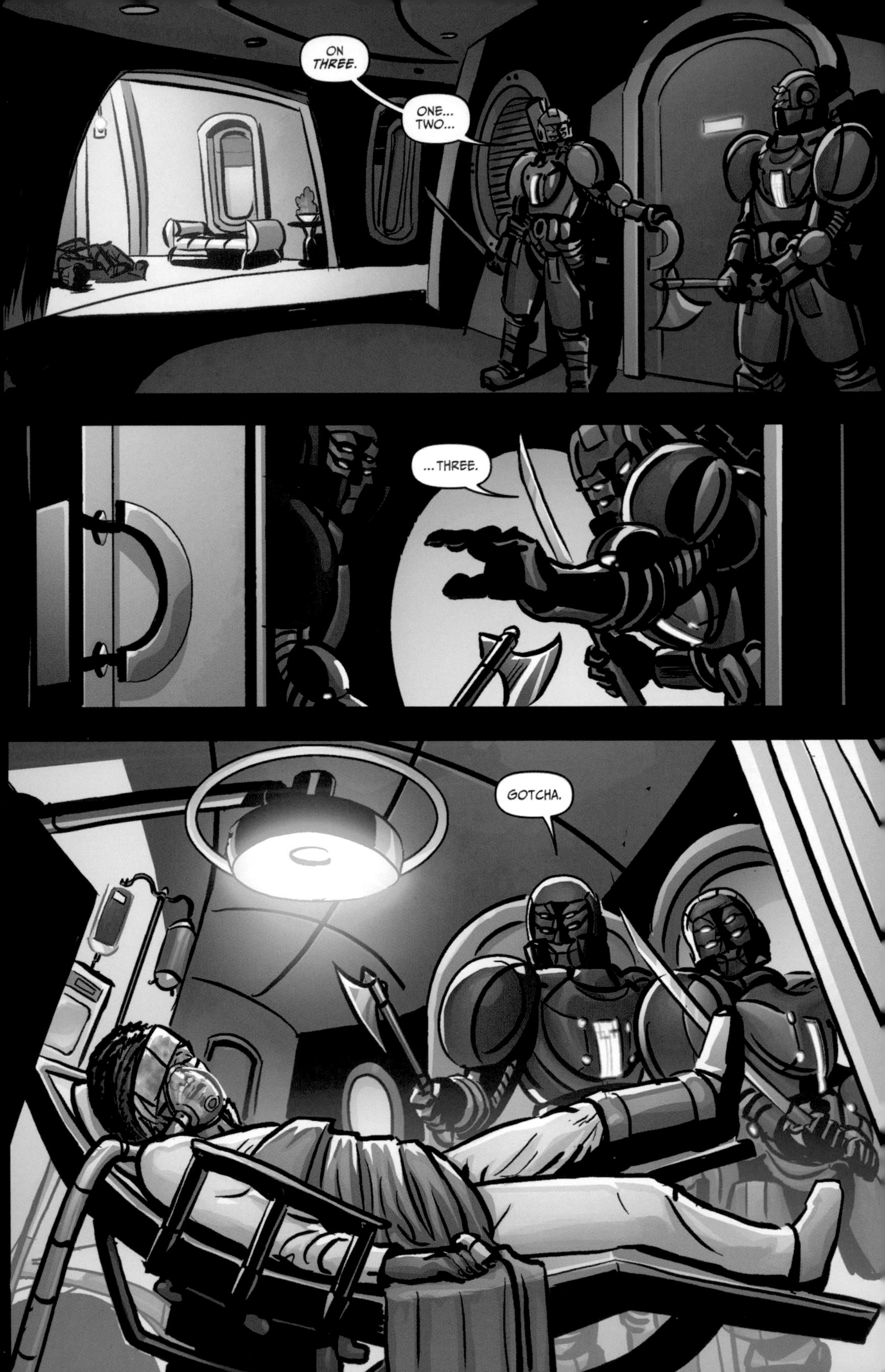
ON *THREE*.
ONE... TWO...
...THREE.
GOTCHA.

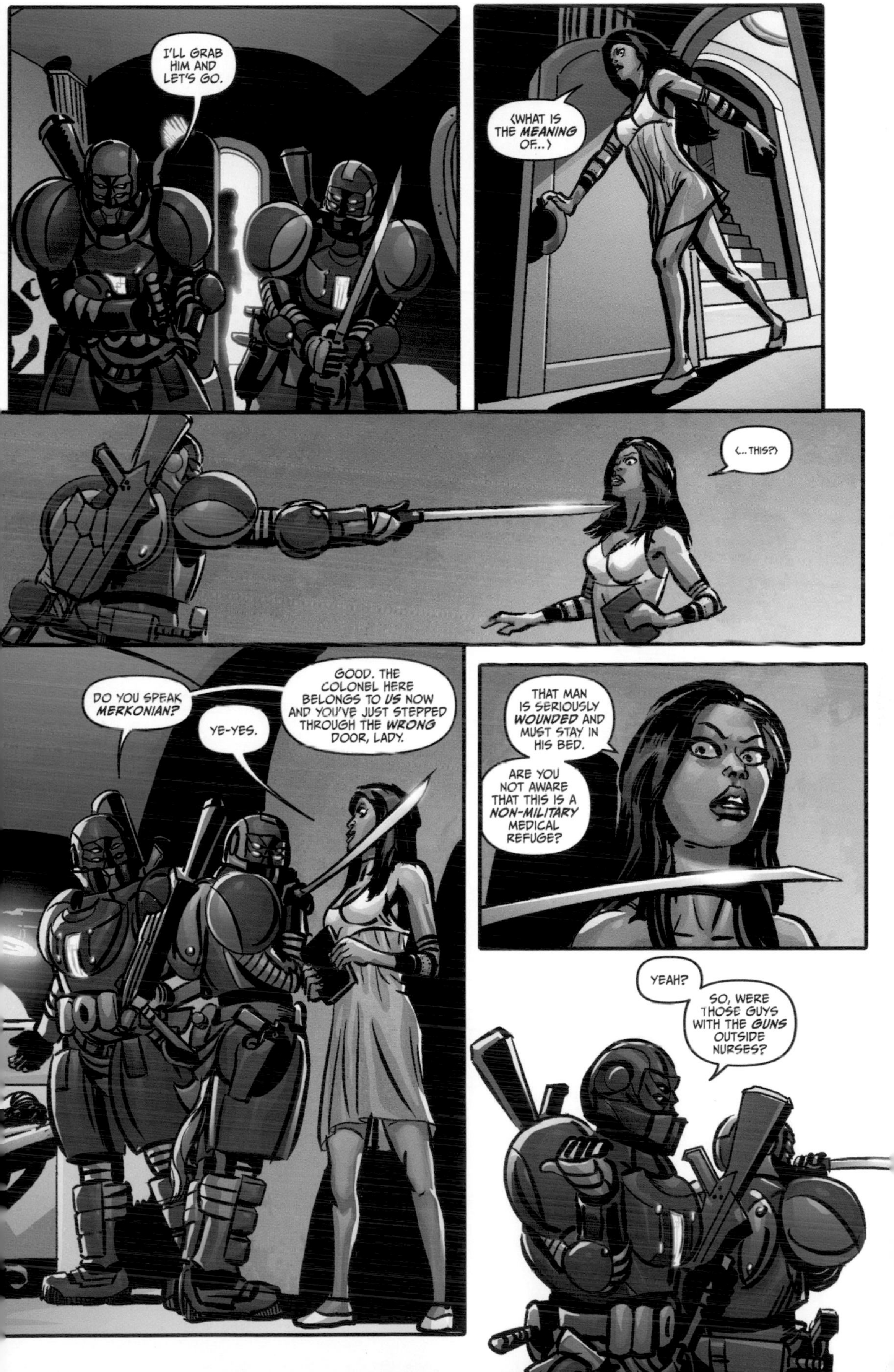
I'LL GRAB HIM AND LET'S GO.
⟨WHAT IS THE MEANING OF...⟩
⟨...THIS?⟩
DO YOU SPEAK MERKONIAN?
YE-YES.
GOOD. THE COLONEL HERE BELONGS TO US NOW AND YOU'VE JUST STEPPED THROUGH THE WRONG DOOR, LADY.
THAT MAN IS SERIOUSLY WOUNDED AND MUST STAY IN HIS BED.
ARE YOU NOT AWARE THAT THIS IS A NON-MILITARY MEDICAL REFUGE?
YEAH?
SO, WERE THOSE GUYS WITH THE GUNS OUTSIDE NURSES?

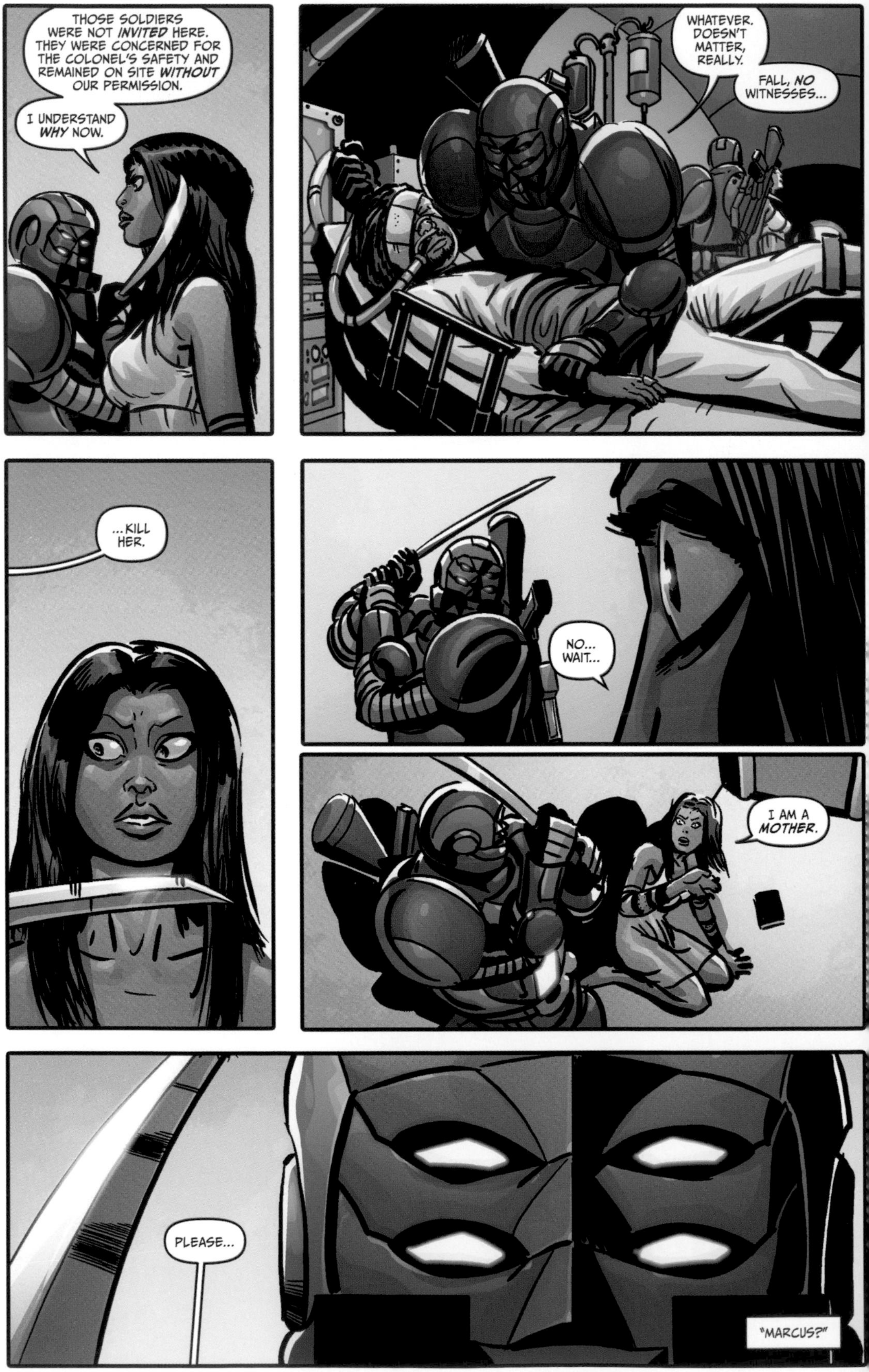
THOSE SOLDIERS WERE NOT INVITED HERE. THEY WERE CONCERNED FOR THE COLONEL'S SAFETY AND REMAINED ON SITE WITHOUT OUR PERMISSION.
I UNDERSTAND WHY NOW.
WHATEVER. DOESN'T MATTER, REALLY.
FALL, NO WITNESSES...
...KILL HER.
NO... WAIT...
I AM A MOTHER.
PLEASE...
"MARCUS?"

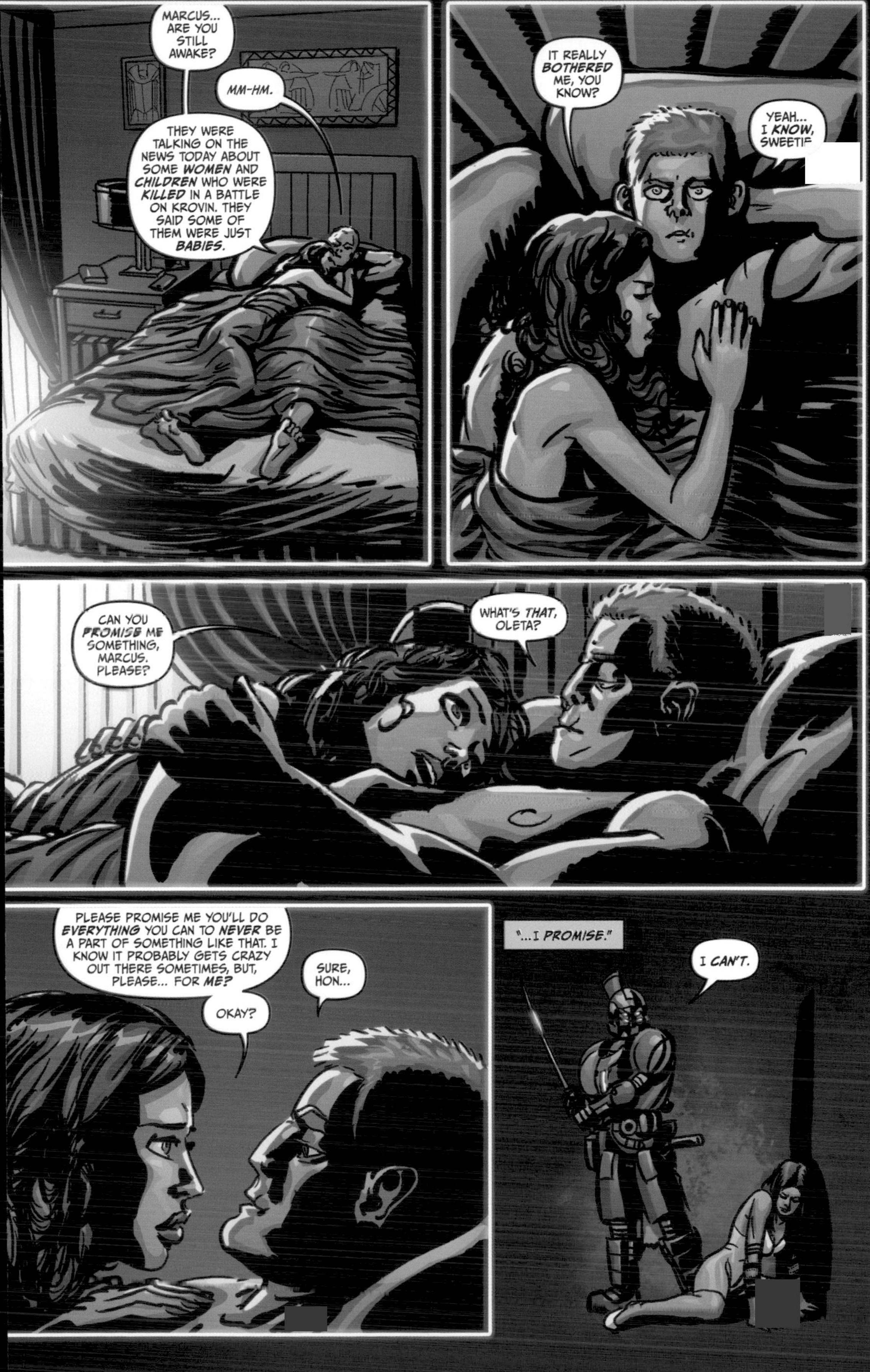
MARCUS... ARE YOU STILL AWAKE?
MM-HM.
THEY WERE TALKING ON THE NEWS TODAY ABOUT SOME WOMEN AND CHILDREN WHO WERE KILLED IN A BATTLE ON KROVIN. THEY SAID SOME OF THEM WERE JUST BABIES.
IT REALLY BOTHERED ME, YOU KNOW?
YEAH... I KNOW, SWEETI
CAN YOU PROMISE ME SOMETHING, MARCUS. PLEASE?
WHAT'S THAT, OLETA?
PLEASE PROMISE ME YOU'LL DO EVERYTHING YOU CAN TO NEVER BE A PART OF SOMETHING LIKE THAT. I KNOW IT PROBABLY GETS CRAZY OUT THERE SOMETIMES, BUT, PLEASE... FOR ME?
OKAY?
SURE, HON...
"...I PROMISE."
I CAN'T.

GODDAMMIT, FALL! WE CAN'T LEAVE *ANY* WITNESSES.

KILL HER AND LET'S GO! THAT'S AN *ORDER!*

NO, COLE. I *WON'T* DO IT. I...

...I JUST WON'T.

WHAT THE *HELL* IS YOUR PROBLEM? ALL YOU'VE BEEN LIVIN' FOR LATELY IS *KILLIN'* KROVINITES.

WELL, *SHE'S* ONE, GODDAMMIT... *KILL HER!*

NO.

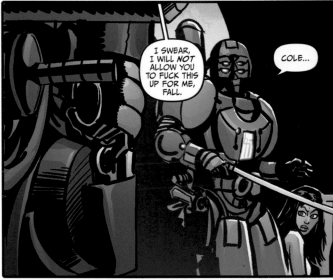

I SWEAR, I WILL *NOT* ALLOW YOU TO FUCK THIS UP FOR ME, FALL.

COLE...

AAGK!

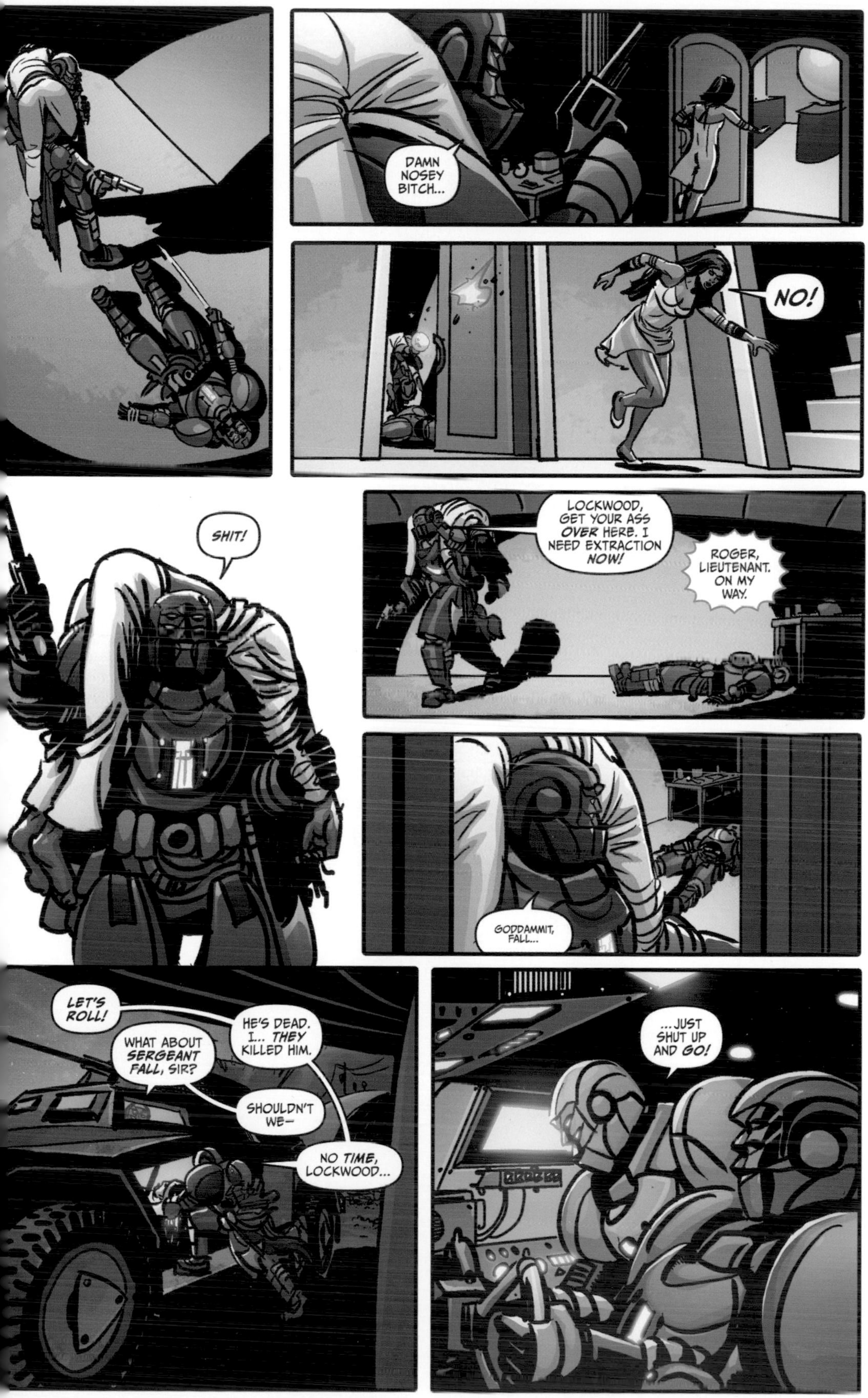
DAMN NOSEY BITCH...
NO!
SHIT!
LOCKWOOD, GET YOUR ASS OVER HERE. I NEED EXTRACTION NOW!
ROGER, LIEUTENANT. ON MY WAY.
GODDAMMIT, FALL...
LET'S ROLL!
WHAT ABOUT SERGEANT FALL, SIR?
HE'S DEAD. I... THEY KILLED HIM.
SHOULDN'T WE–
NO TIME, LOCKWOOD...
...JUST SHUT UP AND GO!

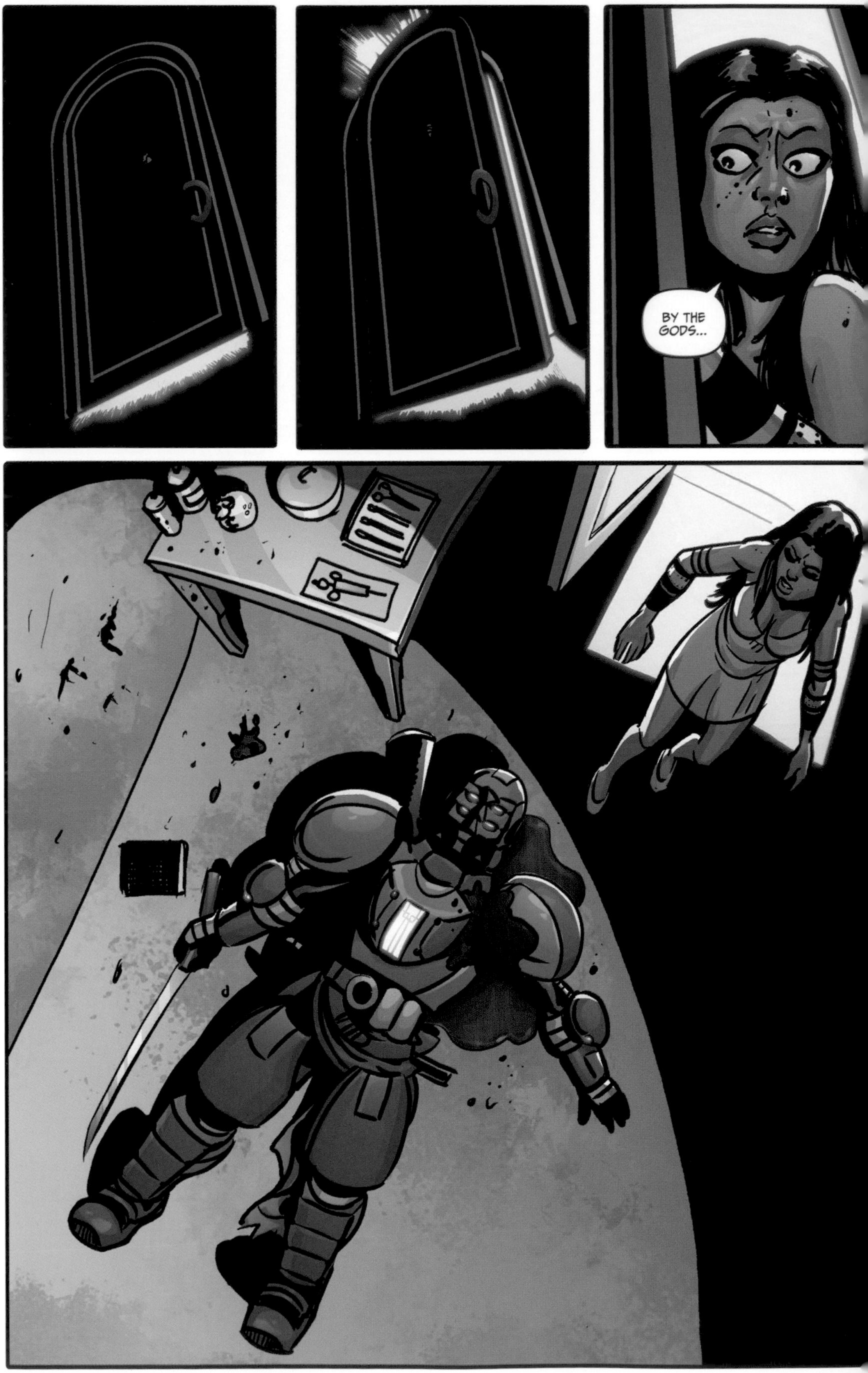
BY THE GODS...

"IN PEACE, SONS BURY THEIR FATHERS.

IN WAR, FATHERS BURY THEIR SONS."

– *HERODOTUS*

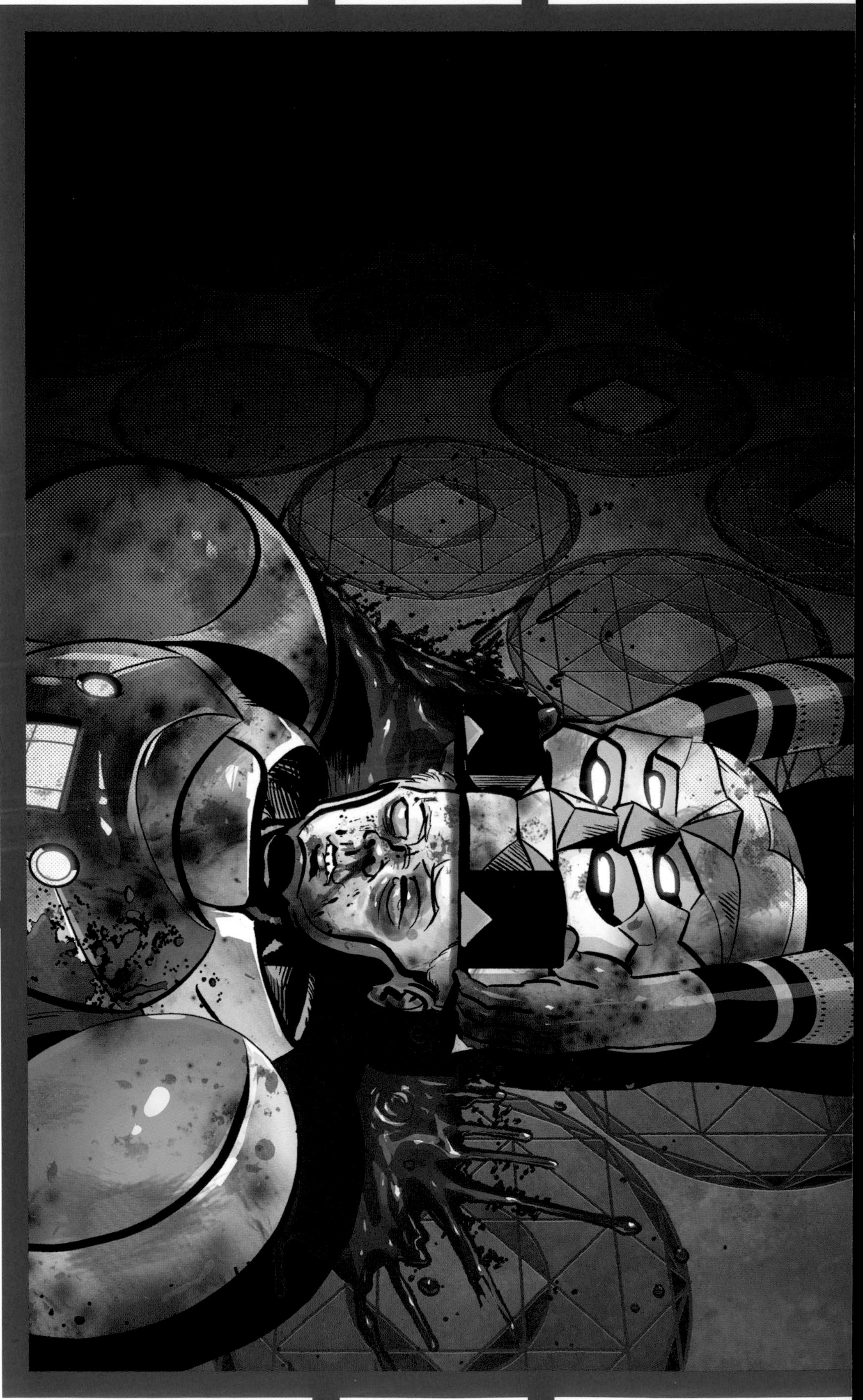

Art by Casey Maloney, Colors by Dusty Yee

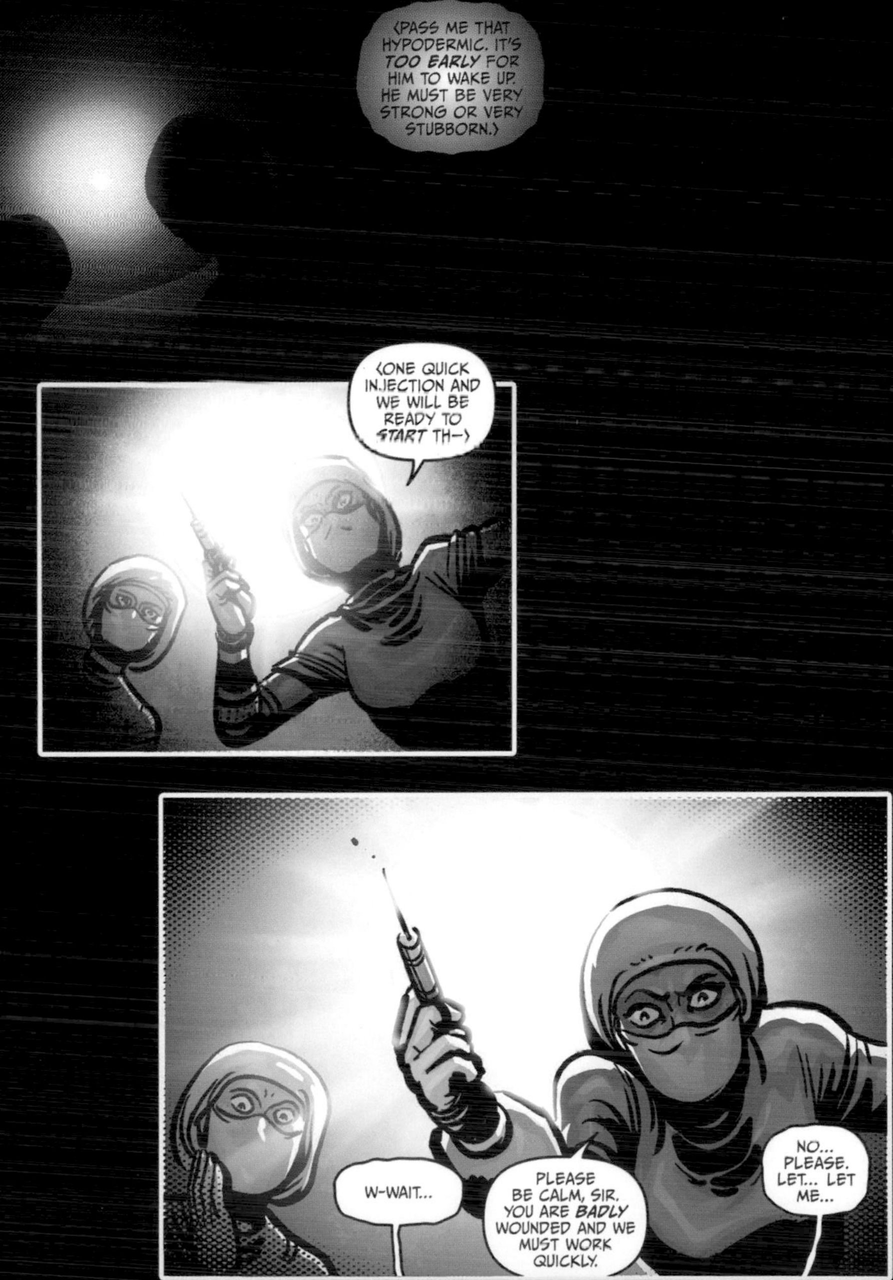

<PASS ME THAT HYPODERMIC. IT'S *TOO EARLY* FOR HIM TO WAKE UP. HE MUST BE VERY STRONG OR VERY STUBBORN.>
<ONE QUICK INJECTION AND WE WILL BE READY TO *START* TH–>
W-WAIT...
PLEASE BE CALM, SIR. YOU ARE *BADLY* WOUNDED AND WE MUST WORK QUICKLY.
NO... PLEASE. LET... LET ME...

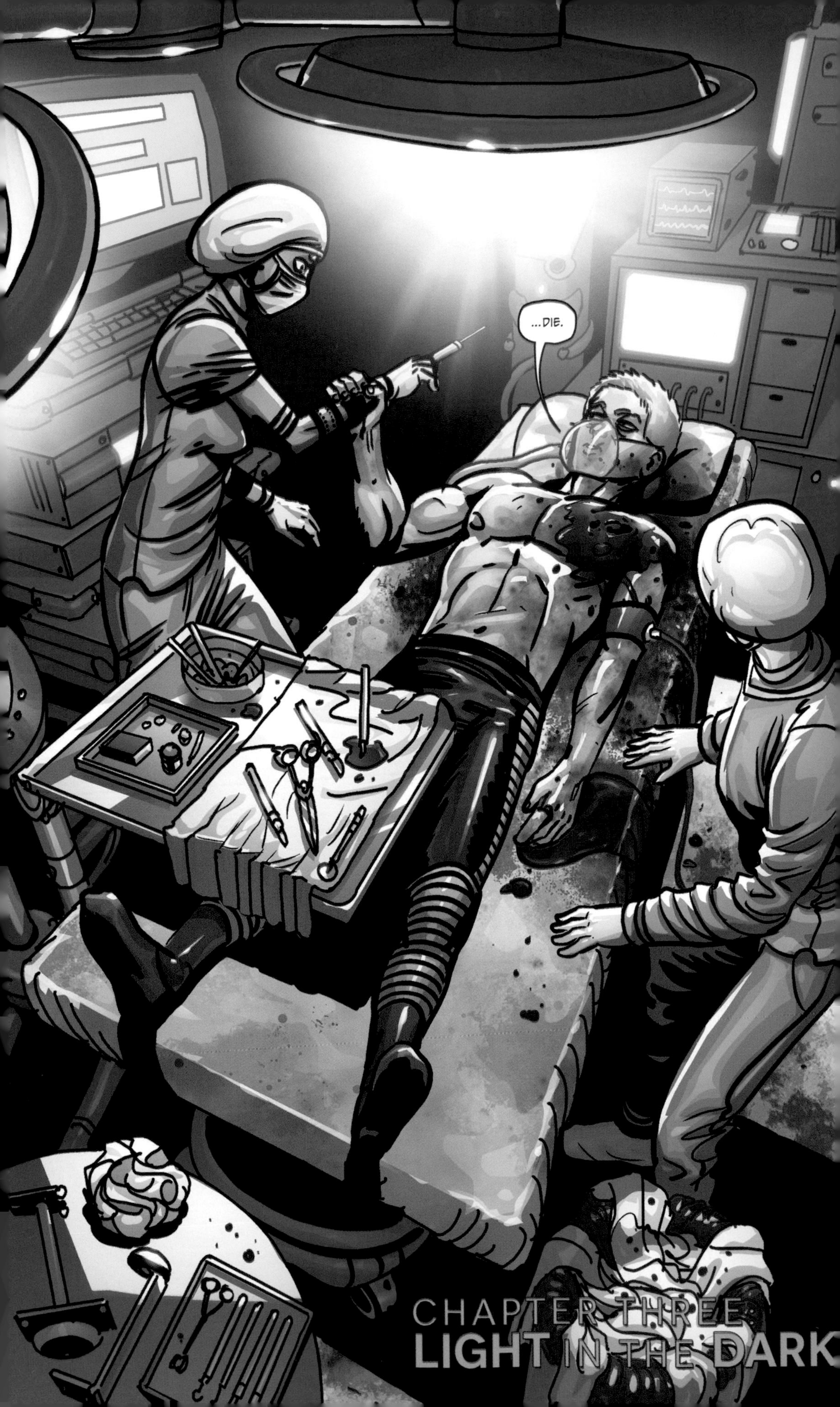
...DIE.
CHAPTER THREE:
LIGHT IN THE DARK

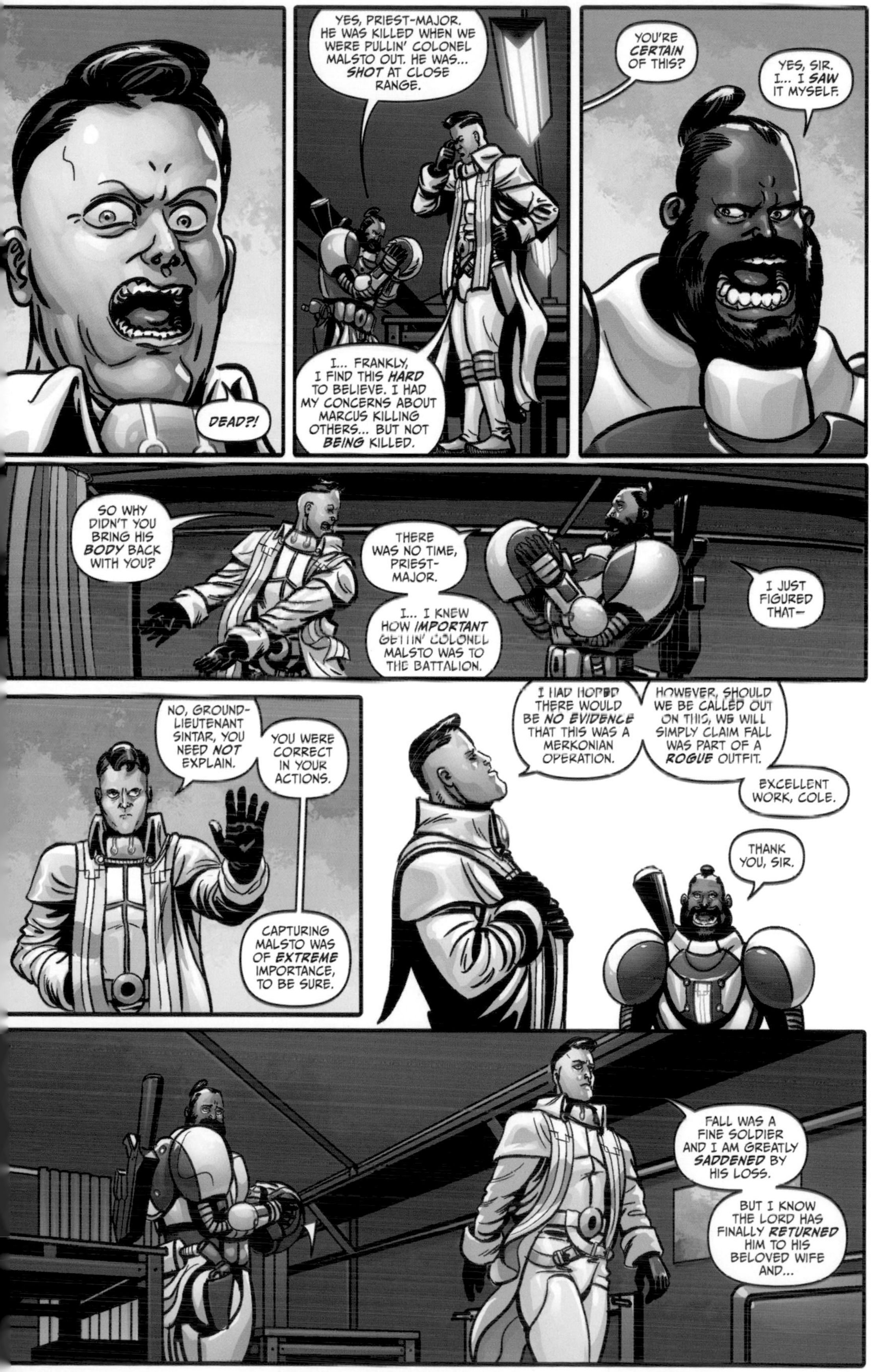

DEAD?!
YES, PRIEST-MAJOR. HE WAS KILLED WHEN WE WERE PULLIN' COLONEL MALSTO OUT. HE WAS... SHOT AT CLOSE RANGE.
I... FRANKLY, I FIND THIS HARD TO BELIEVE. I HAD MY CONCERNS ABOUT MARCUS KILLING OTHERS... BUT NOT BEING KILLED.
YOU'RE CERTAIN OF THIS?
YES, SIR. I... I SAW IT MYSELF.
SO WHY DIDN'T YOU BRING HIS BODY BACK WITH YOU?
THERE WAS NO TIME, PRIEST-MAJOR.
I... I KNEW HOW IMPORTANT GETTIN' COLONEL MALSTO WAS TO THE BATTALION.
I JUST FIGURED THAT—
NO, GROUND-LIEUTENANT SINTAR, YOU NEED NOT EXPLAIN.
YOU WERE CORRECT IN YOUR ACTIONS.
CAPTURING MALSTO WAS OF EXTREME IMPORTANCE, TO BE SURE.
I HAD HOPED THERE WOULD BE NO EVIDENCE THAT THIS WAS A MERKONIAN OPERATION.
HOWEVER, SHOULD WE BE CALLED OUT ON THIS, WE WILL SIMPLY CLAIM FALL WAS PART OF A ROGUE OUTFIT.
EXCELLENT WORK, COLE.
THANK YOU, SIR.
FALL WAS A FINE SOLDIER AND I AM GREATLY SADDENED BY HIS LOSS.
BUT I KNOW THE LORD HAS FINALLY RETURNED HIM TO HIS BELOVED WIFE AND...

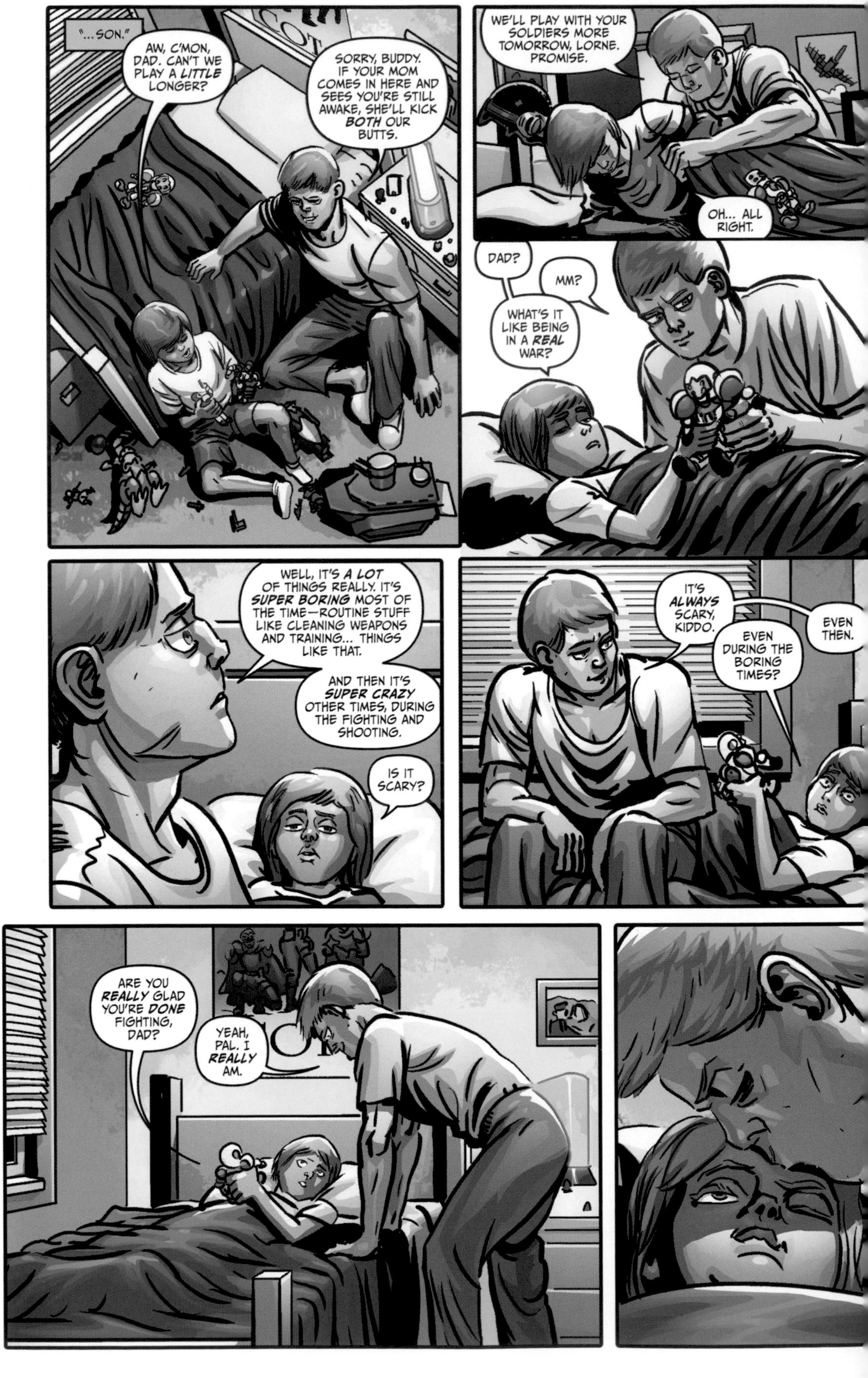
"...SON."
AW, C'MON, DAD. CAN'T WE PLAY A LITTLE LONGER?
SORRY, BUDDY. IF YOUR MOM COMES IN HERE AND SEES YOU'RE STILL AWAKE, SHE'LL KICK BOTH OUR BUTTS.
WE'LL PLAY WITH YOUR SOLDIERS MORE TOMORROW, LORNE. PROMISE.
OH... ALL RIGHT.
DAD?
MM?
WHAT'S IT LIKE BEING IN A REAL WAR?
WELL, IT'S A LOT OF THINGS REALLY. IT'S SUPER BORING MOST OF THE TIME—ROUTINE STUFF LIKE CLEANING WEAPONS AND TRAINING... THINGS LIKE THAT.
AND THEN IT'S SUPER CRAZY OTHER TIMES, DURING THE FIGHTING AND SHOOTING.
IS IT SCARY?
IT'S ALWAYS SCARY, KIDDO.
EVEN DURING THE BORING TIMES?
EVEN THEN.
ARE YOU REALLY GLAD YOU'RE DONE FIGHTING, DAD?
YEAH, PAL. I REALLY AM.

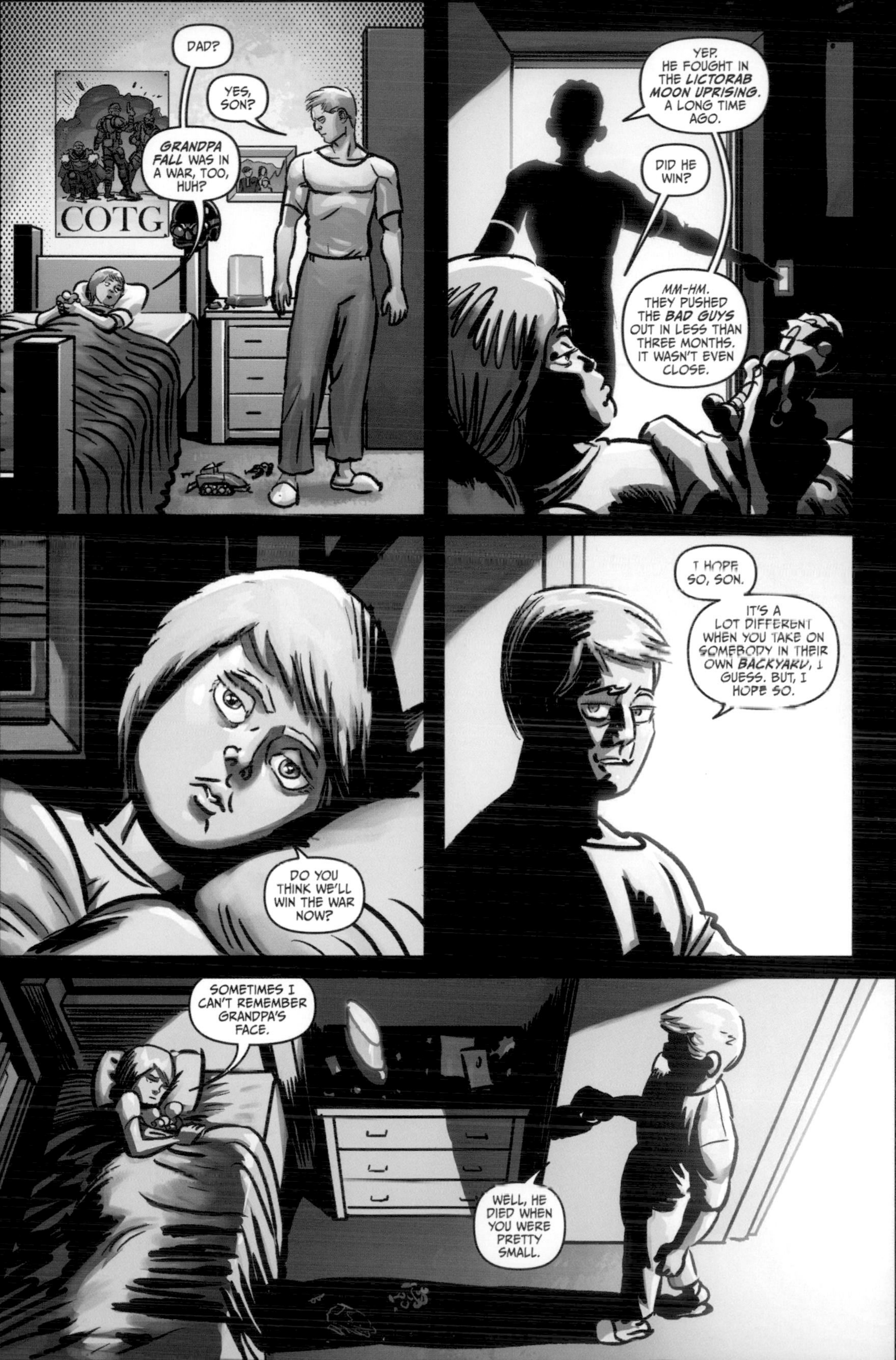
COTG
DAD?
YES, SON?
GRANDPA FALL WAS IN A WAR, TOO, HUH?
YEP. HE FOUGHT IN THE LICTORAB MOON UPRISING. A LONG TIME AGO.
DID HE WIN?
MM-HM. THEY PUSHED THE BAD GUYS OUT IN LESS THAN THREE MONTHS. IT WASN'T EVEN CLOSE.
DO YOU THINK WE'LL WIN THE WAR NOW?
I HOPE SO, SON.
IT'S A LOT DIFFERENT WHEN YOU TAKE ON SOMEBODY IN THEIR OWN BACKYARD, I GUESS. BUT, I HOPE SO.
SOMETIMES I CAN'T REMEMBER GRANDPA'S FACE.
WELL, HE DIED WHEN YOU WERE PRETTY SMALL.

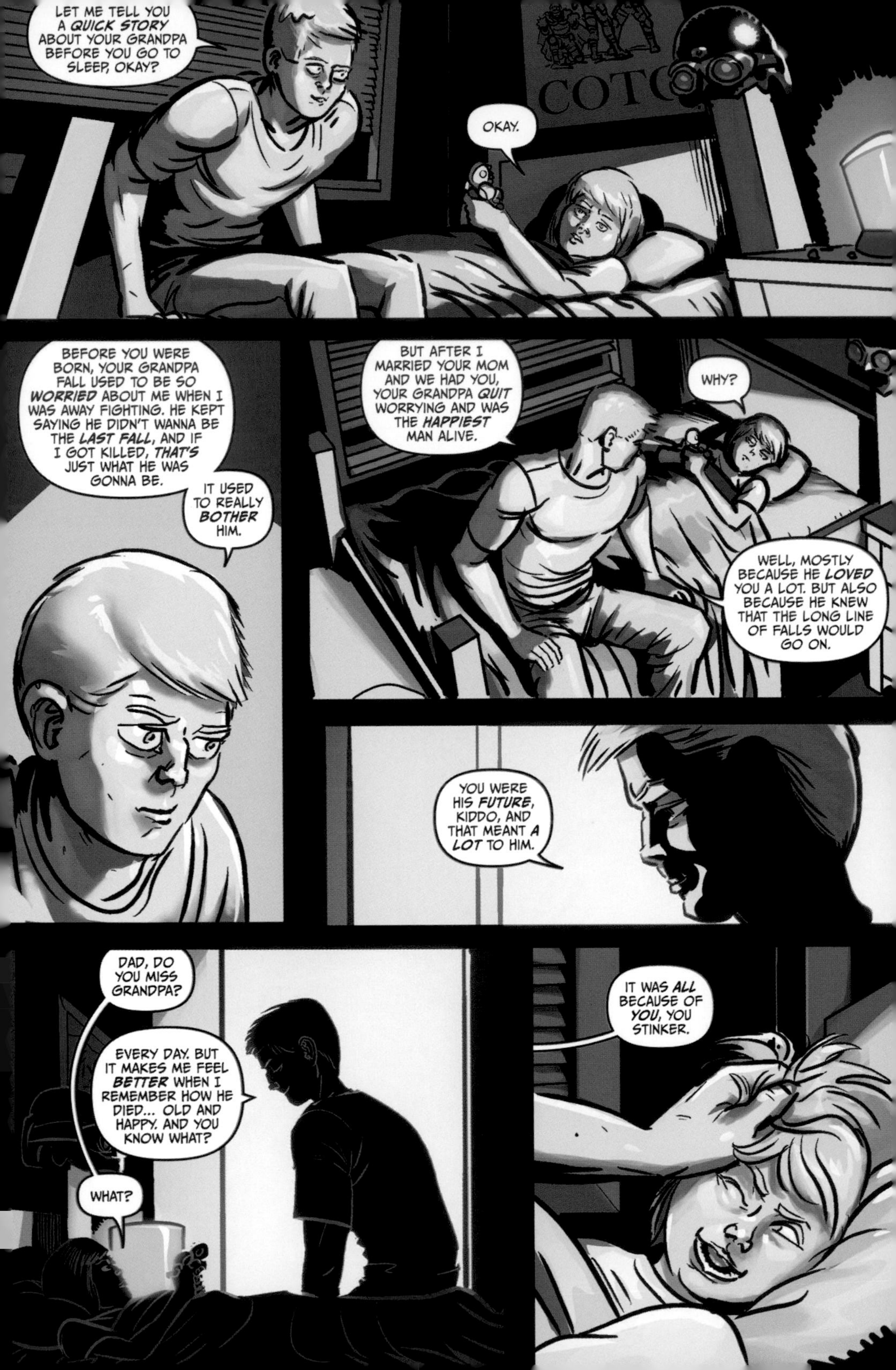
LET ME TELL YOU A QUICK STORY ABOUT YOUR GRANDPA BEFORE YOU GO TO SLEEP, OKAY?
COTC
OKAY.
BEFORE YOU WERE BORN, YOUR GRANDPA FALL USED TO BE SO WORRIED ABOUT ME WHEN I WAS AWAY FIGHTING. HE KEPT SAYING HE DIDN'T WANNA BE THE LAST FALL, AND IF I GOT KILLED, THAT'S JUST WHAT HE WAS GONNA BE.
IT USED TO REALLY BOTHER HIM.
BUT AFTER I MARRIED YOUR MOM AND WE HAD YOU, YOUR GRANDPA QUIT WORRYING AND WAS THE HAPPIEST MAN ALIVE.
WHY?
WELL, MOSTLY BECAUSE HE LOVED YOU A LOT. BUT ALSO BECAUSE HE KNEW THAT THE LONG LINE OF FALLS WOULD GO ON.
YOU WERE HIS FUTURE, KIDDO, AND THAT MEANT A LOT TO HIM.
DAD, DO YOU MISS GRANDPA?
EVERY DAY. BUT IT MAKES ME FEEL BETTER WHEN I REMEMBER HOW HE DIED... OLD AND HAPPY. AND YOU KNOW WHAT?
WHAT?
IT WAS ALL BECAUSE OF YOU, YOU STINKER.

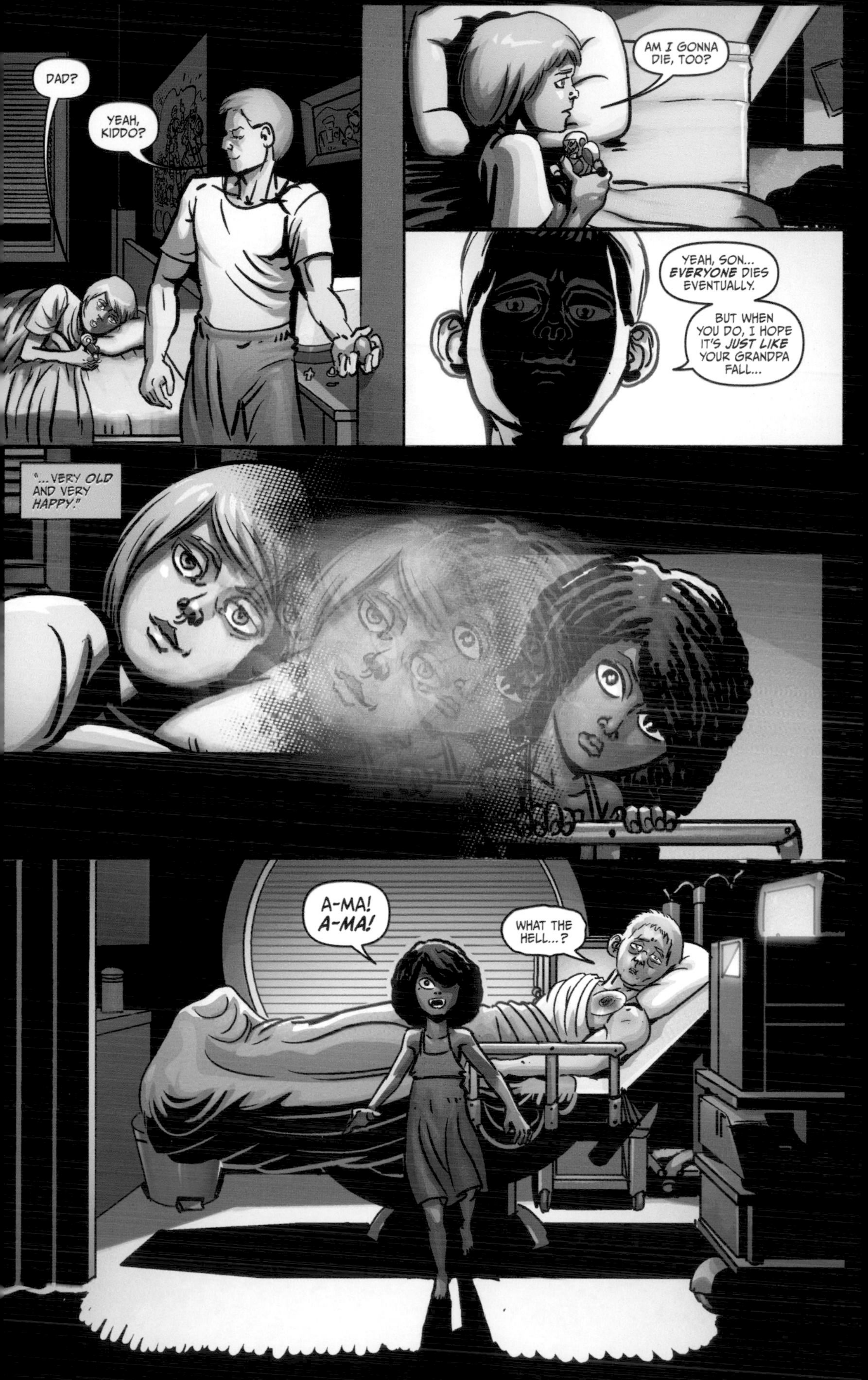
DAD?
YEAH, KIDDO?
AM I GONNA DIE, TOO?
YEAH, SON... EVERYONE DIES EVENTUALLY.
BUT WHEN YOU DO, I HOPE IT'S JUST LIKE YOUR GRANDPA FALL...
"...VERY OLD AND VERY HAPPY."
A-MA! A-MA!
WHAT THE HELL...?

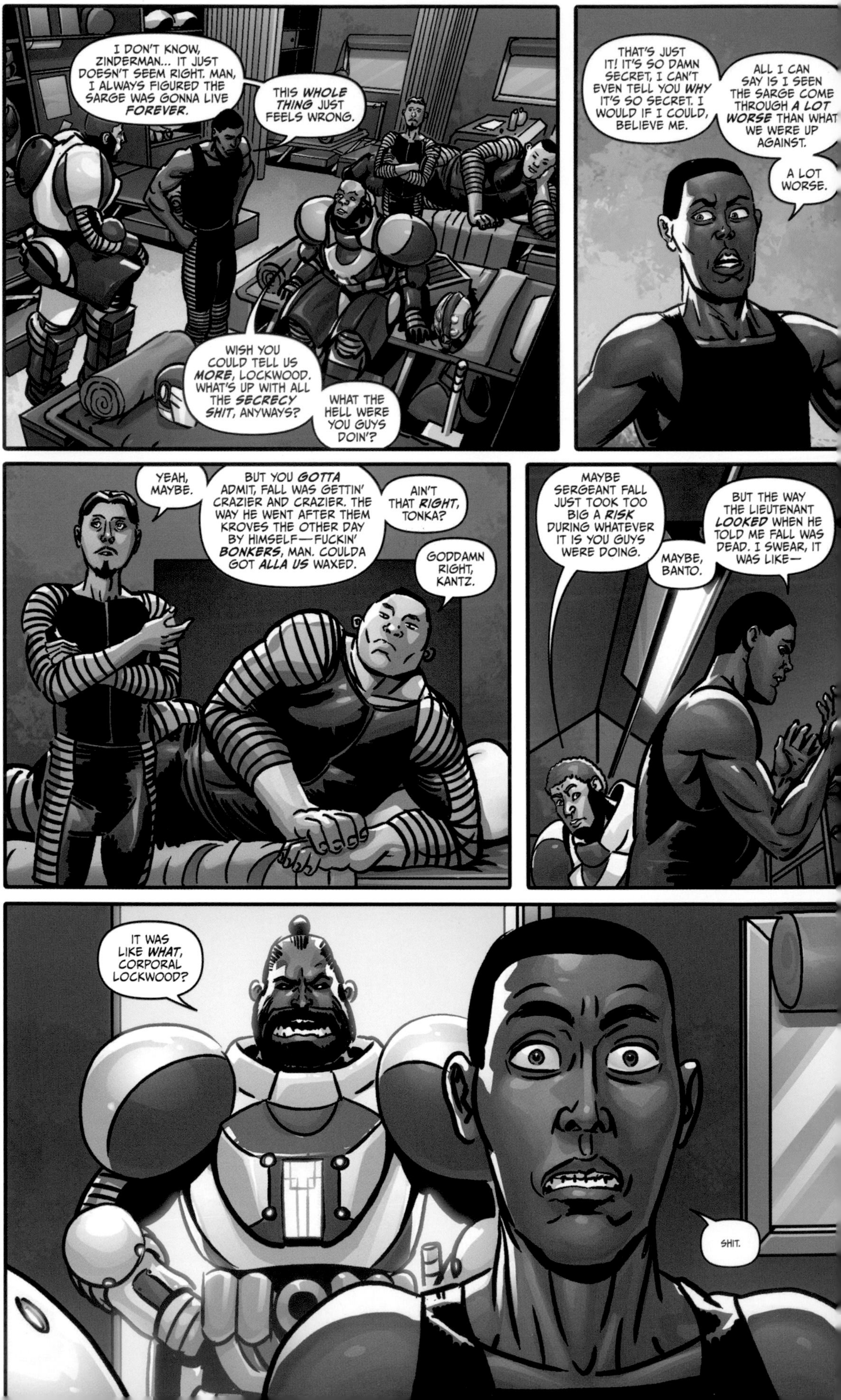

I DON'T KNOW, ZINDERMAN... IT JUST DOESN'T SEEM RIGHT. MAN, I ALWAYS FIGURED THE SARGE WAS GONNA LIVE *FOREVER.*
THIS *WHOLE THING* JUST FEELS WRONG.
WISH YOU COULD TELL US *MORE,* LOCKWOOD. WHAT'S UP WITH ALL THE *SECRECY SHIT,* ANYWAYS?
WHAT THE HELL WERE YOU GUYS DOIN'?
THAT'S JUST IT! IT'S SO DAMN SECRET, I CAN'T EVEN TELL YOU *WHY* IT'S SO SECRET. I WOULD IF I COULD, BELIEVE ME.
ALL I CAN SAY IS I SEEN THE SARGE COME THROUGH *A LOT WORSE* THAN WHAT WE WERE UP AGAINST.
A LOT WORSE.
YEAH, MAYBE.
BUT YOU *GOTTA* ADMIT, FALL WAS GETTIN' CRAZIER AND CRAZIER. THE WAY HE WENT AFTER THEM KROVES THE OTHER DAY BY HIMSELF—FUCKIN' *BONKERS,* MAN. COULDA GOT *ALLA US* WAXED.
AIN'T THAT *RIGHT,* TONKA?
GODDAMN RIGHT, KANTZ.
MAYBE SERGEANT FALL JUST TOOK TOO BIG A *RISK* DURING WHATEVER IT IS YOU GUYS WERE DOING.
MAYBE, BANTO.
BUT THE WAY THE LIEUTENANT *LOOKED* WHEN HE TOLD ME FALL WAS DEAD. I SWEAR, IT WAS LIKE—
IT WAS LIKE *WHAT,* CORPORAL LOCKWOOD?
SHIT.

SHIT? IS THAT WHAT YOU *SAID*... SHIT?

FUNNY, 'CAUSE THAT'S *EXACTLY* WHAT I WAS GONNA SAY THIS TENT LOOKS AND SMELLS LIKE—SHIT!

LOCKWOOD, YOU ARE IN CHARGE OF THIS *GAGGLE*, CORRECT?

YES, SIR.

AND I AM YOUR *COMMANDING OFFICER*, YES?

YES, SIR.

THEN *WHY THE HELL* ARE THESE SOLDIERS *STANDIN' AROUND* WITH THEIR THUMBS *UP* THEIR FUCKIN' ASSES?!

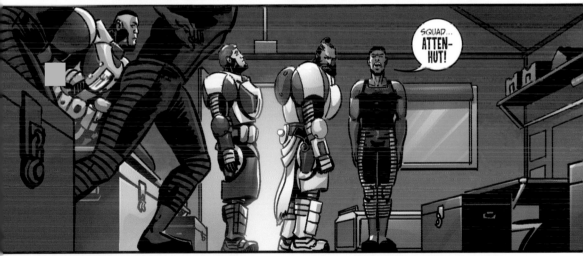

SQUAD... *ATTEN-HUT!*

YEAH...

...THAT'S *MORE LIKE* IT.

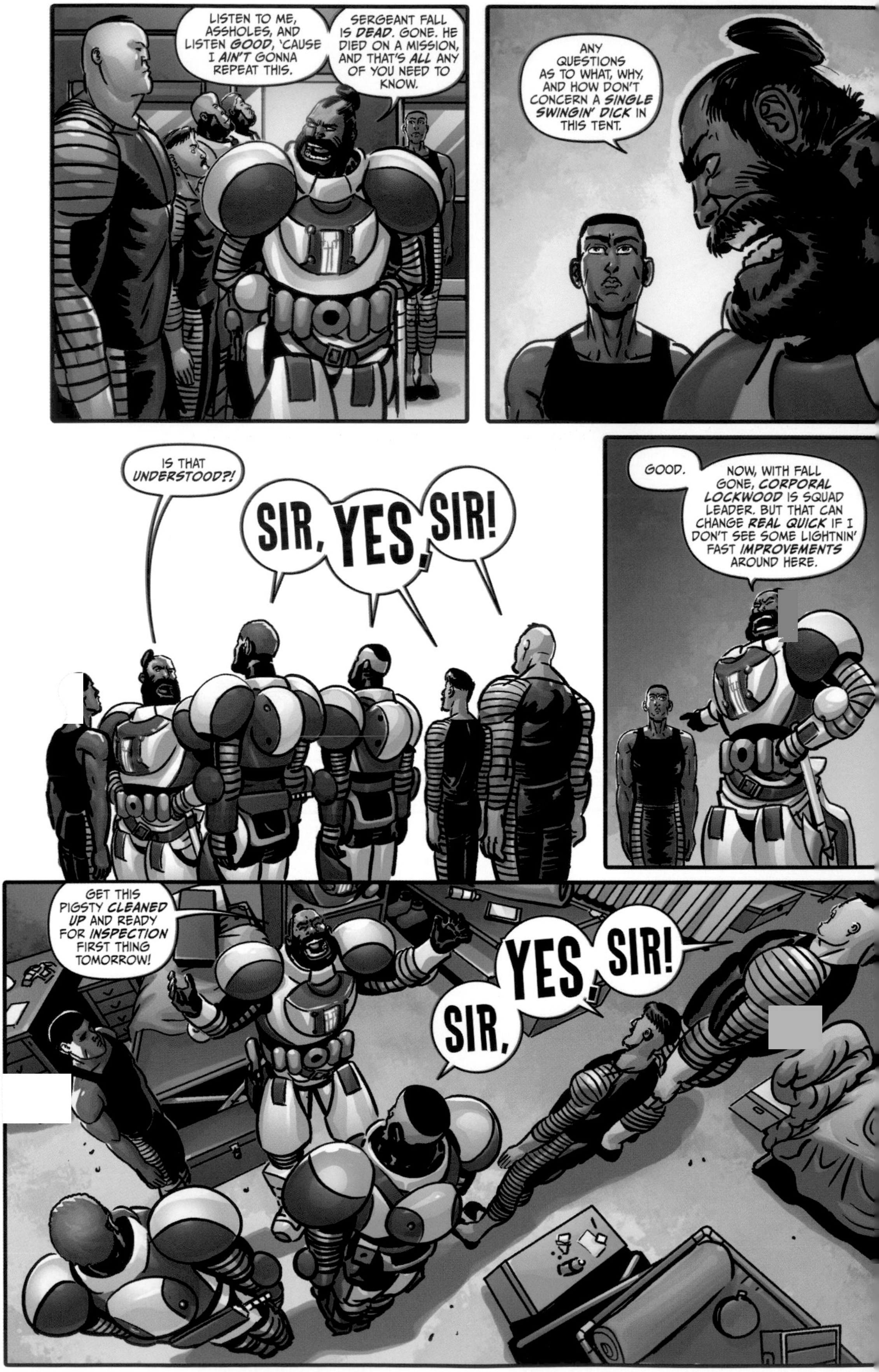
LISTEN TO ME, ASSHOLES, AND LISTEN GOOD, 'CAUSE I AIN'T GONNA REPEAT THIS.
SERGEANT FALL IS DEAD. GONE. HE DIED ON A MISSION, AND THAT'S ALL ANY OF YOU NEED TO KNOW.
ANY QUESTIONS AS TO WHAT, WHY, AND HOW DON'T CONCERN A SINGLE SWINGIN' DICK IN THIS TENT.
IS THAT UNDERSTOOD?!
SIR, YES, SIR!
GOOD.
NOW, WITH FALL GONE, CORPORAL LOCKWOOD IS SQUAD LEADER. BUT THAT CAN CHANGE REAL QUICK IF I DON'T SEE SOME LIGHTNIN' FAST IMPROVEMENTS AROUND HERE.
GET THIS PIGSTY CLEANED UP AND READY FOR INSPECTION FIRST THING TOMORROW!
SIR, YES, SIR!

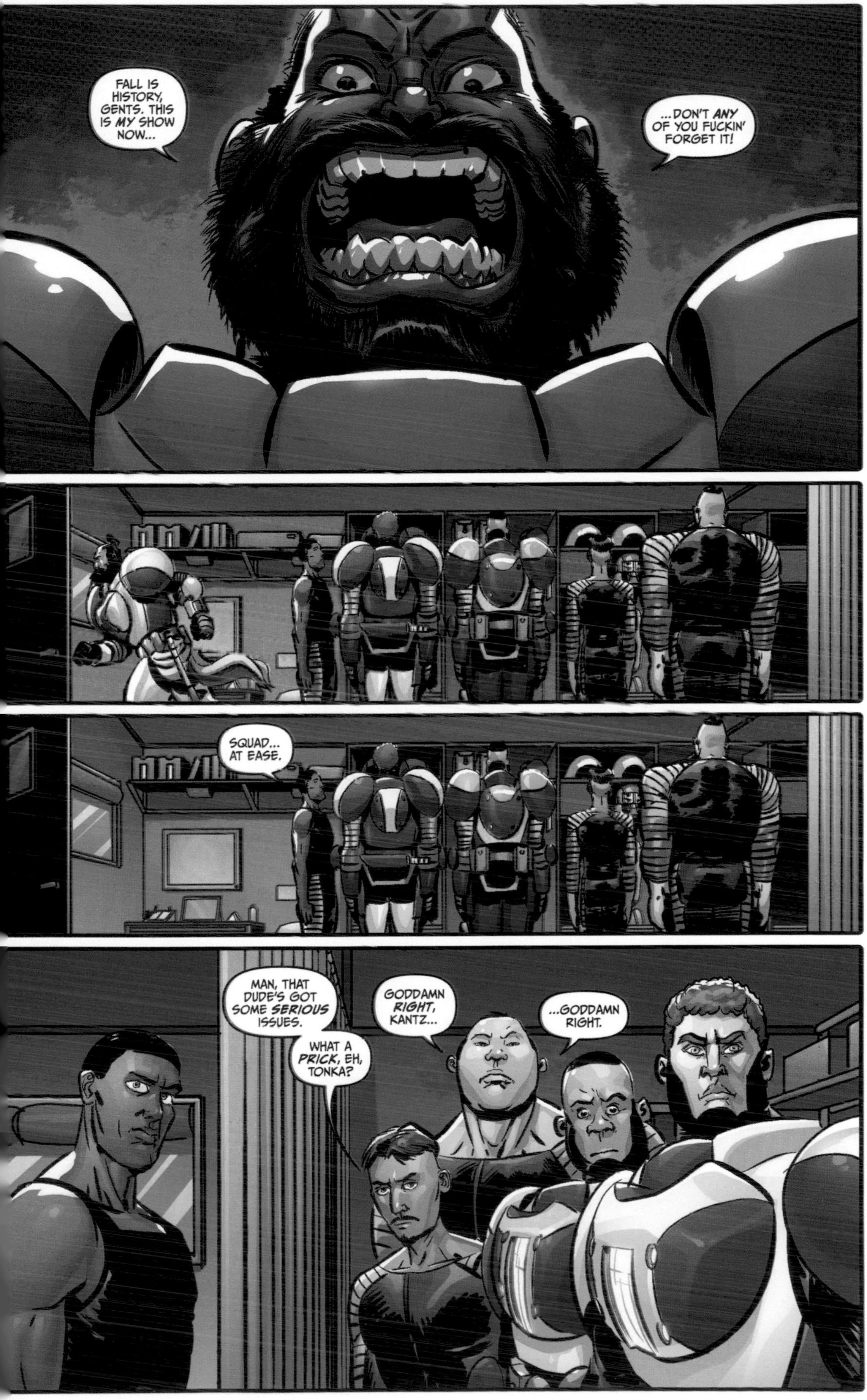

FALL IS HISTORY, GENTS. THIS IS *MY* SHOW NOW...
...DON'T *ANY* OF YOU FUCKIN' FORGET IT!
SQUAD... AT EASE.
MAN, THAT DUDE'S GOT SOME *SERIOUS* ISSUES.
WHAT A *PRICK*, EH, TONKA?
GODDAMN *RIGHT*, KANTZ...
...GODDAMN RIGHT.

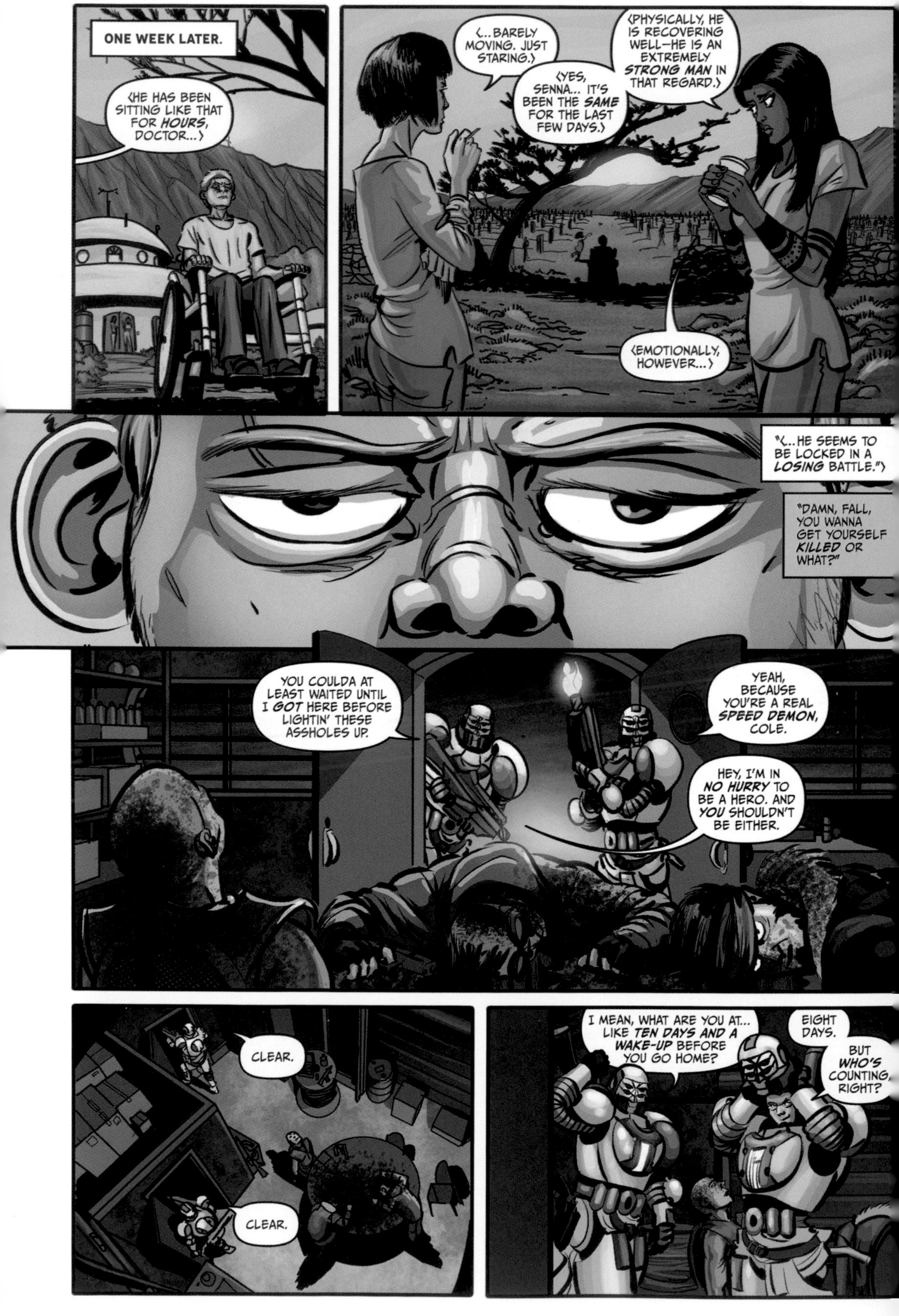
ONE WEEK LATER.
‹HE HAS BEEN SITTING LIKE THAT FOR HOURS, DOCTOR...›
‹...BARELY MOVING. JUST STARING.›
‹YES, SENNA... IT'S BEEN THE SAME FOR THE LAST FEW DAYS.›
‹PHYSICALLY, HE IS RECOVERING WELL—HE IS AN EXTREMELY STRONG MAN IN THAT REGARD.›
‹EMOTIONALLY, HOWEVER...›
"‹...HE SEEMS TO BE LOCKED IN A LOSING BATTLE."›
"DAMN, FALL, YOU WANNA GET YOURSELF KILLED OR WHAT?"
YOU COULDA AT LEAST WAITED UNTIL I GOT HERE BEFORE LIGHTIN' THESE ASSHOLES UP.
YEAH, BECAUSE YOU'RE A REAL SPEED DEMON, COLE.
HEY, I'M IN NO HURRY TO BE A HERO. AND YOU SHOULDN'T BE EITHER.
CLEAR.
CLEAR.
I MEAN, WHAT ARE YOU AT... LIKE TEN DAYS AND A WAKE-UP BEFORE YOU GO HOME?
EIGHT DAYS.
BUT WHO'S COUNTING, RIGHT?

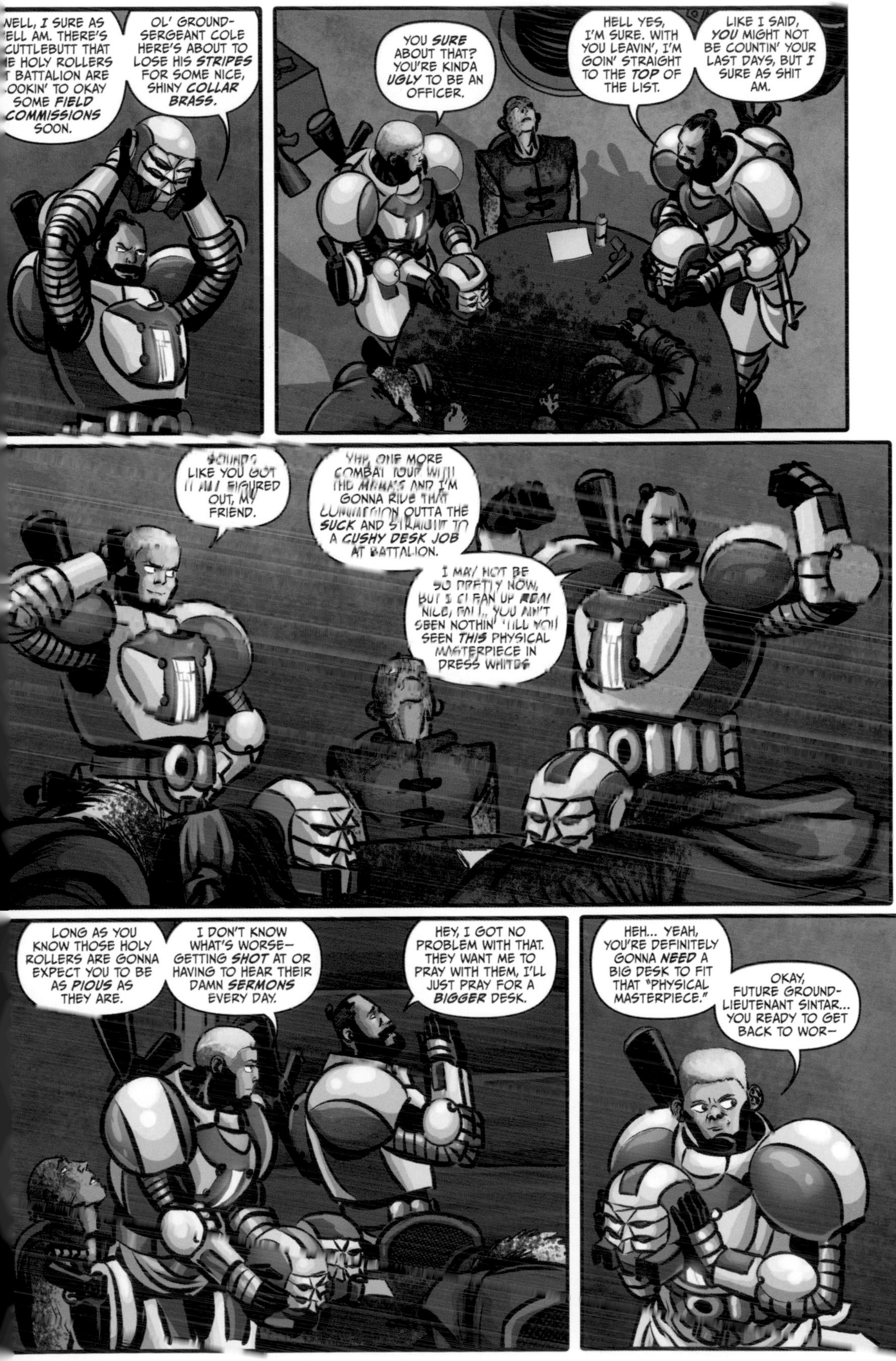
WELL, I SURE AS
ELL AM. THERE'S
CUTTLEBUTT THAT
E HOLY ROLLERS
BATTALION ARE
OOKIN' TO OKAY
SOME FIELD
COMMISSIONS
SOON.
OL' GROUND-SERGEANT COLE HERE'S ABOUT TO LOSE HIS STRIPES FOR SOME NICE, SHINY COLLAR BRASS.
YOU SURE ABOUT THAT? YOU'RE KINDA UGLY TO BE AN OFFICER.
HELL YES, I'M SURE. WITH YOU LEAVIN', I'M GOIN' STRAIGHT TO THE TOP OF THE LIST.
LIKE I SAID, YOU MIGHT NOT BE COUNTIN' YOUR LAST DAYS, BUT I SURE AS SHIT AM.
SOUNDS LIKE YOU GOT IT ALL FIGURED OUT, MY FRIEND.
YUP, ONE MORE COMBAT TOUR WITH THE AND I'M GONNA RIDE THAT COMMISSION OUTTA THE SUCK AND STRAIGHT TO A CUSHY DESK JOB AT BATTALION.
I MAY NOT BE SO PRETTY NOW, BUT I CLEAN UP REAL NICE, PAL... YOU AIN'T SEEN NOTHIN' 'TILL YOU SEEN THIS PHYSICAL MASTERPIECE IN DRESS WHITES
LONG AS YOU KNOW THOSE HOLY ROLLERS ARE GONNA EXPECT YOU TO BE AS PIOUS AS THEY ARE.
I DON'T KNOW WHAT'S WORSE— GETTING SHOT AT OR HAVING TO HEAR THEIR DAMN SERMONS EVERY DAY.
HEY, I GOT NO PROBLEM WITH THAT. THEY WANT ME TO PRAY WITH THEM, I'LL JUST PRAY FOR A BIGGER DESK.
HEH... YEAH, YOU'RE DEFINITELY GONNA NEED A BIG DESK TO FIT THAT "PHYSICAL MASTERPIECE."
OKAY, FUTURE GROUND-LIEUTENANT SINTAR... YOU READY TO GET BACK TO WOR—

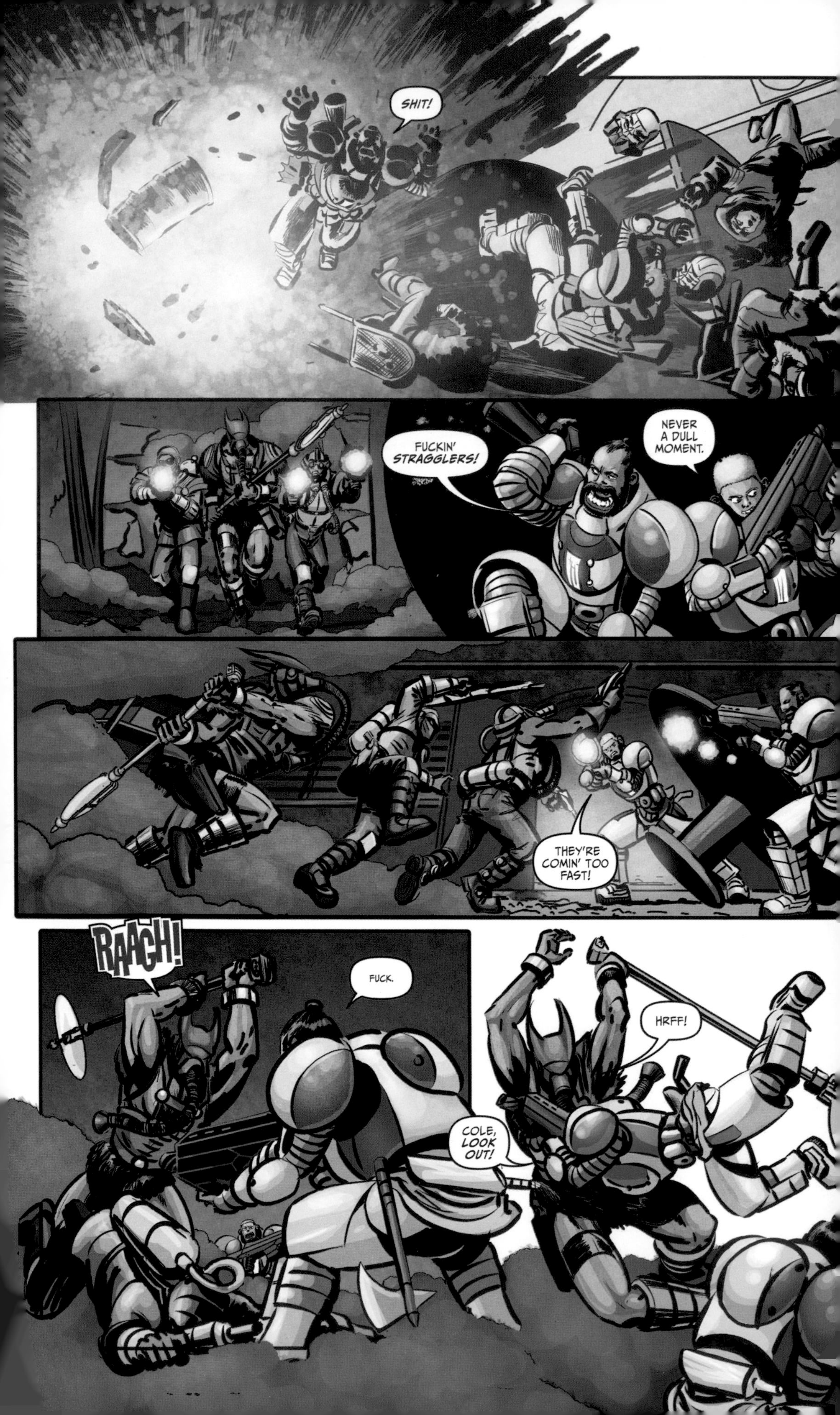
SHIT!
FUCKIN' STRAGGLERS!
NEVER A DULL MOMENT.
THEY'RE COMIN' TOO FAST!
RAAGH!
FUCK.
HRFF!
COLE, LOOK OUT!

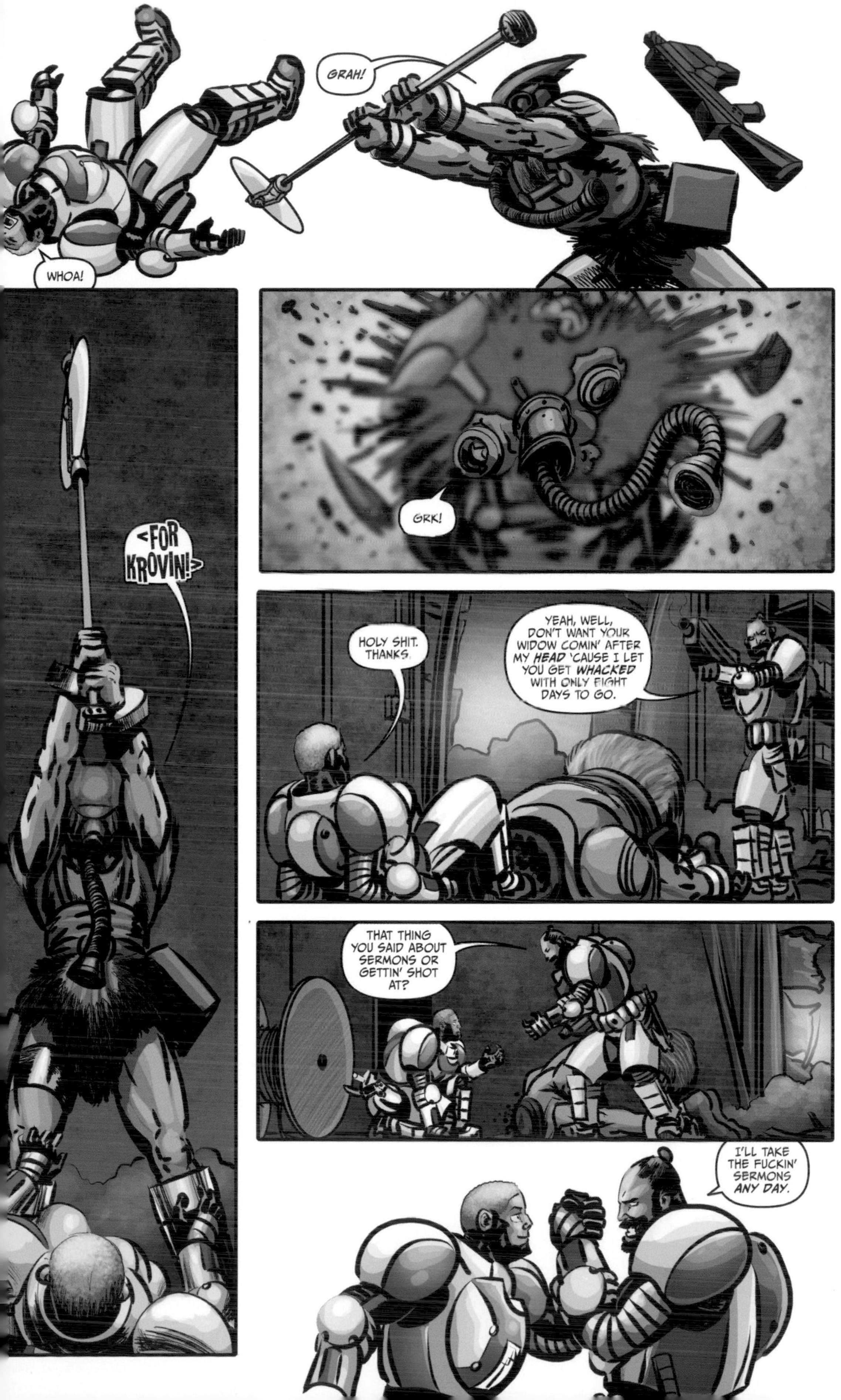

GRAH!
WHOA!
<FOR KROVIN!>
GRK!
HOLY SHIT. THANKS.
YEAH, WELL, DON'T WANT YOUR WIDOW COMIN' AFTER MY HEAD 'CAUSE I LET YOU GET WHACKED WITH ONLY EIGHT DAYS TO GO.
THAT THING YOU SAID ABOUT SERMONS OR GETTIN' SHOT AT?
I'LL TAKE THE FUCKIN' SERMONS ANY DAY.

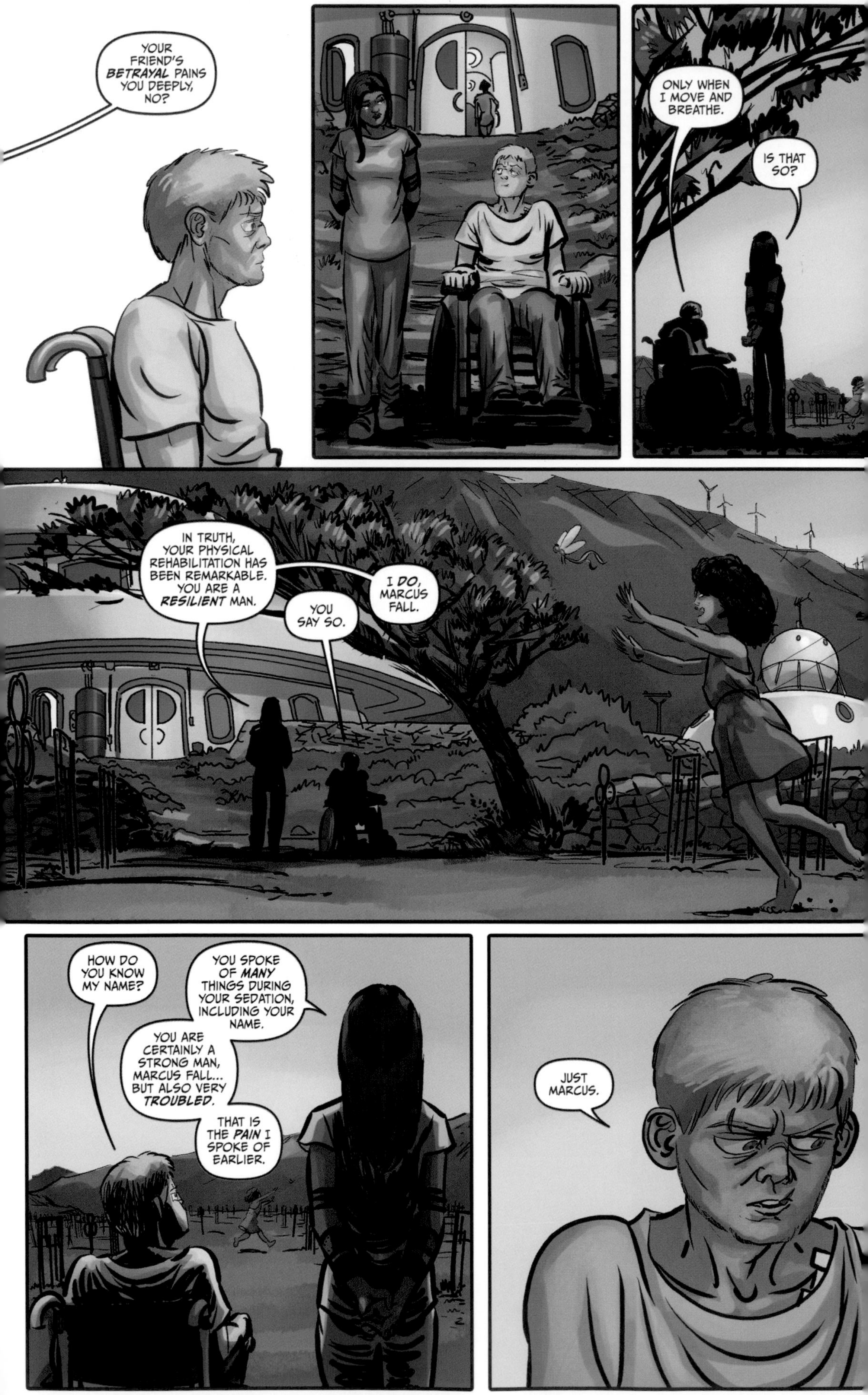
YOUR FRIEND'S BETRAYAL PAINS YOU DEEPLY, NO?
ONLY WHEN I MOVE AND BREATHE.
IS THAT SO?
IN TRUTH, YOUR PHYSICAL REHABILITATION HAS BEEN REMARKABLE. YOU ARE A RESILIENT MAN.
YOU SAY SO.
I DO, MARCUS FALL.
HOW DO YOU KNOW MY NAME?
YOU SPOKE OF MANY THINGS DURING YOUR SEDATION, INCLUDING YOUR NAME.
YOU ARE CERTAINLY A STRONG MAN, MARCUS FALL... BUT ALSO VERY TROUBLED.
THAT IS THE PAIN I SPOKE OF EARLIER.
JUST MARCUS.

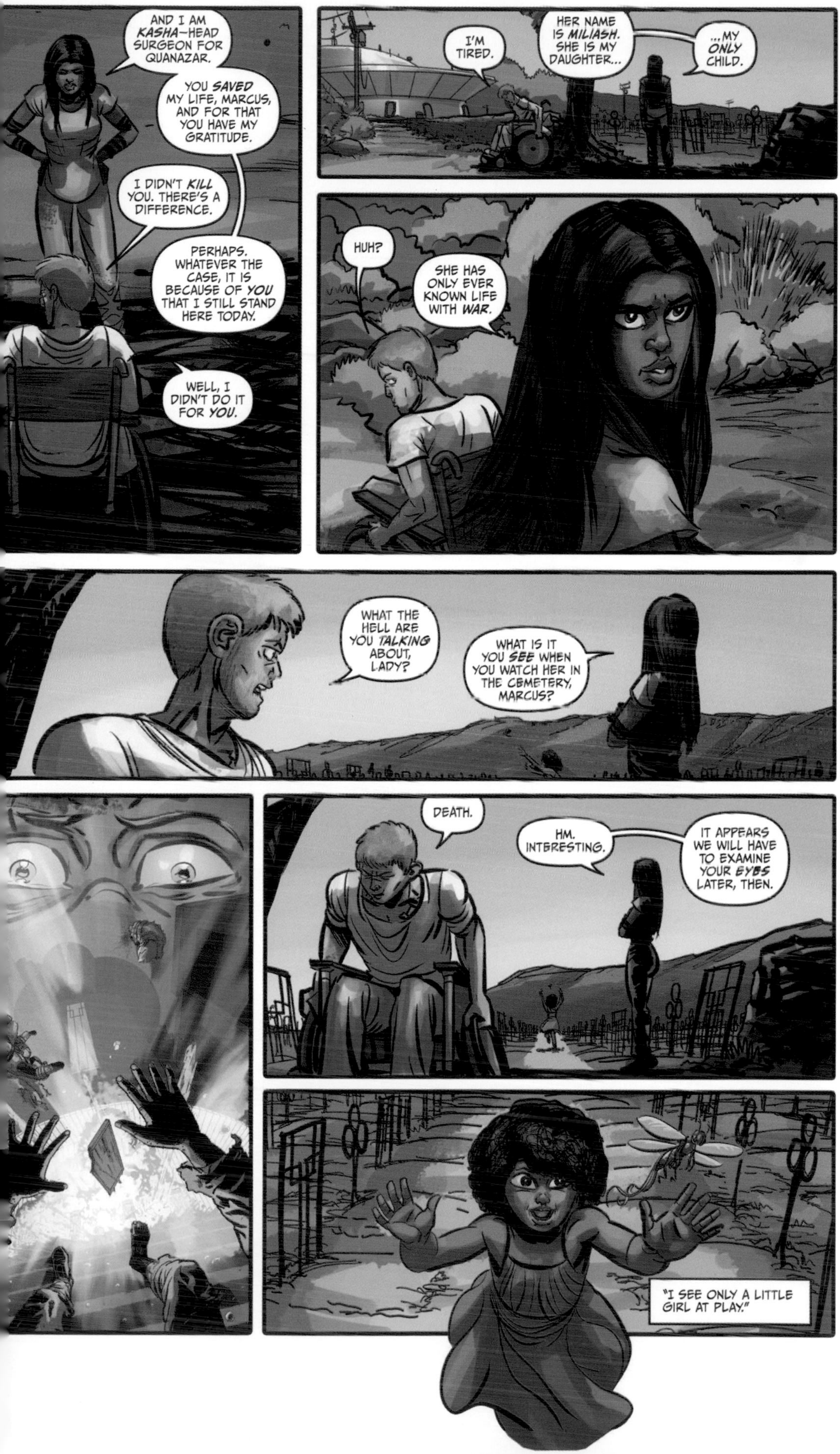
AND I AM KASHA—HEAD SURGEON FOR QUANAZAR.
YOU SAVED MY LIFE, MARCUS, AND FOR THAT YOU HAVE MY GRATITUDE.
I DIDN'T KILL YOU. THERE'S A DIFFERENCE.
PERHAPS. WHATEVER THE CASE, IT IS BECAUSE OF YOU THAT I STILL STAND HERE TODAY.
WELL, I DIDN'T DO IT FOR YOU.
I'M TIRED.
HER NAME IS MILIASH. SHE IS MY DAUGHTER...
...MY ONLY CHILD.
HUH?
SHE HAS ONLY EVER KNOWN LIFE WITH WAR.
WHAT THE HELL ARE YOU TALKING ABOUT, LADY?
WHAT IS IT YOU SEE WHEN YOU WATCH HER IN THE CEMETERY, MARCUS?
DEATH.
HM. INTERESTING.
IT APPEARS WE WILL HAVE TO EXAMINE YOUR EYES LATER, THEN.
"I SEE ONLY A LITTLE GIRL AT PLAY."

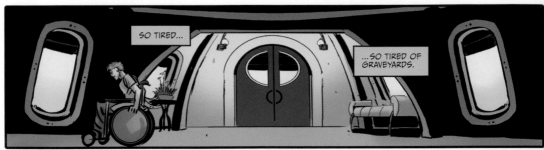

SO TIRED...

...SO TIRED OF GRAVEYARDS.

"DON'T YOU THINK IT'S A BIT *MORBID*, MARCUS..."

...HAVING A PICNIC IN A *CEMETERY*?

RRRRRMMMM!

NAH, HON—FOLKS LIKE MY DAD SERVED SO WE COULD *HAVE* THIS PICNIC. IT'D BE *MORE* MORBID IF WE *DIDN'T* CELEBRATE THAT.

WE'RE ENJOYING THE FREEDOM THEY FOUGHT FOR. TRUST ME—TO A SOLDIER, *THAT'S* RESPECT.

I SUPPOSE. I JUST DON'T WANT TO BE DISRESPECTFUL.

FALL

A Life of
Service and Honor

YES, SIR, SERGEANT FALL, SIR.

STOW THAT "SIR" BUSINESS, WOMAN—I'M NO OFFICER. I *WORK* FOR A LIVING.

SO YOU SAY.

YOU KNOW... I HOPE IT'S THE *SAME* IF ANYTHING EVER HAPPENS TO ME, MARCUS—IF I DIE *BEFORE* YOU, I MEAN.

OKAY, *NOW* WE'RE GETTING MORBID.

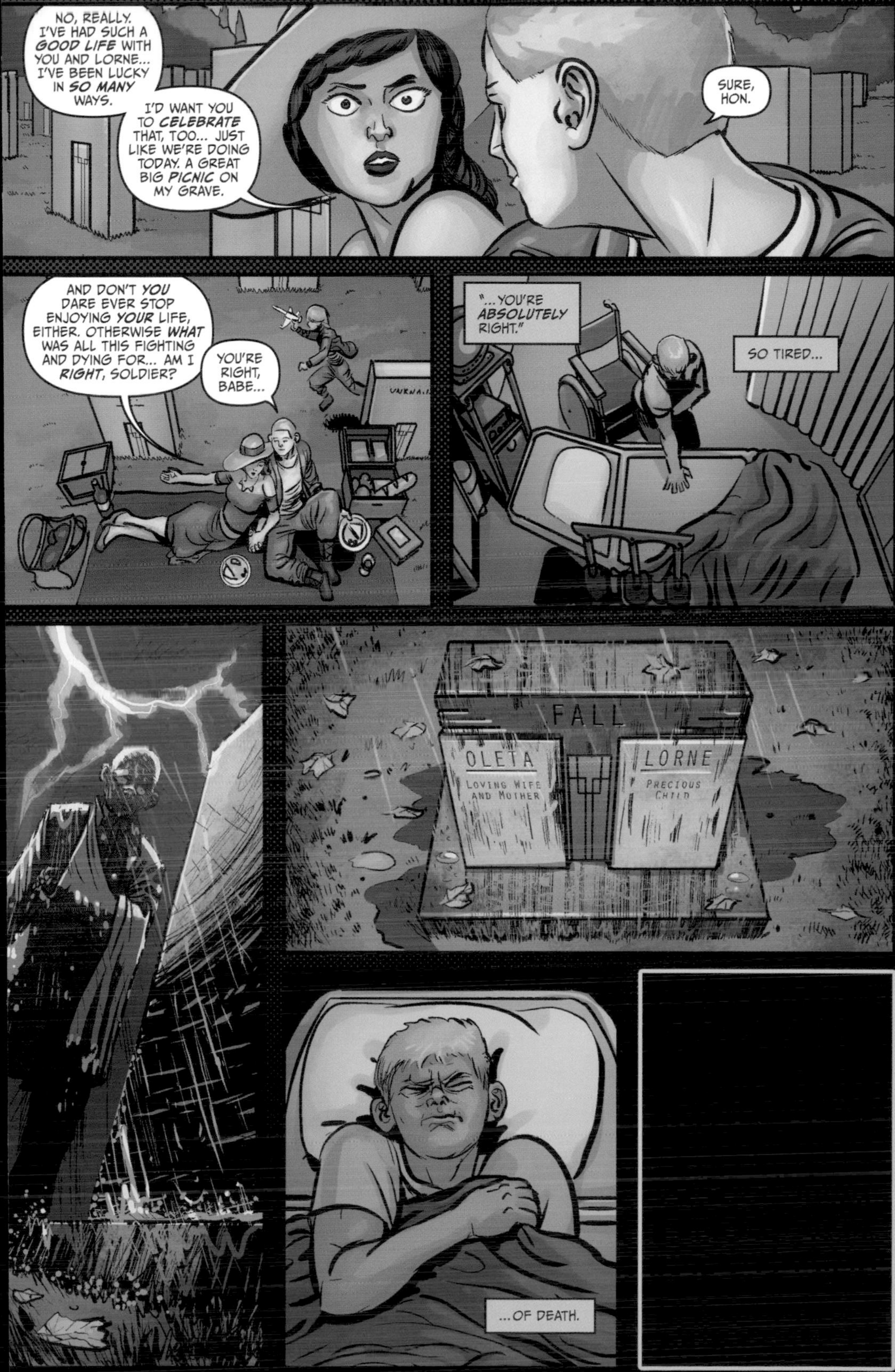
NO, REALLY. I'VE HAD SUCH A GOOD LIFE WITH YOU AND LORNE... I'VE BEEN LUCKY IN SO MANY WAYS.
I'D WANT YOU TO CELEBRATE THAT, TOO... JUST LIKE WE'RE DOING TODAY. A GREAT BIG PICNIC ON MY GRAVE.
SURE, HON.
AND DON'T YOU DARE EVER STOP ENJOYING YOUR LIFE, EITHER. OTHERWISE WHAT WAS ALL THIS FIGHTING AND DYING FOR... AM I RIGHT, SOLDIER?
YOU'RE RIGHT, BABE...
"...YOU'RE ABSOLUTELY RIGHT."
SO TIRED...
FALL
OLETA
LOVING WIFE AND MOTHER
LORNE
PRECIOUS CHILD
...OF DEATH.

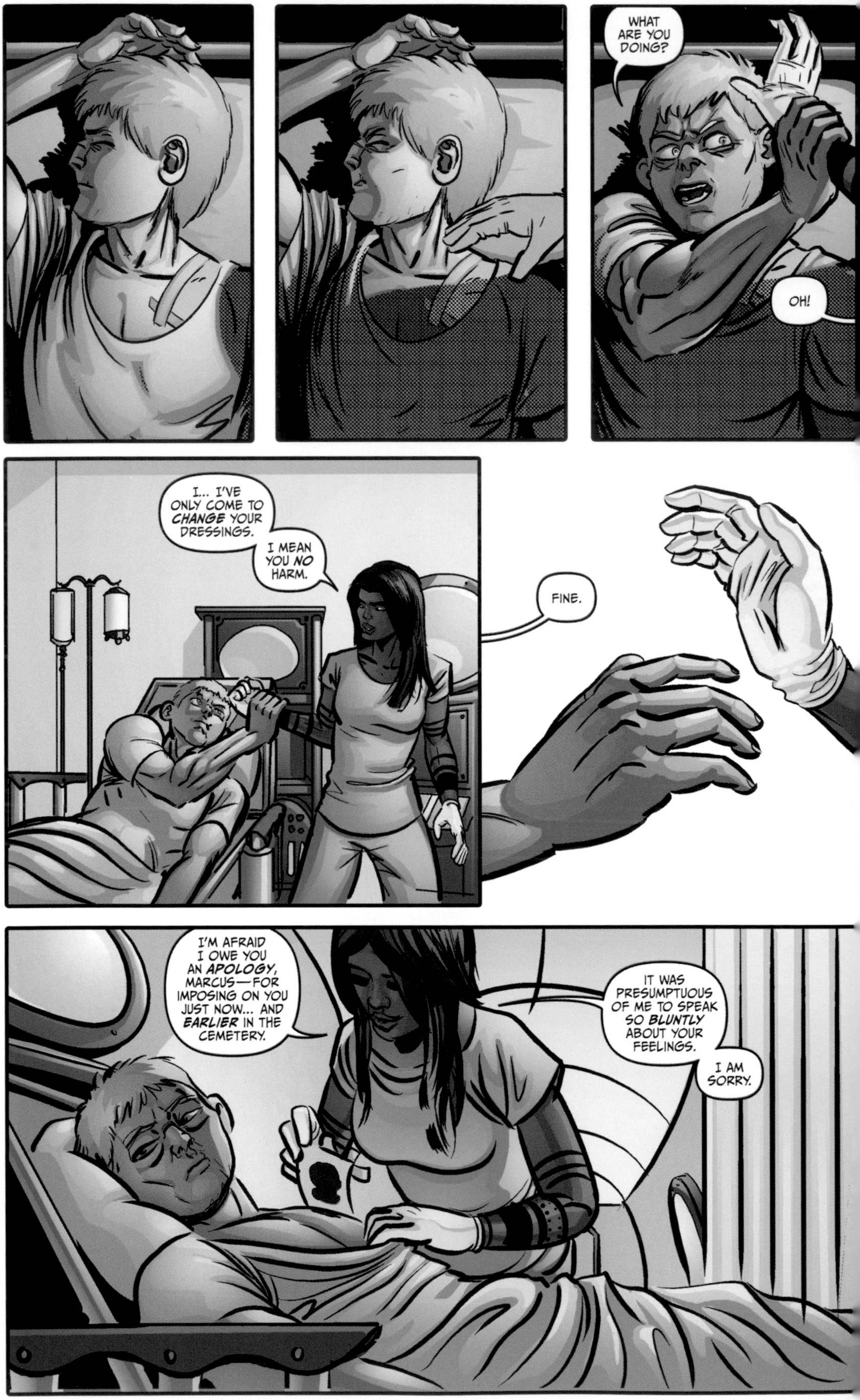
WHAT ARE YOU DOING?
OH!
I... I'VE ONLY COME TO CHANGE YOUR DRESSINGS.
I MEAN YOU NO HARM.
FINE.
I'M AFRAID I OWE YOU AN APOLOGY, MARCUS—FOR IMPOSING ON YOU JUST NOW... AND EARLIER IN THE CEMETERY.
IT WAS PRESUMPTUOUS OF ME TO SPEAK SO BLUNTLY ABOUT YOUR FEELINGS.
I AM SORRY.

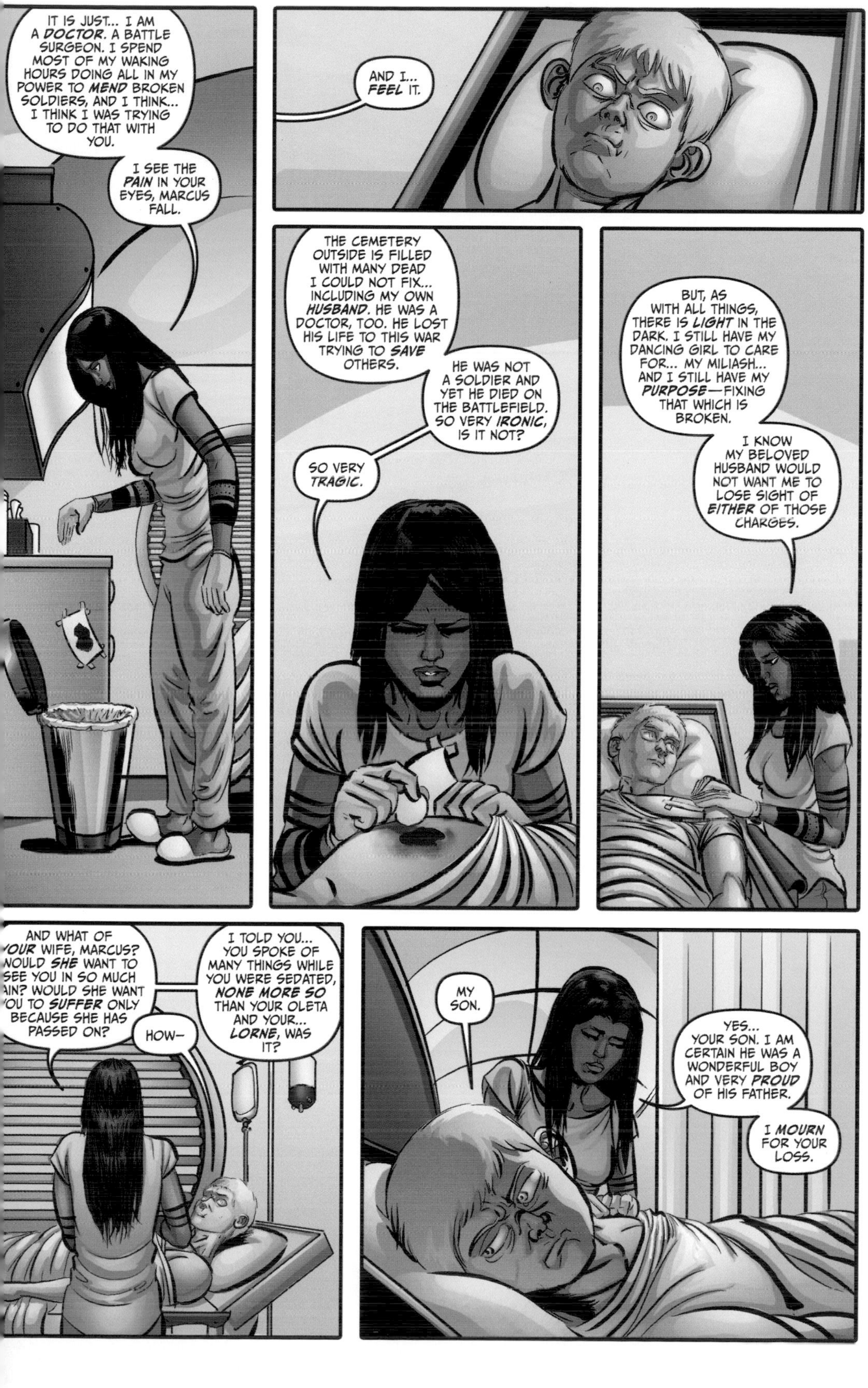
IT IS JUST... I AM A DOCTOR. A BATTLE SURGEON. I SPEND MOST OF MY WAKING HOURS DOING ALL IN MY POWER TO MEND BROKEN SOLDIERS, AND I THINK... I THINK I WAS TRYING TO DO THAT WITH YOU.
I SEE THE PAIN IN YOUR EYES, MARCUS FALL.
AND I... FEEL IT.
THE CEMETERY OUTSIDE IS FILLED WITH MANY DEAD I COULD NOT FIX... INCLUDING MY OWN HUSBAND. HE WAS A DOCTOR, TOO. HE LOST HIS LIFE TO THIS WAR TRYING TO SAVE OTHERS.
HE WAS NOT A SOLDIER AND YET HE DIED ON THE BATTLEFIELD. SO VERY IRONIC, IS IT NOT?
SO VERY TRAGIC.
BUT, AS WITH ALL THINGS, THERE IS LIGHT IN THE DARK. I STILL HAVE MY DANCING GIRL TO CARE FOR... MY MILIASH... AND I STILL HAVE MY PURPOSE—FIXING THAT WHICH IS BROKEN.
I KNOW MY BELOVED HUSBAND WOULD NOT WANT ME TO LOSE SIGHT OF EITHER OF THOSE CHARGES.
AND WHAT OF YOUR WIFE, MARCUS? WOULD SHE WANT TO SEE YOU IN SO MUCH PAIN? WOULD SHE WANT YOU TO SUFFER ONLY BECAUSE SHE HAS PASSED ON?
HOW—
I TOLD YOU... YOU SPOKE OF MANY THINGS WHILE YOU WERE SEDATED, NONE MORE SO THAN YOUR OLETA AND YOUR... LORNE, WAS IT?
MY SON.
YES... YOUR SON. I AM CERTAIN HE WAS A WONDERFUL BOY AND VERY PROUD OF HIS FATHER.
I MOURN FOR YOUR LOSS.

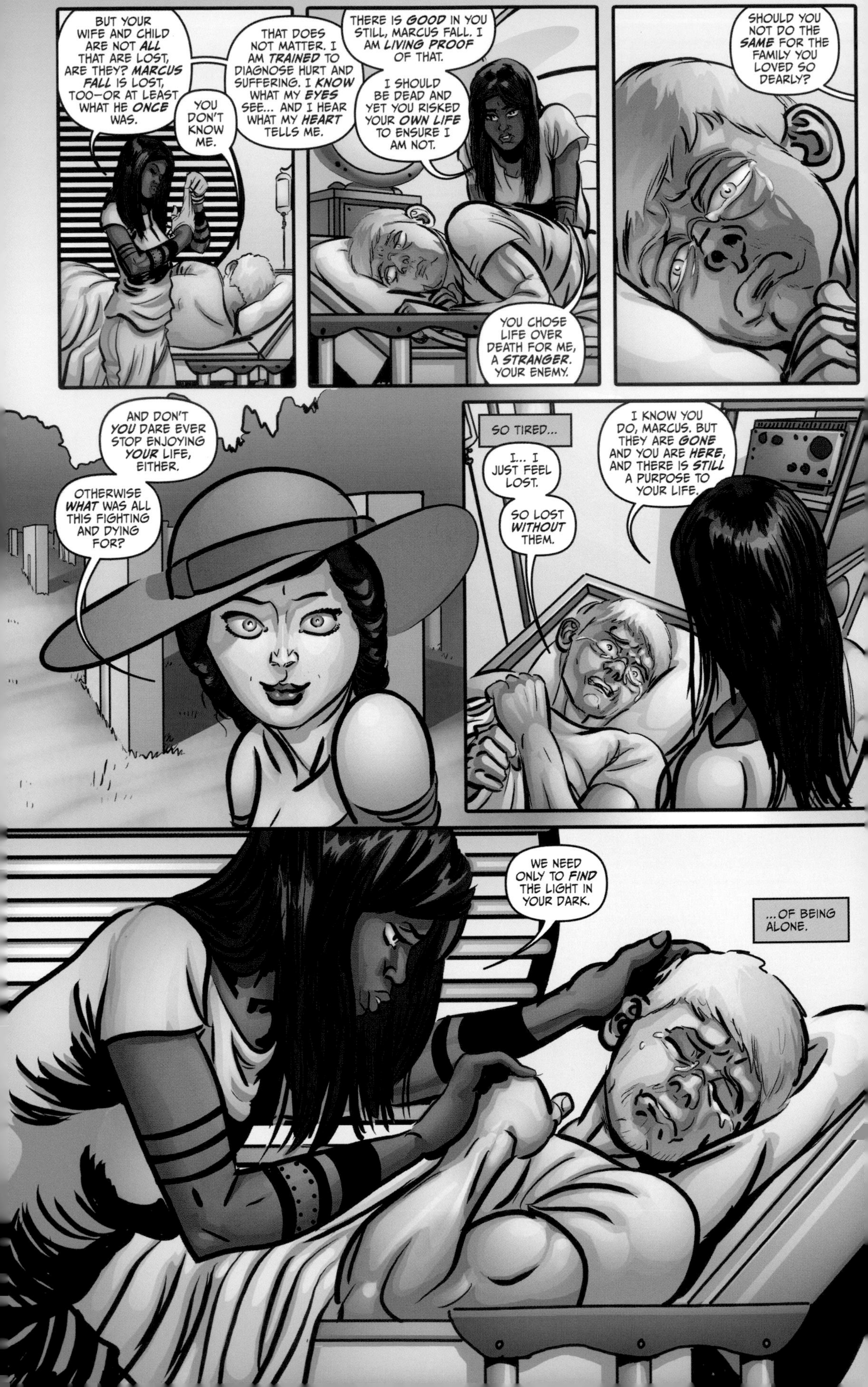

BUT YOUR WIFE AND CHILD ARE NOT ALL THAT ARE LOST, ARE THEY? MARCUS FALL IS LOST, TOO—OR AT LEAST WHAT HE ONCE WAS.
YOU DON'T KNOW ME.
THAT DOES NOT MATTER. I AM TRAINED TO DIAGNOSE HURT AND SUFFERING. I KNOW WHAT MY EYES SEE... AND I HEAR WHAT MY HEART TELLS ME.
THERE IS GOOD IN YOU STILL, MARCUS FALL. I AM LIVING PROOF OF THAT.
I SHOULD BE DEAD AND YET YOU RISKED YOUR OWN LIFE TO ENSURE I AM NOT.
YOU CHOSE LIFE OVER DEATH FOR ME, A STRANGER. YOUR ENEMY.
SHOULD YOU NOT DO THE SAME FOR THE FAMILY YOU LOVED SO DEARLY?
AND DON'T YOU DARE EVER STOP ENJOYING YOUR LIFE, EITHER.
OTHERWISE WHAT WAS ALL THIS FIGHTING AND DYING FOR?
SO TIRED...
I... I JUST FEEL LOST.
SO LOST WITHOUT THEM.
I KNOW YOU DO, MARCUS. BUT THEY ARE GONE AND YOU ARE HERE, AND THERE IS STILL A PURPOSE TO YOUR LIFE.
WE NEED ONLY TO FIND THE LIGHT IN YOUR DARK.
...OF BEING ALONE.

"IN THE COUNCILS OF GOVERNMENT,

WE MUST GUARD AGAINST THE

ACQUISITION OF UNWARRANTED

INFLUENCE, WHETHER SOUGHT

OR UNSOUGHT, BY THE MILITARY-

INDUSTRIAL COMPLEX."

- PRESIDENT DWIGHT D. EISENHOWER

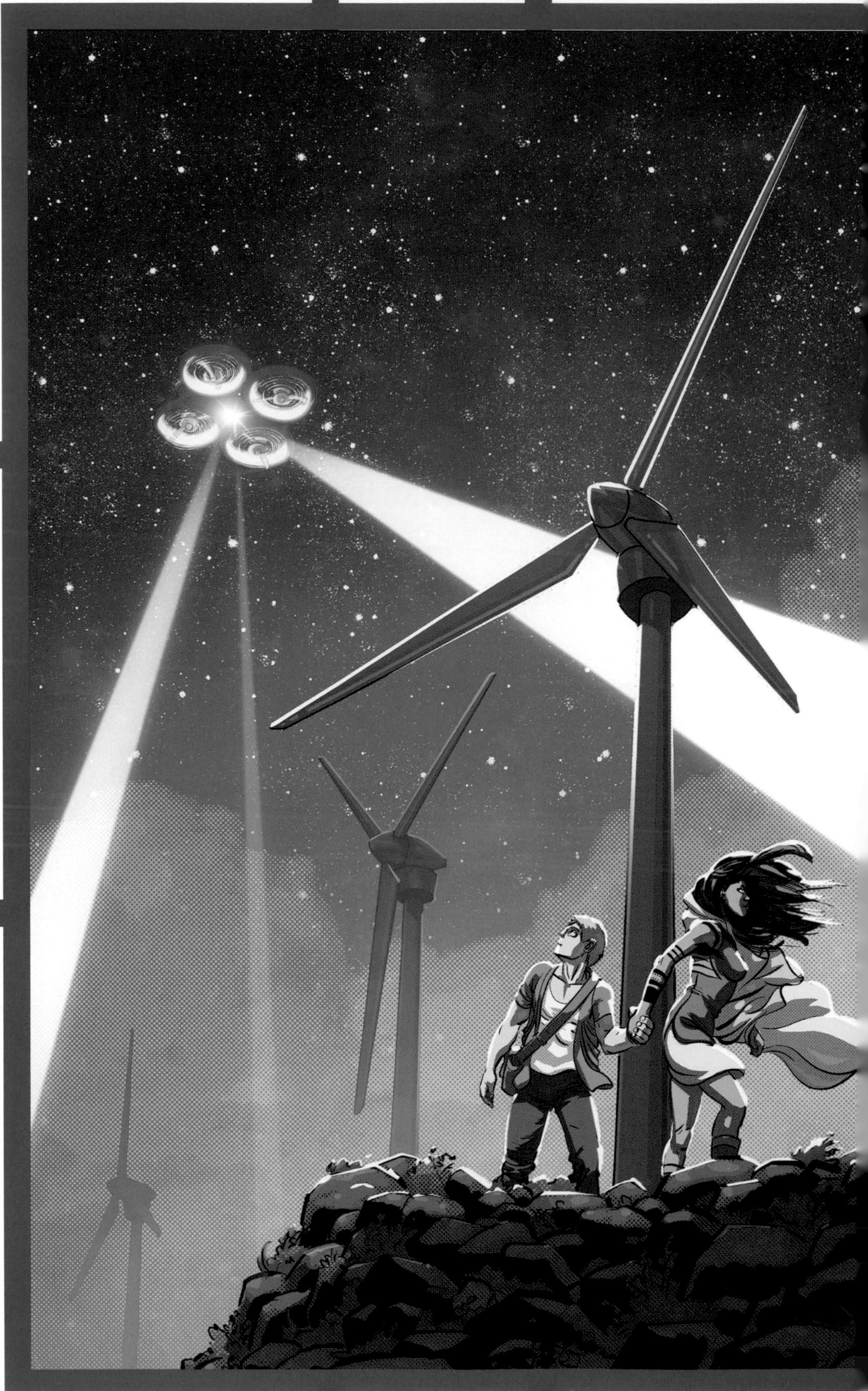

Art by Casey Maloney, Colors by Dusty Yee

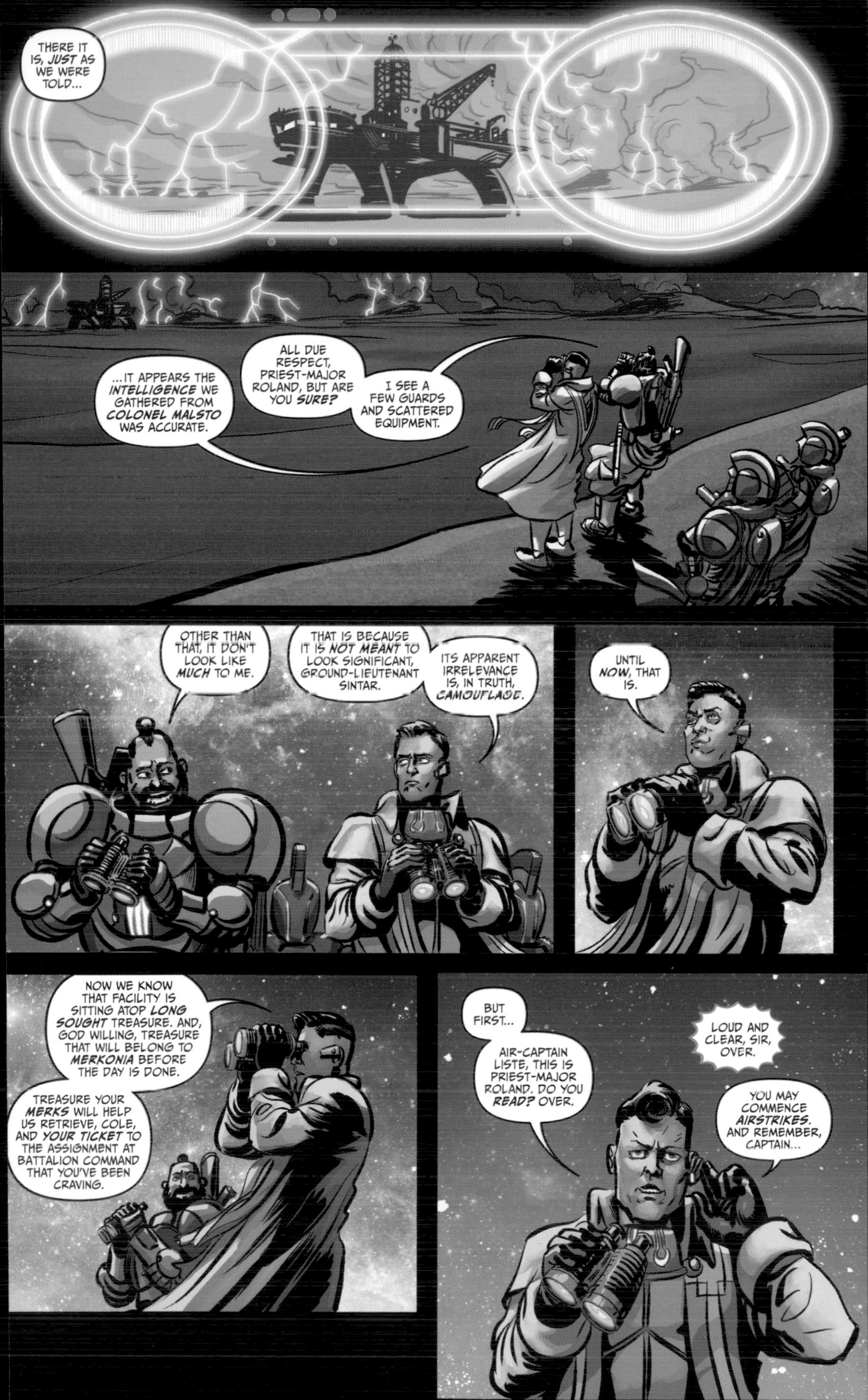
THERE IT IS, JUST AS WE WERE TOLD...
...IT APPEARS THE INTELLIGENCE WE GATHERED FROM COLONEL MALSTO WAS ACCURATE.
ALL DUE RESPECT, PRIEST-MAJOR ROLAND, BUT ARE YOU SURE?
I SEE A FEW GUARDS AND SCATTERED EQUIPMENT.
OTHER THAN THAT, IT DON'T LOOK LIKE MUCH TO ME.
THAT IS BECAUSE IT IS NOT MEANT TO LOOK SIGNIFICANT, GROUND-LIEUTENANT SINTAR.
ITS APPARENT IRRELEVANCE IS, IN TRUTH, CAMOUFLAGE.
UNTIL NOW, THAT IS.
NOW WE KNOW THAT FACILITY IS SITTING ATOP LONG SOUGHT TREASURE. AND, GOD WILLING, TREASURE THAT WILL BELONG TO MERKONIA BEFORE THE DAY IS DONE.
TREASURE YOUR MERKS WILL HELP US RETRIEVE, COLE, AND YOUR TICKET TO THE ASSIGNMENT AT BATTALION COMMAND THAT YOU'VE BEEN CRAVING.
BUT FIRST...
AIR-CAPTAIN LISTE, THIS IS PRIEST-MAJOR ROLAND. DO YOU READ? OVER.
LOUD AND CLEAR, SIR, OVER.
YOU MAY COMMENCE AIRSTRIKES. AND REMEMBER, CAPTAIN...

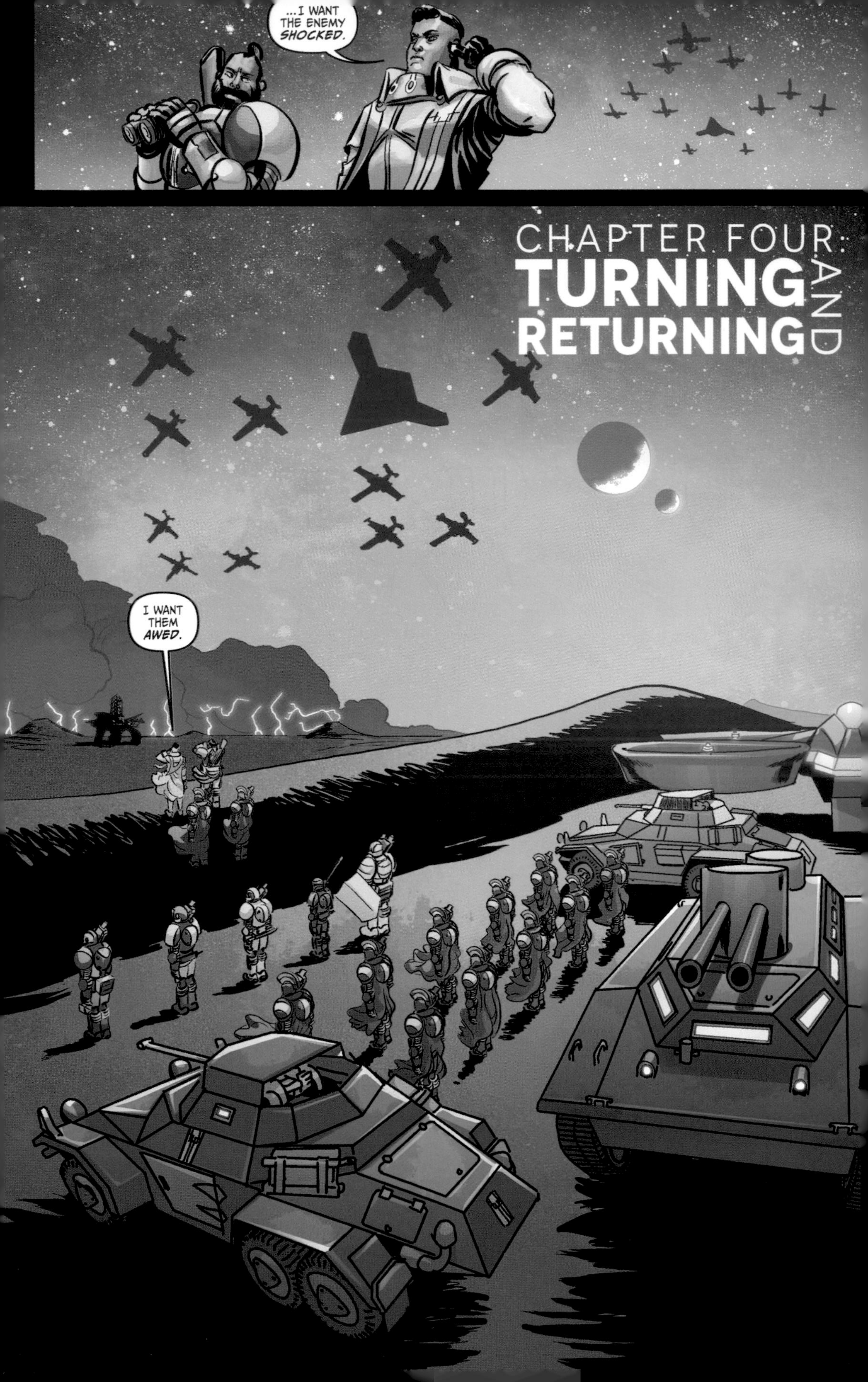
...I WANT THE ENEMY SHOCKED.
CHAPTER FOUR:
TURNING AND RETURNING
I WANT THEM AWED.

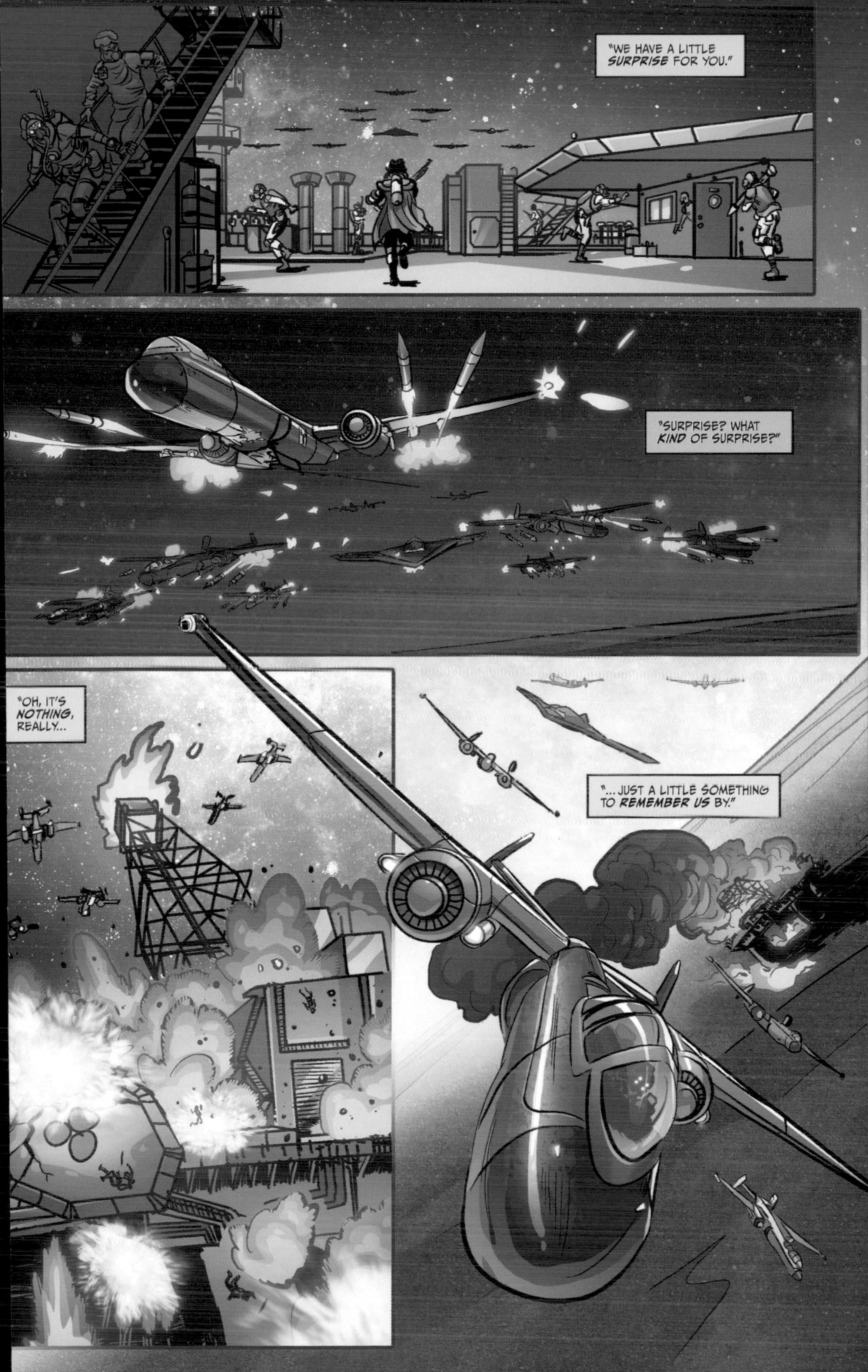

"WE HAVE A LITTLE SURPRISE FOR YOU."
"SURPRISE? WHAT KIND OF SURPRISE?"
"OH, IT'S NOTHING, REALLY...
"...JUST A LITTLE SOMETHING TO REMEMBER US BY."

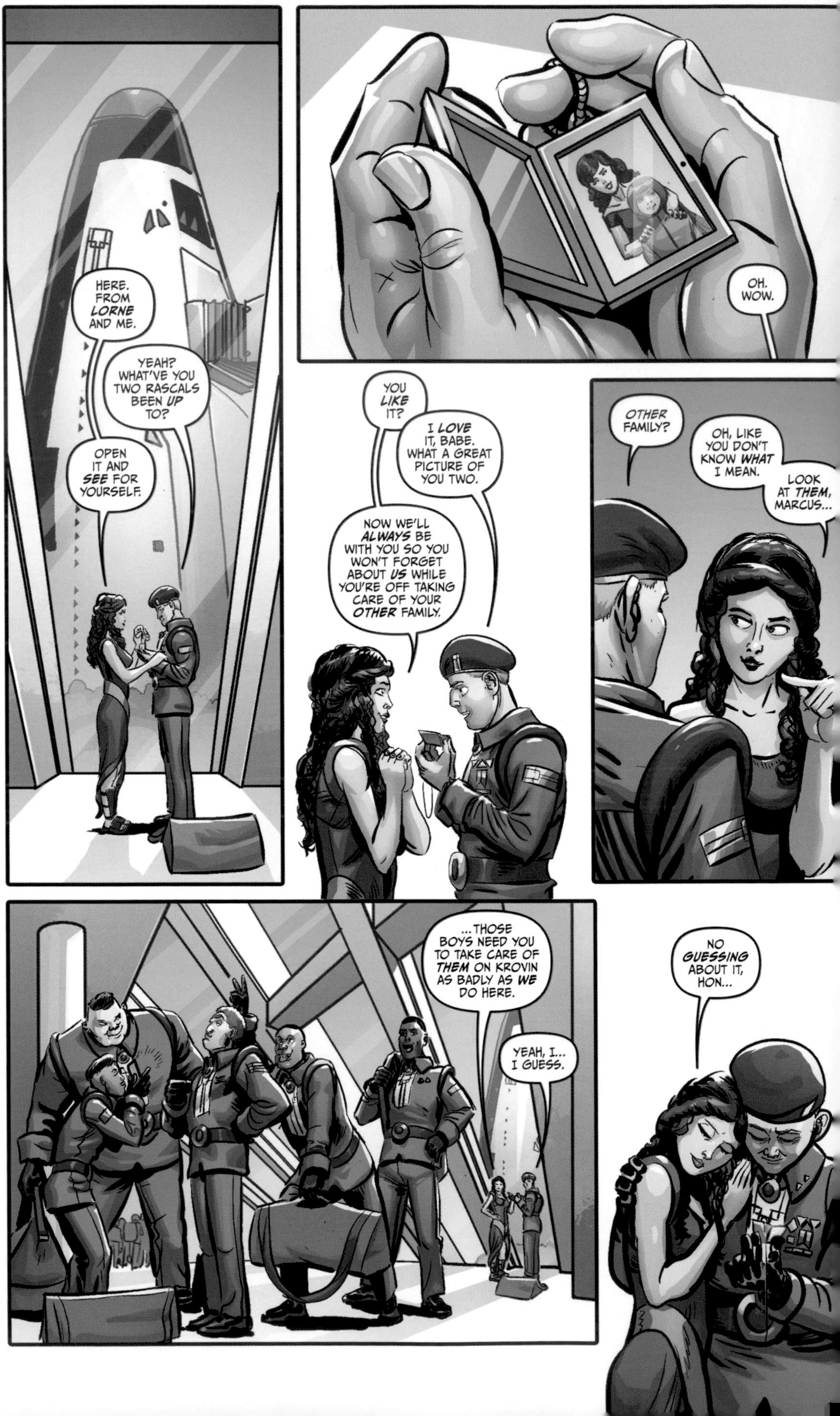
HERE. FROM LORNE AND ME.
YEAH? WHAT'VE YOU TWO RASCALS BEEN UP TO?
OPEN IT AND SEE FOR YOURSELF.
OH. WOW.
YOU LIKE IT?
I LOVE IT, BABE. WHAT A GREAT PICTURE OF YOU TWO.
NOW WE'LL ALWAYS BE WITH YOU SO YOU WON'T FORGET ABOUT US WHILE YOU'RE OFF TAKING CARE OF YOUR OTHER FAMILY.
OTHER FAMILY?
OH, LIKE YOU DON'T KNOW WHAT I MEAN.
LOOK AT THEM, MARCUS...
...THOSE BOYS NEED YOU TO TAKE CARE OF THEM ON KROVIN AS BADLY AS WE DO HERE.
YEAH, I... I GUESS.
NO GUESSING ABOUT IT, HON...

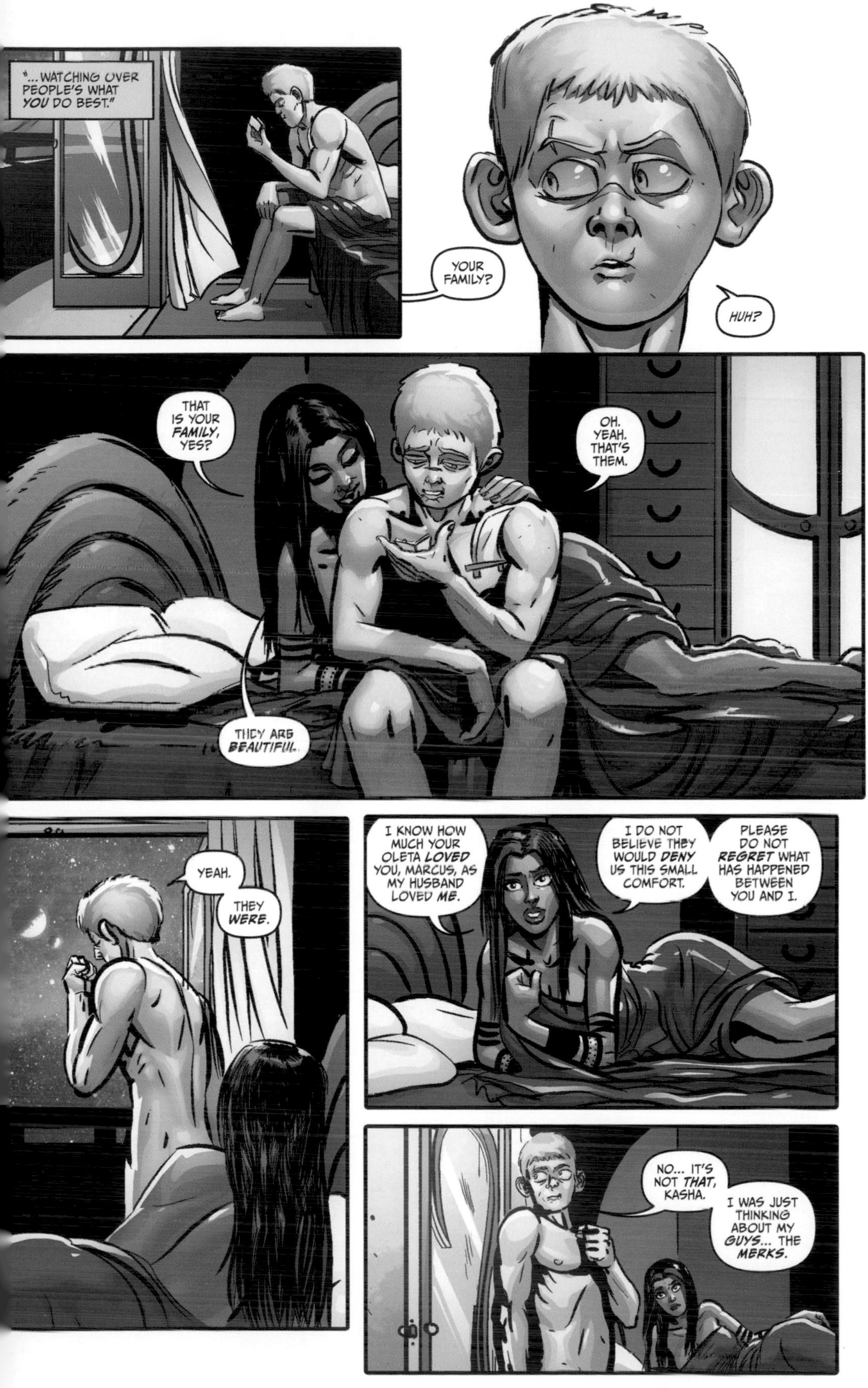
"...WATCHING OVER PEOPLE'S WHAT YOU DO BEST."
YOUR FAMILY?
HUH?
THAT IS YOUR FAMILY, YES?
OH. YEAH. THAT'S THEM.
THEY ARE BEAUTIFUL.
YEAH.
THEY WERE.
I KNOW HOW MUCH YOUR OLETA LOVED YOU, MARCUS, AS MY HUSBAND LOVED ME.
I DO NOT BELIEVE THEY WOULD DENY US THIS SMALL COMFORT.
PLEASE DO NOT REGRET WHAT HAS HAPPENED BETWEEN YOU AND I.
NO... IT'S NOT THAT, KASHA.
I WAS JUST THINKING ABOUT MY GUYS... THE MERKS.

"JUST WONDERING IF THEY'RE ALL *OKAY*."

MAN, THIS IS *NOT OKAY*.

I MEAN, WHAT'S THE *POINT* OF BLOWIN' THE HELL OUTTA A RUSTY OLD REFINERY UNLESS THE BRASS *KNOW* SOMETHIN' WE DON'T.

AND WHAT'S UP WITH ALL THE *HOLY GUARD* FREAKS?

"WE NEVER HAD *THIS MANY* PRIEST PUPPIES ON AN OP WITH US BEFORE."

LOCK IT UP, GUYS. THE *LIEUTENANT'S* COMING.

SPEAKING OF FREAKY...

QUIET, BANTO!

ALL RIGHT, *MERKS, OUR* TURN!

THE FLYBOYS *SOFTENED UP* THE KROVES PRETTY DAMN GOOD BUT WE ALL KNOW THERE'S BOUND TO BE *MORE* RATS HOLED UP IN THAT NEST JUST *WAITIN'* TO TAKE A BITE OUTTA US GROUND SLOGGERS.

LET'S MAKE SURE THAT *DON'T* HAPPEN.

WE GOT OUR ORDERS AND THEY'RE *REAL* SIMPLE.

WE *FIND* THE STRAGGLERS, WE HIT 'EM *FAST*, WE HIT 'EM *HARD*... WE SMASH *EVERY* LAST ONE OF 'EM!

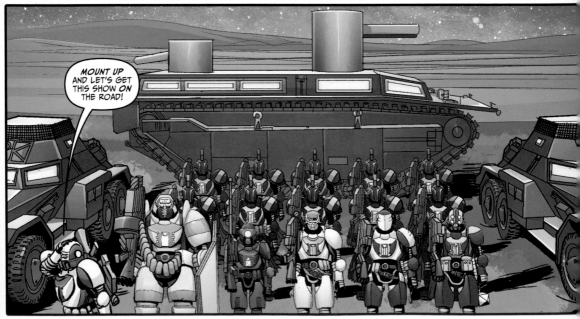

MOUNT UP AND LET'S GET THIS SHOW *ON* THE ROAD!

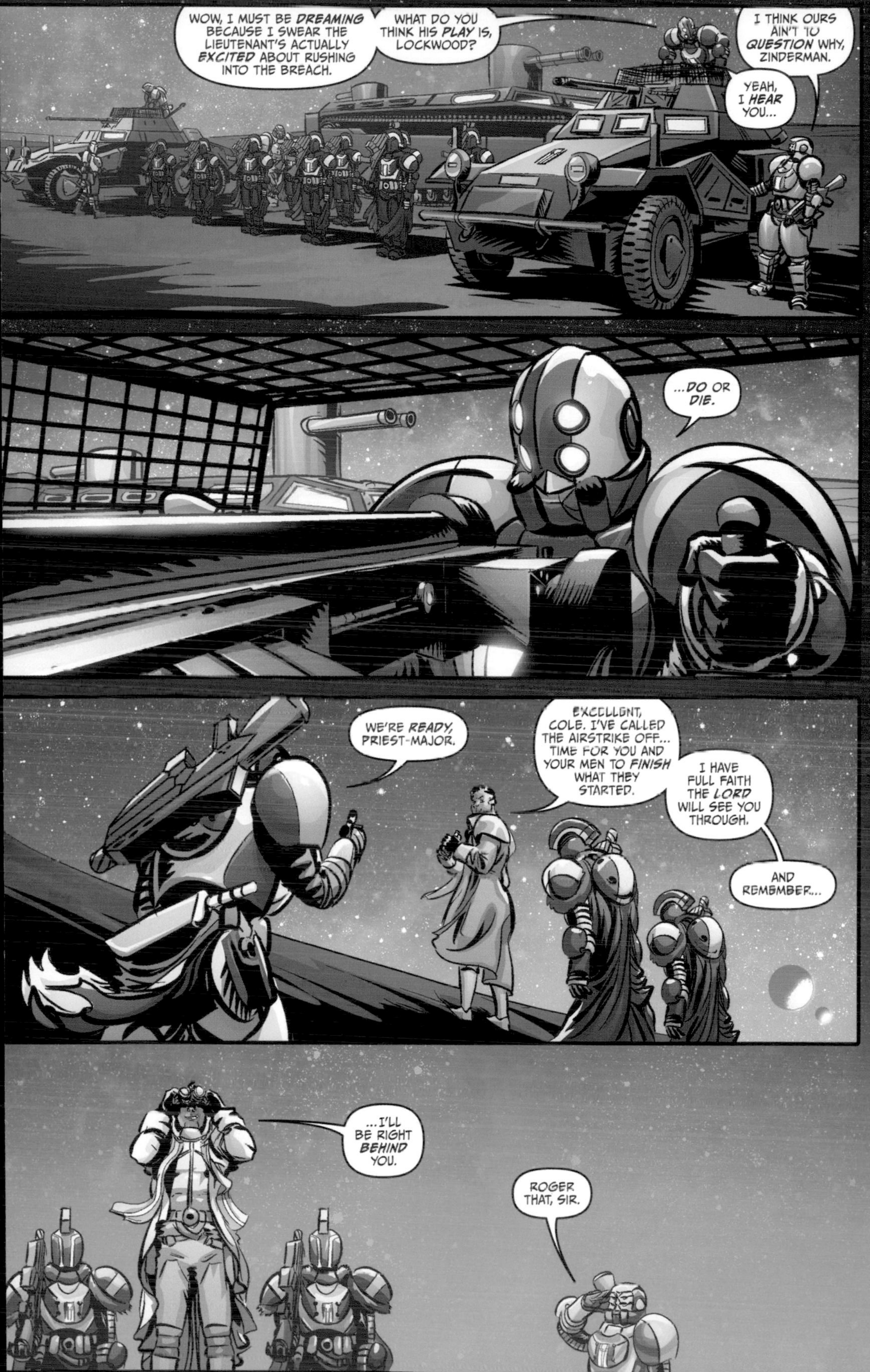
WOW, I MUST BE DREAMING BECAUSE I SWEAR THE LIEUTENANT'S ACTUALLY EXCITED ABOUT RUSHING INTO THE BREACH.
WHAT DO YOU THINK HIS PLAY IS, LOCKWOOD?
I THINK OURS AIN'T TO QUESTION WHY, ZINDERMAN.
YEAH, I HEAR YOU...
...DO OR DIE.
WE'RE READY, PRIEST-MAJOR.
EXCELLENT, COLE. I'VE CALLED THE AIRSTRIKE OFF... TIME FOR YOU AND YOUR MEN TO FINISH WHAT THEY STARTED.
I HAVE FULL FAITH THE LORD WILL SEE YOU THROUGH.
AND REMEMBER...
...I'LL BE RIGHT BEHIND YOU.
ROGER THAT, SIR.

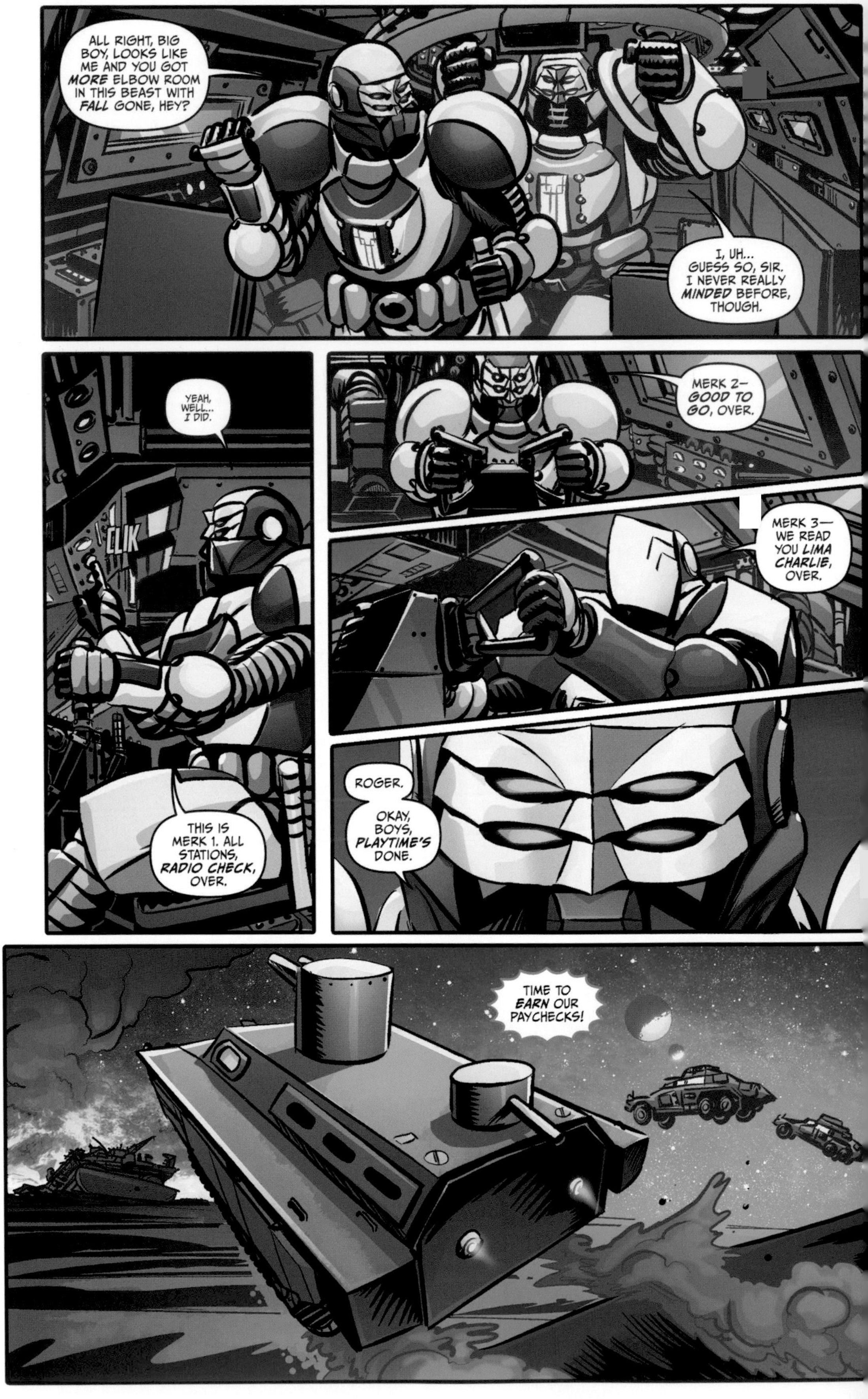
ALL RIGHT, BIG BOY, LOOKS LIKE ME AND YOU GOT MORE ELBOW ROOM IN THIS BEAST WITH FALL GONE, HEY?
I, UH... GUESS SO, SIR. I NEVER REALLY MINDED BEFORE, THOUGH.
YEAH, WELL... I DID.
CLIK
THIS IS MERK 1. ALL STATIONS, RADIO CHECK, OVER.
MERK 2— GOOD TO GO, OVER.
MERK 3— WE READ YOU LIMA CHARLIE, OVER.
ROGER.
OKAY, BOYS, PLAYTIME'S DONE.
TIME TO EARN OUR PAYCHECKS!

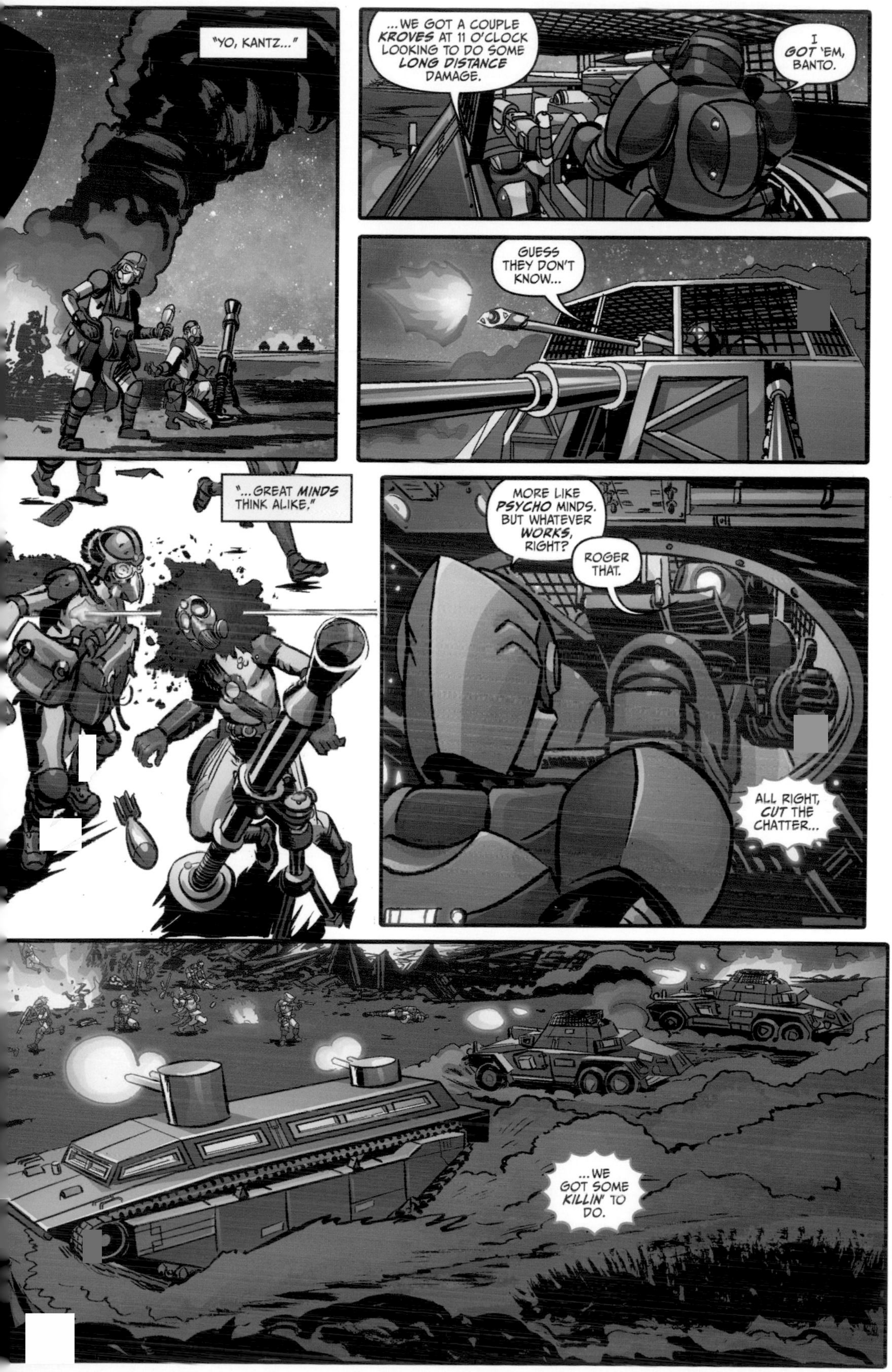

"YO, KANTZ..."
...WE GOT A COUPLE KROVES AT 11 O'CLOCK LOOKING TO DO SOME LONG DISTANCE DAMAGE.
I GOT 'EM, BANTO.
GUESS THEY DON'T KNOW...
"...GREAT MINDS THINK ALIKE."
MORE LIKE PSYCHO MINDS. BUT WHATEVER WORKS, RIGHT?
ROGER THAT.
ALL RIGHT, CUT THE CHATTER...
...WE GOT SOME KILLIN' TO DO.

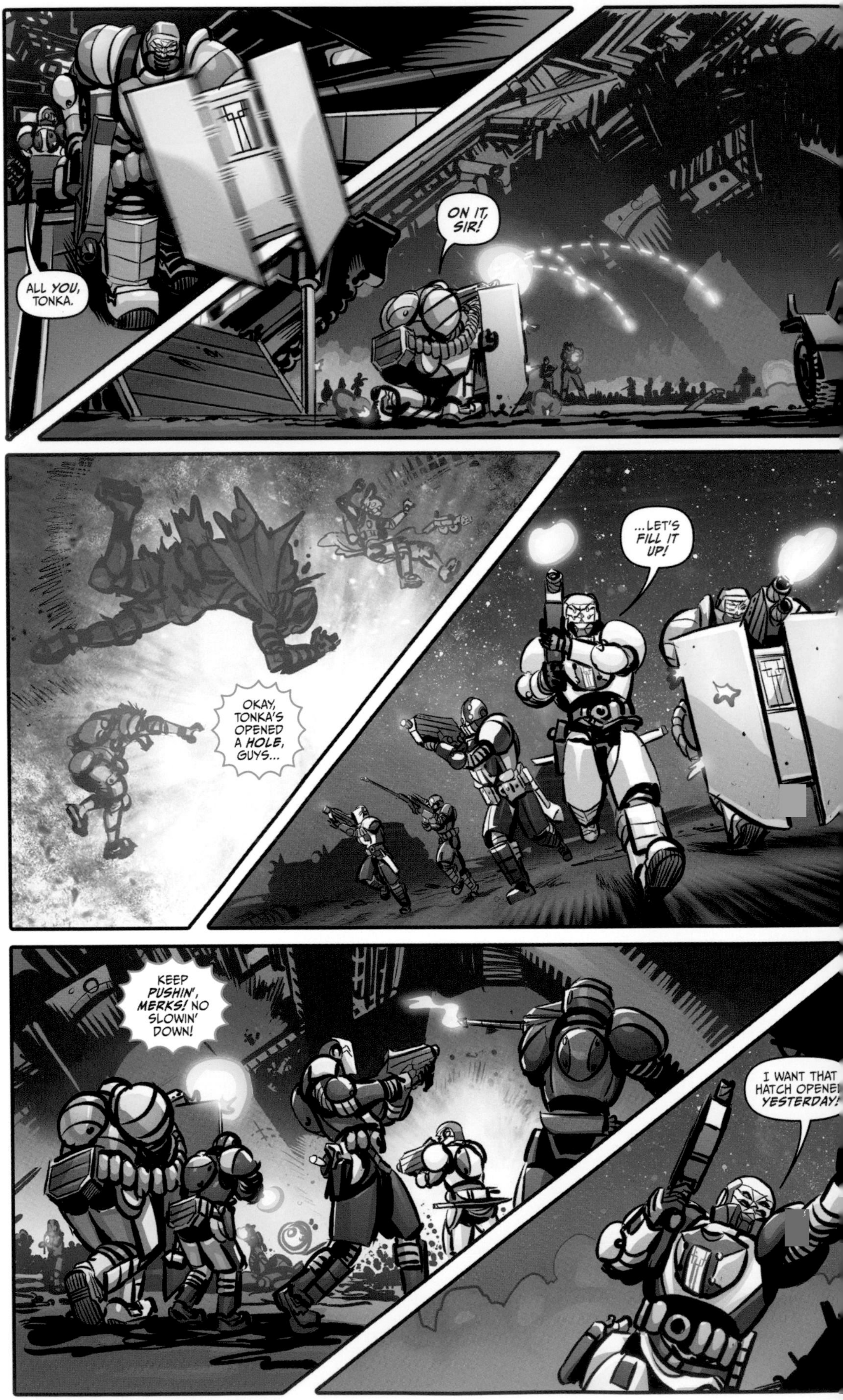
ALL YOU, TONKA.
ON IT, SIR!
OKAY, TONKA'S OPENED A HOLE, GUYS...
...LET'S FILL IT UP!
KEEP PUSHIN', MERKS! NO SLOWIN' DOWN!
I WANT THAT HATCH OPENE YESTERDAY!

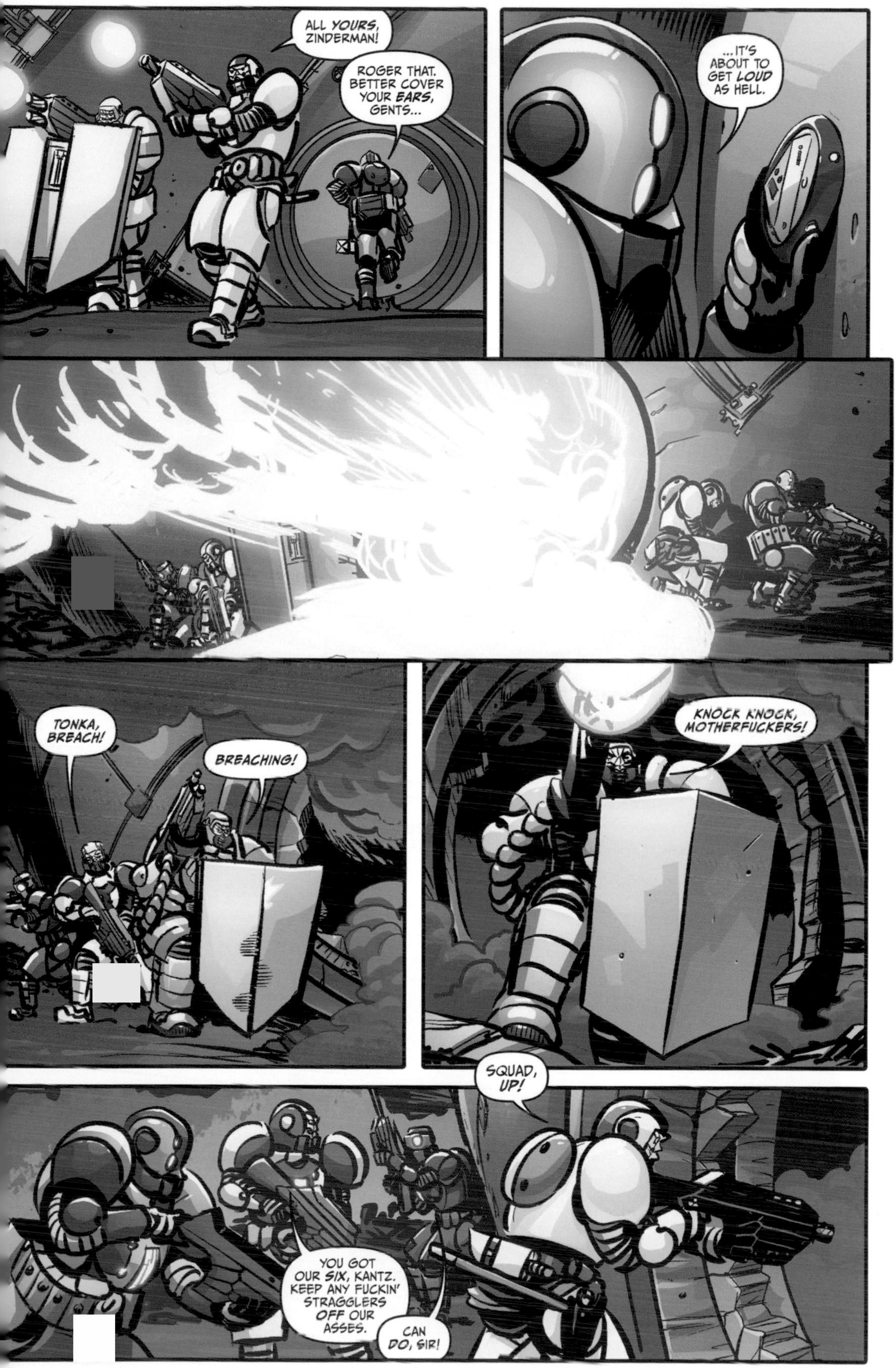
ALL YOURS, ZINDERMAN!
ROGER THAT. BETTER COVER YOUR EARS, GENTS...
...IT'S ABOUT TO GET LOUD AS HELL.
TONKA, BREACH!
BREACHING!
KNOCK KNOCK, MOTHERFUCKERS!
SQUAD, UP!
YOU GOT OUR SIX, KANTZ. KEEP ANY FUCKIN' STRAGGLERS OFF OUR ASSES.
CAN DO, SIR!

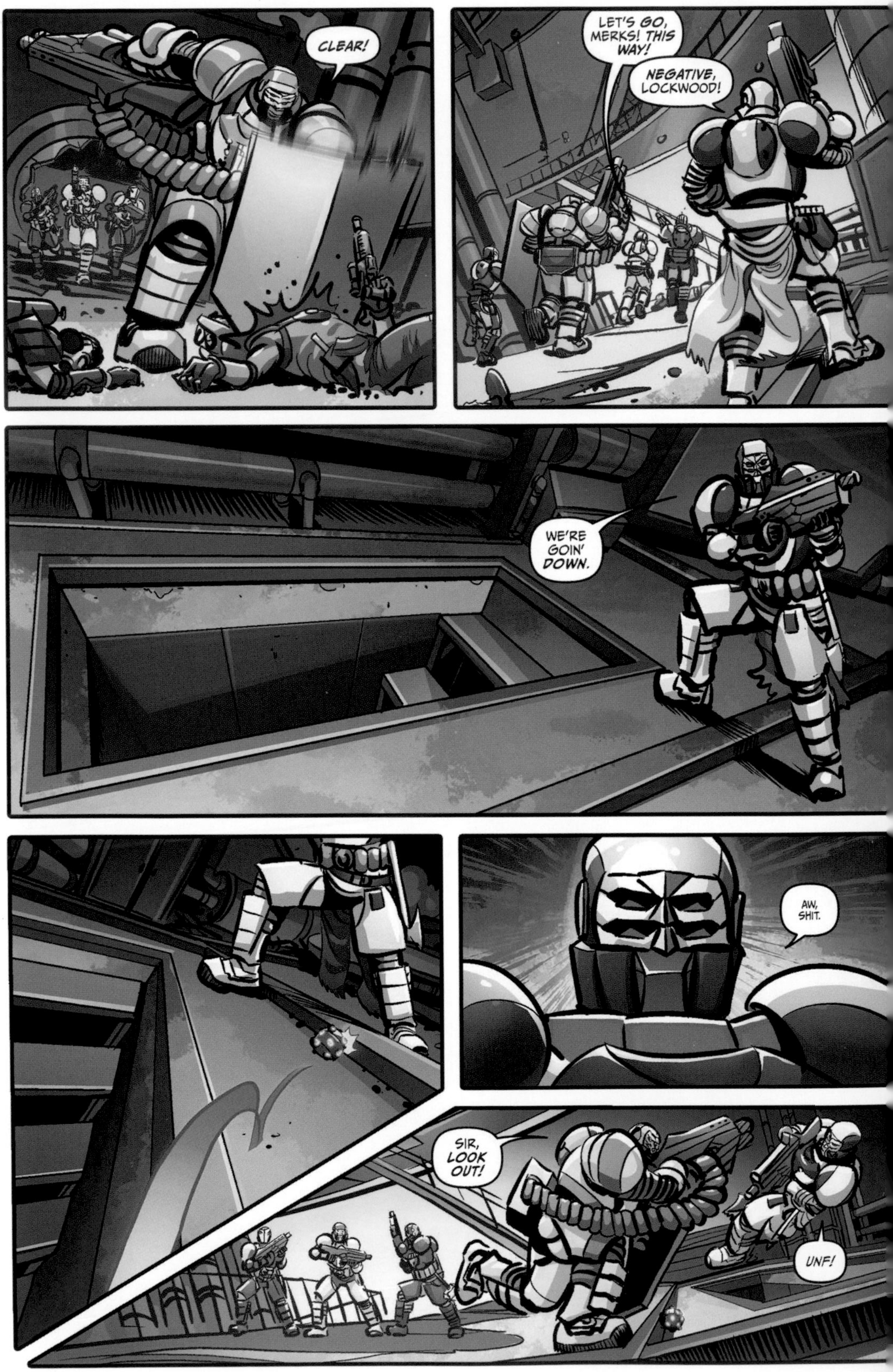
CLEAR!
LET'S GO, MERKS! THIS WAY!
NEGATIVE, LOCKWOOD!
WE'RE GOIN' DOWN.
AW, SHIT.
SIR, LOOK OUT!
UNF!

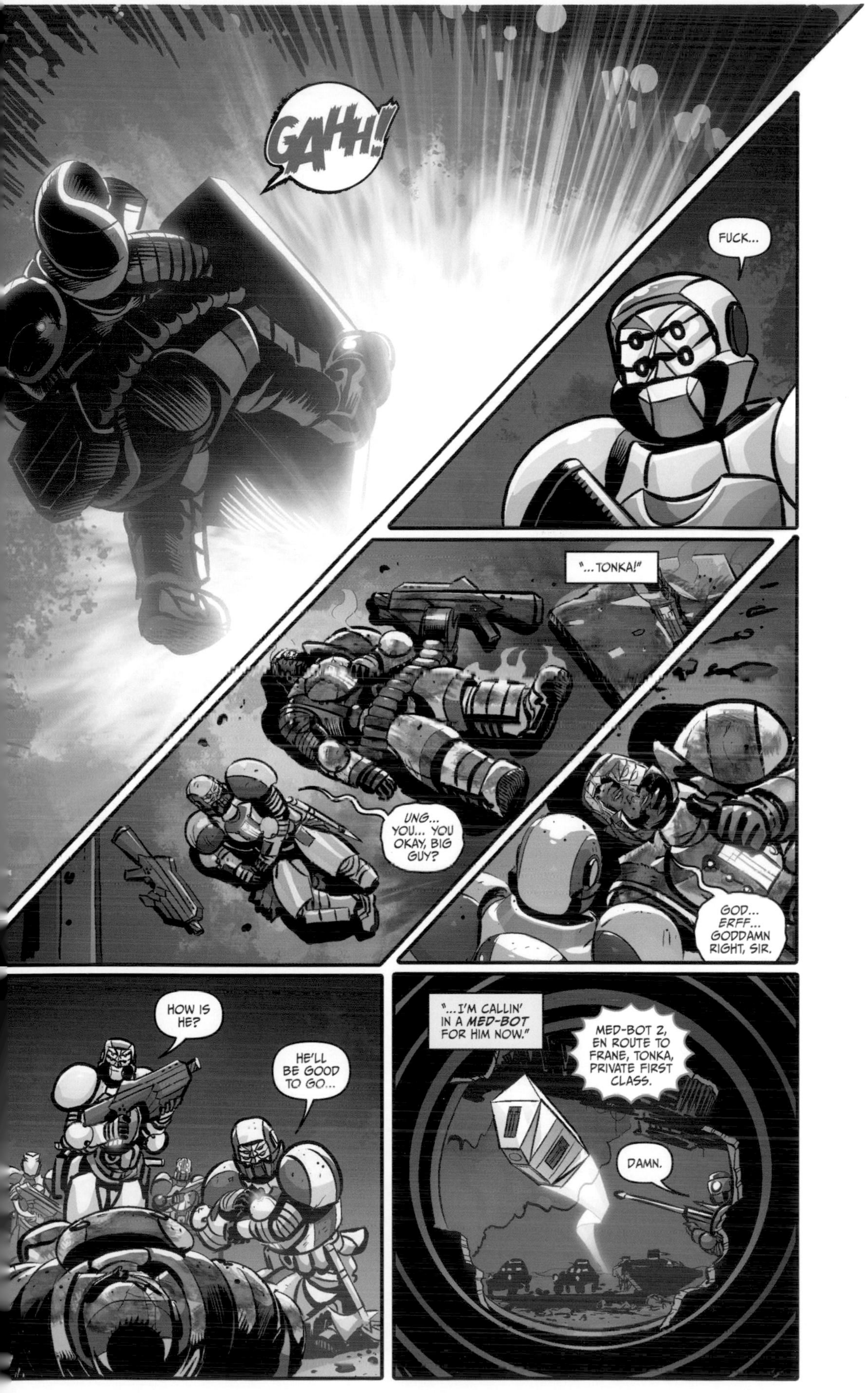
GAHH!
FUCK...
"...TONKA!"
UNG... YOU... YOU OKAY, BIG GUY?
GOD... ERFF... GODDAMN RIGHT, SIR.
HOW IS HE?
HE'LL BE GOOD TO GO...
"...I'M CALLIN' IN A *MED-BOT* FOR HIM NOW."
MED-BOT 2, EN ROUTE TO FRANE, TONKA, PRIVATE FIRST CLASS.
DAMN.

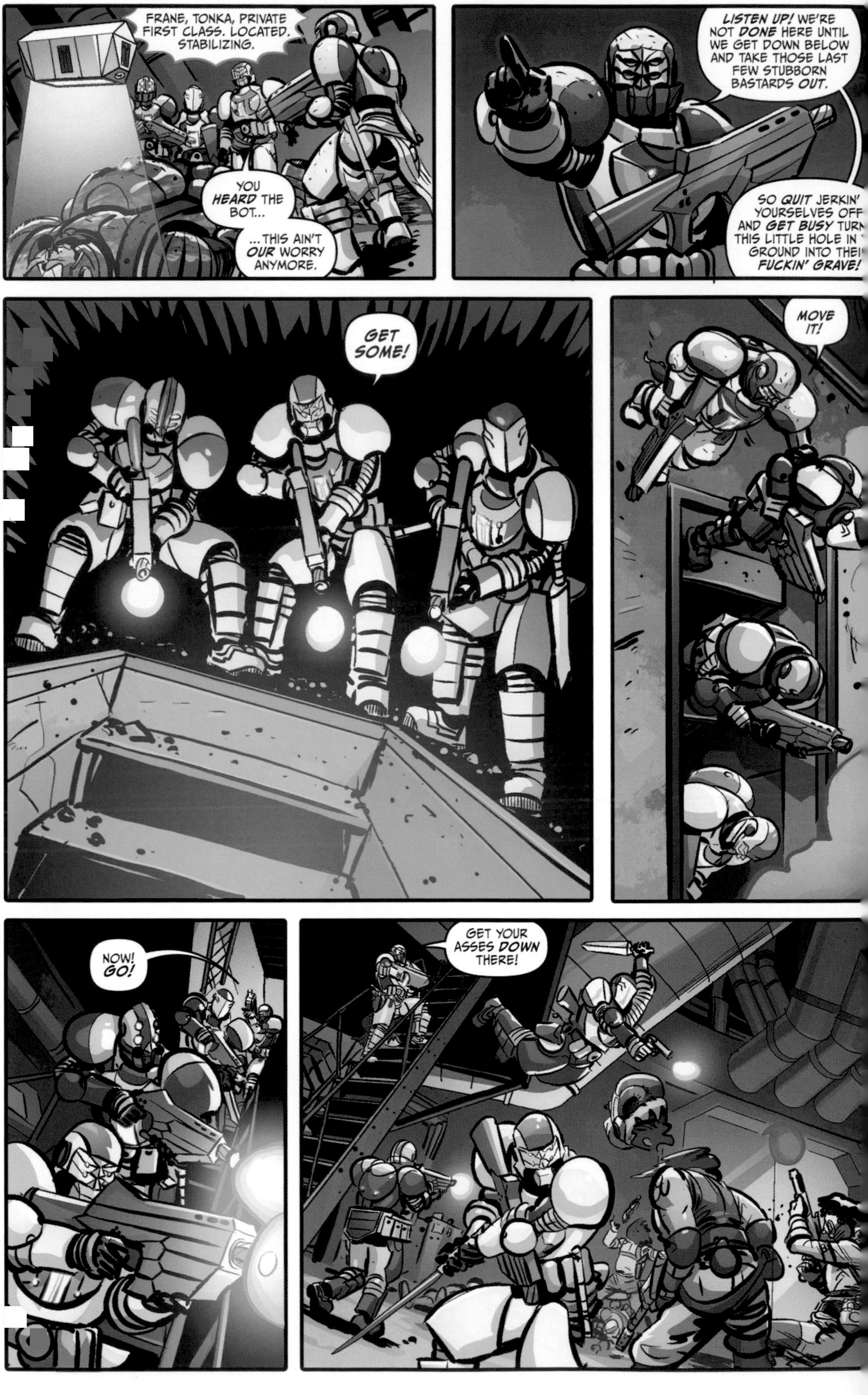
FRANE, TONKA, PRIVATE FIRST CLASS. LOCATED. STABILIZING.
YOU HEARD THE BOT...
...THIS AIN'T OUR WORRY ANYMORE.
LISTEN UP! WE'RE NOT DONE HERE UNTIL WE GET DOWN BELOW AND TAKE THOSE LAST FEW STUBBORN BASTARDS OUT.
SO QUIT JERKIN' YOURSELVES OFF AND GET BUSY TURN THIS LITTLE HOLE IN GROUND INTO THEI FUCKIN' GRAVE!
GET SOME!
MOVE IT!
NOW! GO!
GET YOUR ASSES DOWN THERE!

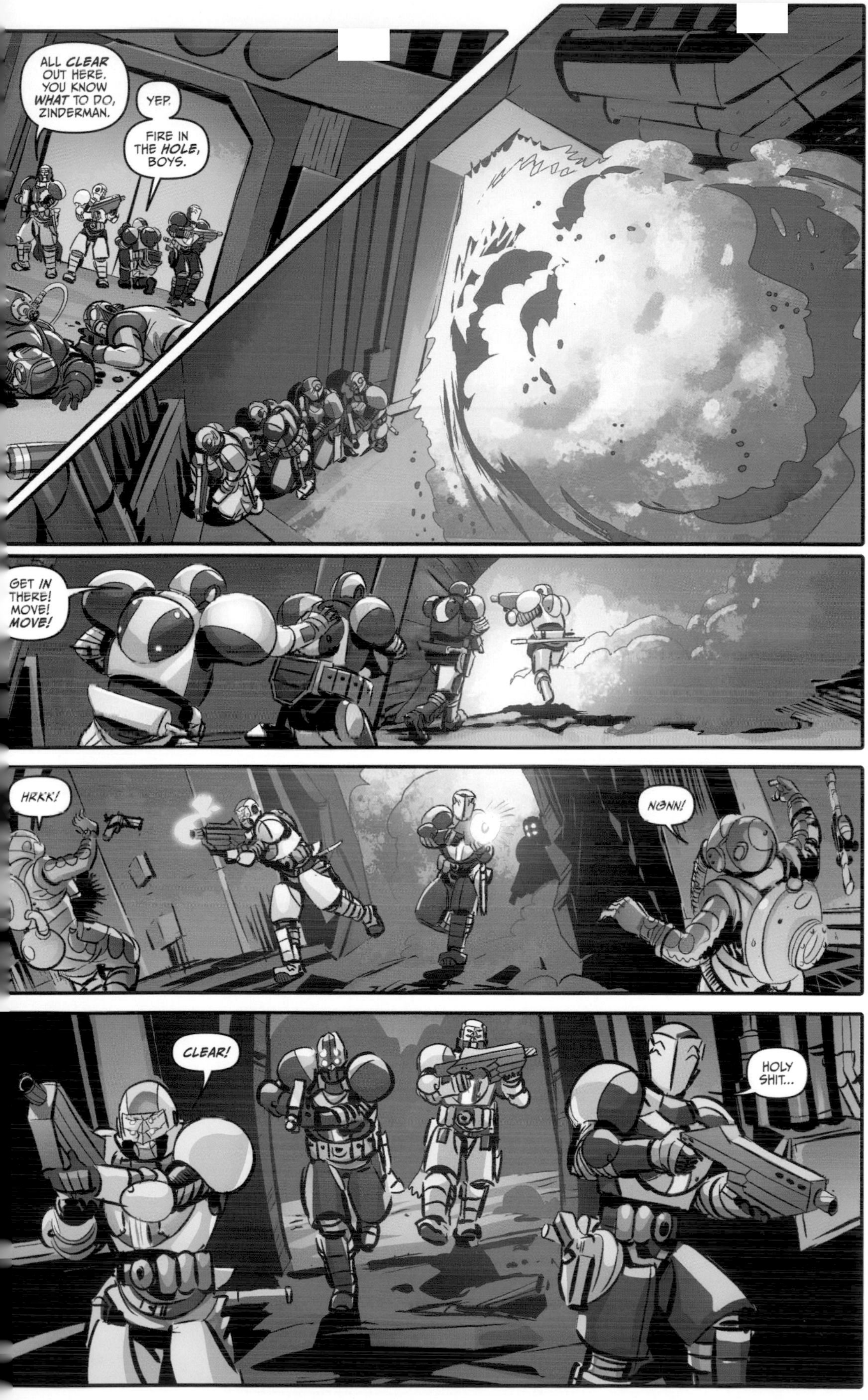
ALL CLEAR OUT HERE. YOU KNOW WHAT TO DO, ZINDERMAN.
YEP.
FIRE IN THE HOLE, BOYS.
GET IN THERE! MOVE! MOVE!
HRKK!
NGNN!
CLEAR!
HOLY SHIT...

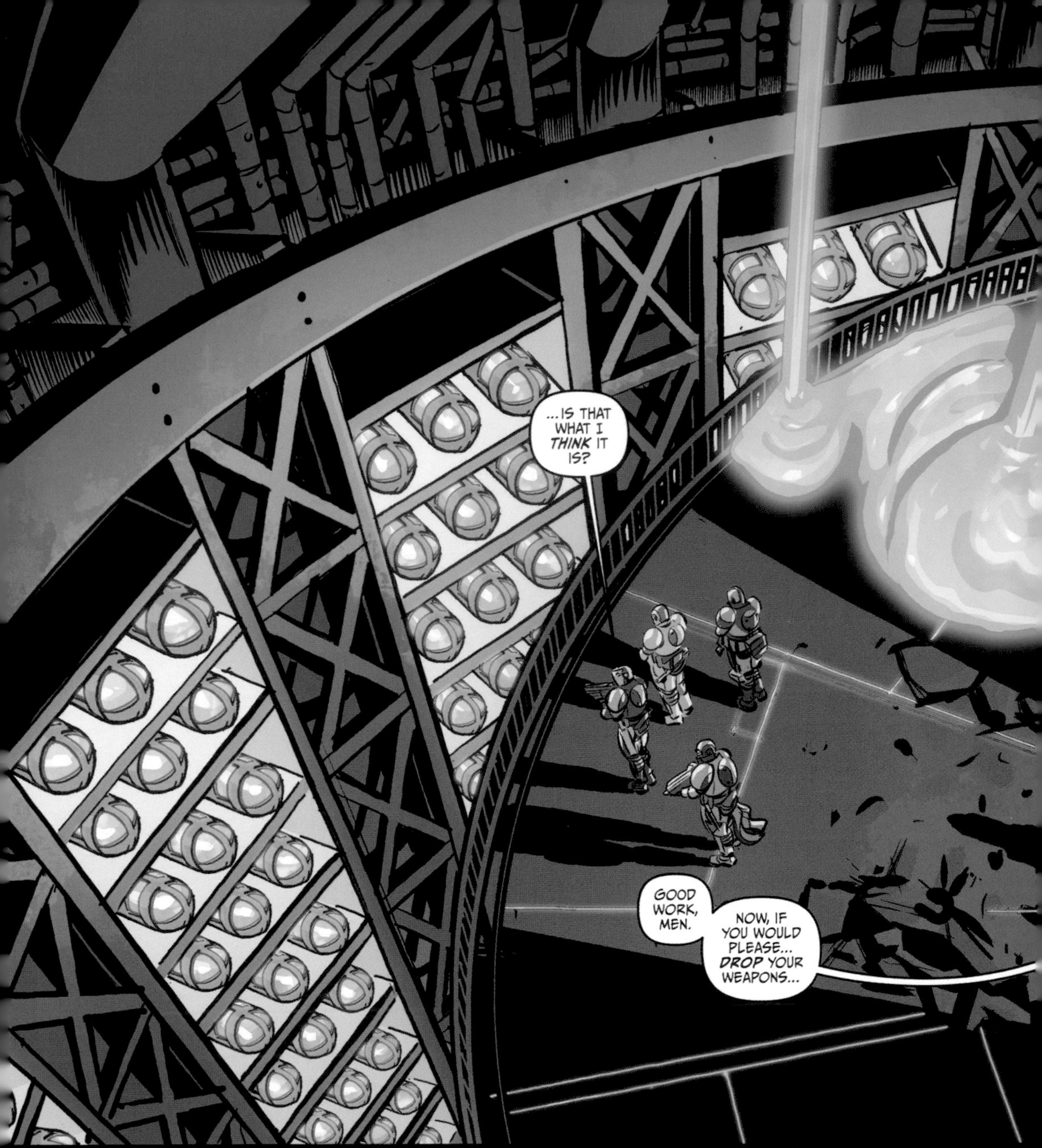
...IS THAT WHAT I THINK IT IS?
GOOD WORK, MEN.
NOW, IF YOU WOULD PLEASE... DROP YOUR WEAPONS...

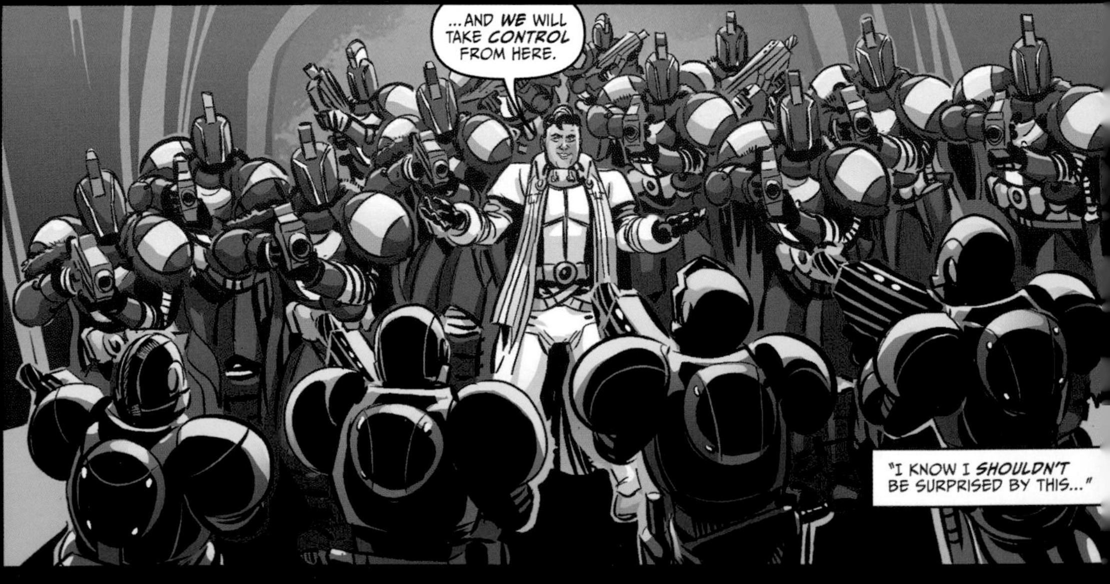
...AND WE WILL TAKE CONTROL FROM HERE.
"I KNOW I SHOULDN'T BE SURPRISED BY THIS..."

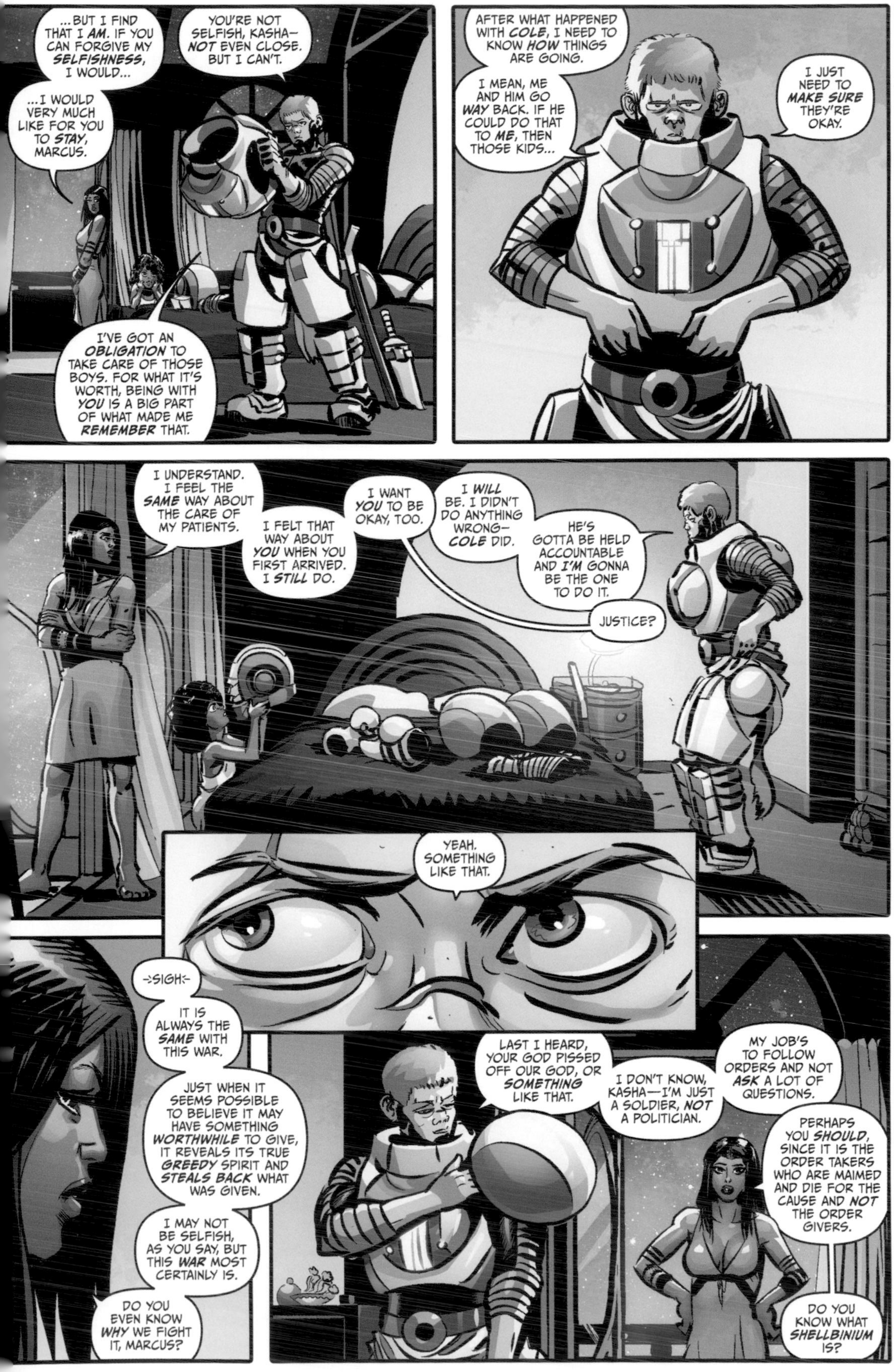
...BUT I FIND THAT I AM. IF YOU CAN FORGIVE MY SELFISHNESS, I WOULD...
...I WOULD VERY MUCH LIKE FOR YOU TO STAY, MARCUS.
YOU'RE NOT SELFISH, KASHA— NOT EVEN CLOSE. BUT I CAN'T.
I'VE GOT AN OBLIGATION TO TAKE CARE OF THOSE BOYS. FOR WHAT IT'S WORTH, BEING WITH YOU IS A BIG PART OF WHAT MADE ME REMEMBER THAT.
AFTER WHAT HAPPENED WITH COLE, I NEED TO KNOW HOW THINGS ARE GOING.
I MEAN, ME AND HIM GO WAY BACK. IF HE COULD DO THAT TO ME, THEN THOSE KIDS...
I JUST NEED TO MAKE SURE THEY'RE OKAY.
I UNDERSTAND. I FEEL THE SAME WAY ABOUT THE CARE OF MY PATIENTS.
I FELT THAT WAY ABOUT YOU WHEN YOU FIRST ARRIVED. I STILL DO.
I WANT YOU TO BE OKAY, TOO.
I WILL BE. I DIDN'T DO ANYTHING WRONG— COLE DID.
HE'S GOTTA BE HELD ACCOUNTABLE AND I'M GONNA BE THE ONE TO DO IT.
JUSTICE?
YEAH. SOMETHING LIKE THAT.
-SIGH-
IT IS ALWAYS THE SAME WITH THIS WAR.
JUST WHEN IT SEEMS POSSIBLE TO BELIEVE IT MAY HAVE SOMETHING WORTHWHILE TO GIVE, IT REVEALS ITS TRUE GREEDY SPIRIT AND STEALS BACK WHAT WAS GIVEN.
I MAY NOT BE SELFISH, AS YOU SAY, BUT THIS WAR MOST CERTAINLY IS.
DO YOU EVEN KNOW WHY WE FIGHT IT, MARCUS?
LAST I HEARD, YOUR GOD PISSED OFF OUR GOD, OR SOMETHING LIKE THAT.
I DON'T KNOW, KASHA—I'M JUST A SOLDIER, NOT A POLITICIAN.
MY JOB'S TO FOLLOW ORDERS AND NOT ASK A LOT OF QUESTIONS.
PERHAPS YOU SHOULD, SINCE IT IS THE ORDER TAKERS WHO ARE MAIMED AND DIE FOR THE CAUSE AND NOT THE ORDER GIVERS.
DO YOU KNOW WHAT SHELLBINIUM IS?

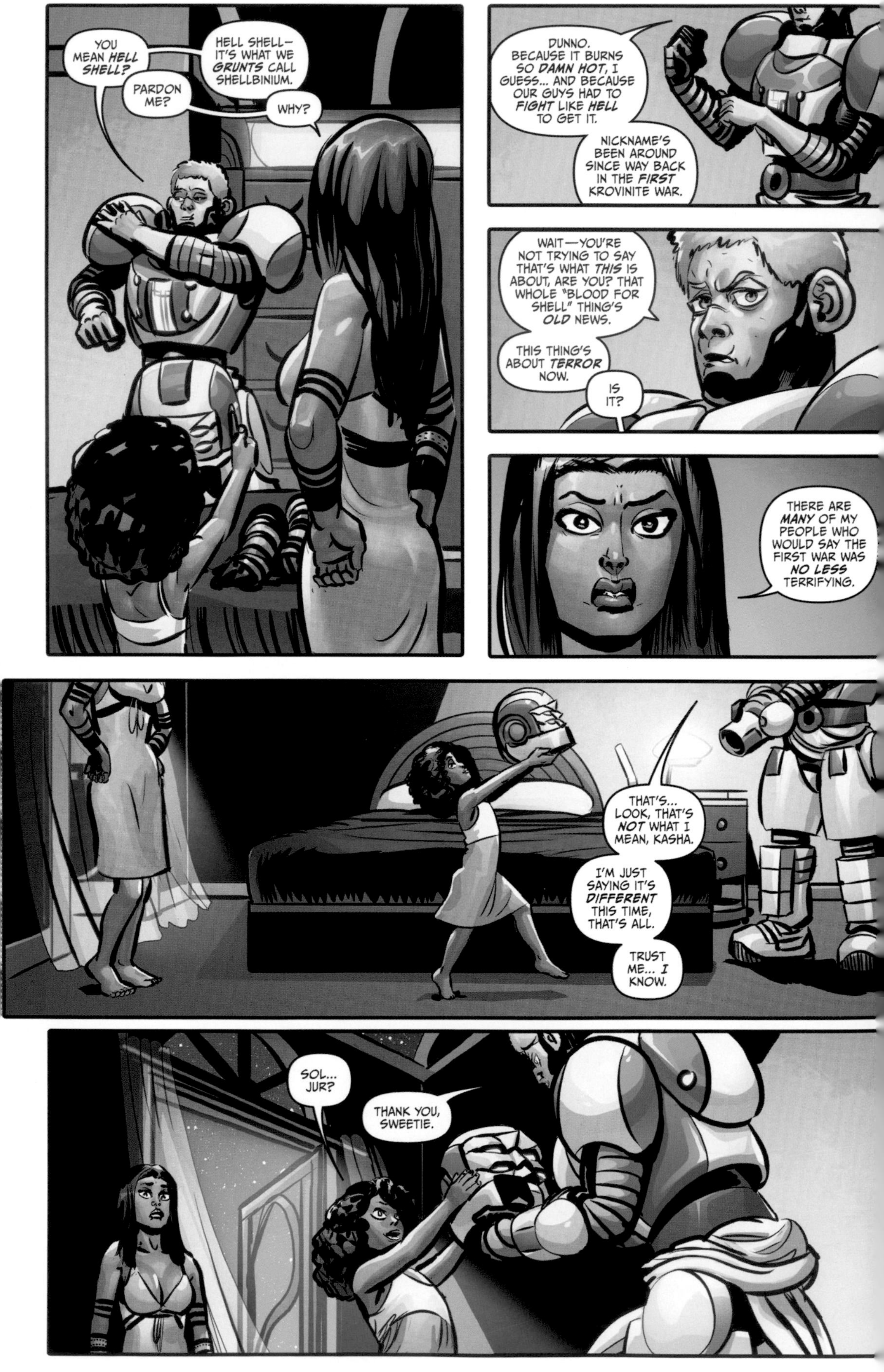
YOU MEAN HELL SHELL?
HELL SHELL— IT'S WHAT WE GRUNTS CALL SHELLBINIUM.
PARDON ME?
WHY?
DUNNO. BECAUSE IT BURNS SO DAMN HOT, I GUESS... AND BECAUSE OUR GUYS HAD TO FIGHT LIKE HELL TO GET IT.
NICKNAME'S BEEN AROUND SINCE WAY BACK IN THE FIRST KROVINITE WAR.
WAIT—YOU'RE NOT TRYING TO SAY THAT'S WHAT THIS IS ABOUT, ARE YOU? THAT WHOLE "BLOOD FOR SHELL" THING'S OLD NEWS.
THIS THING'S ABOUT TERROR NOW.
IS IT?
THERE ARE MANY OF MY PEOPLE WHO WOULD SAY THE FIRST WAR WAS NO LESS TERRIFYING.
THAT'S... LOOK, THAT'S NOT WHAT I MEAN, KASHA.
I'M JUST SAYING IT'S DIFFERENT THIS TIME, THAT'S ALL.
TRUST ME... I KNOW.
SOL... JUR?
THANK YOU, SWEETIE.

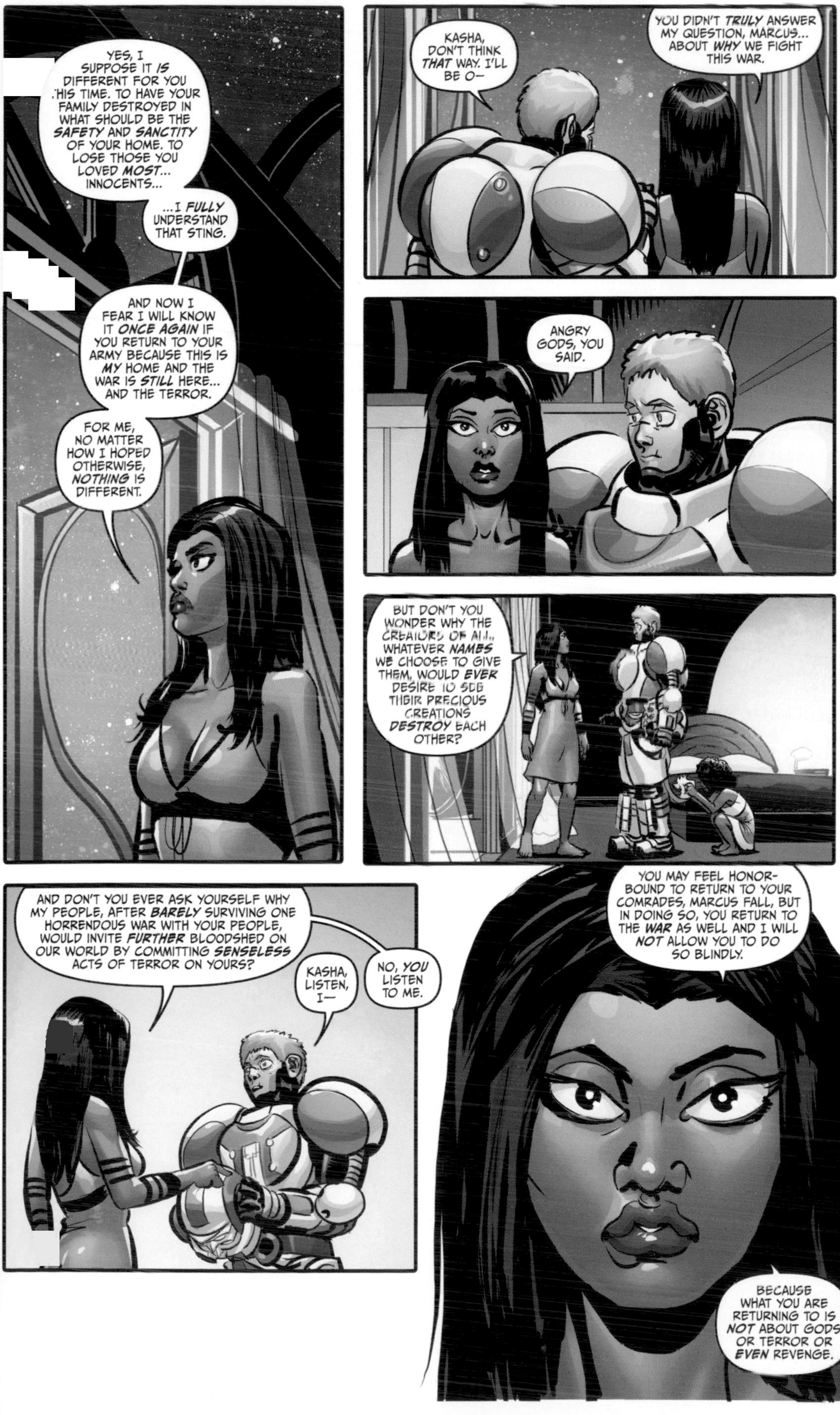

YES, I SUPPOSE IT *IS* DIFFERENT FOR YOU THIS TIME. TO HAVE YOUR FAMILY DESTROYED IN WHAT SHOULD BE THE *SAFETY* AND *SANCTITY* OF YOUR HOME. TO LOSE THOSE YOU LOVED *MOST*... INNOCENTS...
...I *FULLY* UNDERSTAND THAT STING.
AND NOW I FEAR I WILL KNOW IT *ONCE AGAIN* IF YOU RETURN TO YOUR ARMY BECAUSE THIS IS *MY* HOME AND THE WAR IS *STILL* HERE... AND THE TERROR.
FOR ME, NO MATTER HOW I HOPED OTHERWISE, *NOTHING* IS DIFFERENT.
KASHA, DON'T THINK *THAT* WAY. I'LL BE O—
YOU DIDN'T *TRULY* ANSWER MY QUESTION, MARCUS... ABOUT *WHY* WE FIGHT THIS WAR.
ANGRY GODS, YOU SAID.
BUT DON'T YOU WONDER WHY THE CREATORS OF ALL, WHATEVER *NAMES* WE CHOOSE TO GIVE THEM, WOULD *EVER* DESIRE TO SEE THEIR PRECIOUS CREATIONS *DESTROY* EACH OTHER?
AND DON'T YOU EVER ASK YOURSELF WHY MY PEOPLE, AFTER *BARELY* SURVIVING ONE HORRENDOUS WAR WITH YOUR PEOPLE, WOULD INVITE *FURTHER* BLOODSHED ON OUR WORLD BY COMMITTING *SENSELESS* ACTS OF TERROR ON YOURS?
KASHA, LISTEN, I—
NO, *YOU* LISTEN TO ME.
YOU MAY FEEL HONOR-BOUND TO RETURN TO YOUR COMRADES, MARCUS FALL, BUT IN DOING SO, YOU RETURN TO THE *WAR* AS WELL AND I WILL *NOT* ALLOW YOU TO DO SO BLINDLY.
BECAUSE WHAT YOU ARE RETURNING TO IS *NOT* ABOUT GODS OR TERROR OR *EVEN* REVENGE.

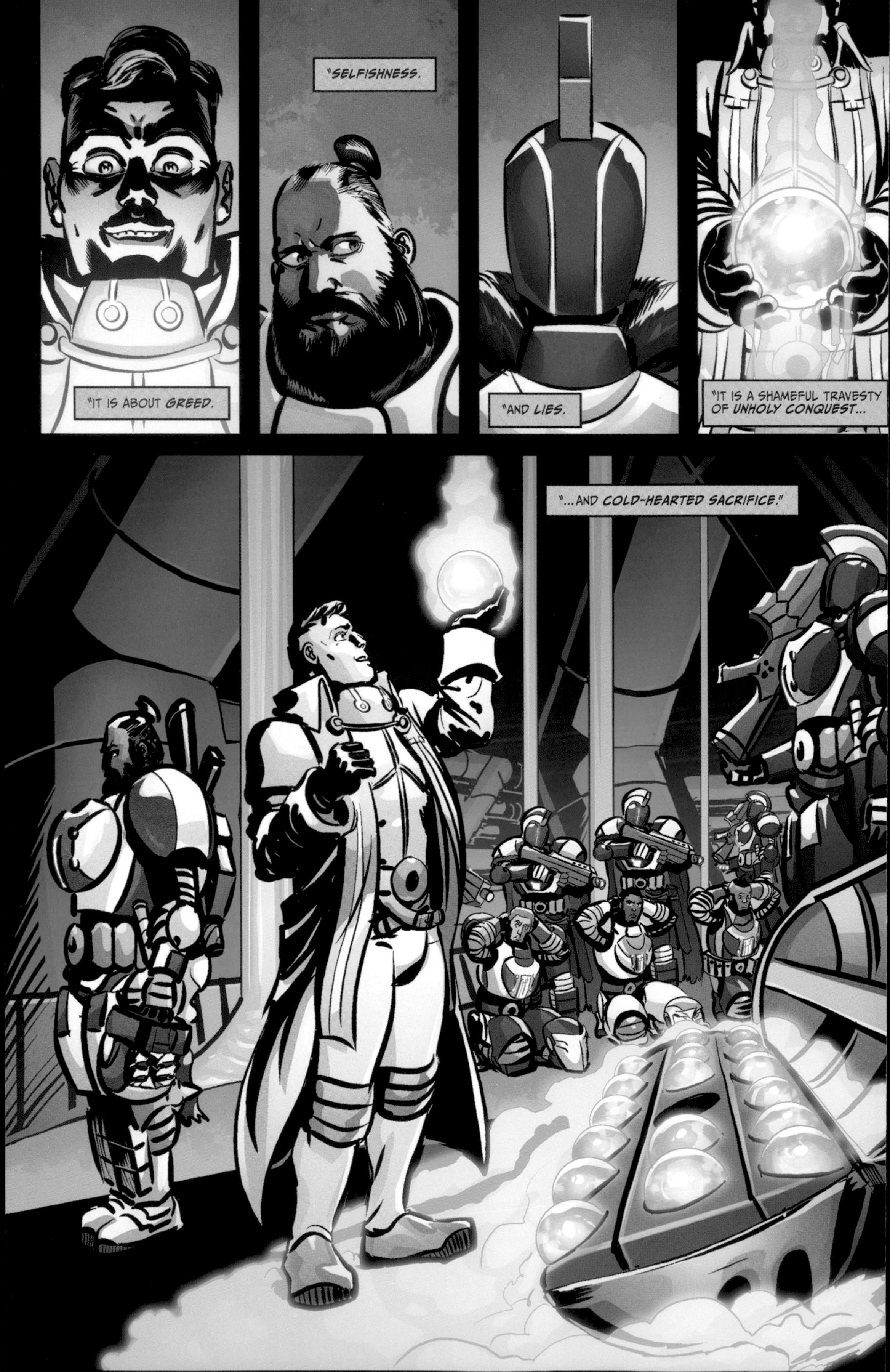
"IT IS ABOUT GREED.
"SELFISHNESS.
"AND LIES.
"IT IS A SHAMEFUL TRAVESTY OF UNHOLY CONQUEST...
"...AND COLD-HEARTED SACRIFICE."

"WAR IS A RACKET. IT ALWAYS HAS

BEEN... IT IS CONDUCTED FOR THE

BENEFIT OF THE VERY FEW, AT THE

EXPENSE OF THE VERY MANY."

– MAJOR GENERAL
SMEDLEY D. BUTLER, USMC

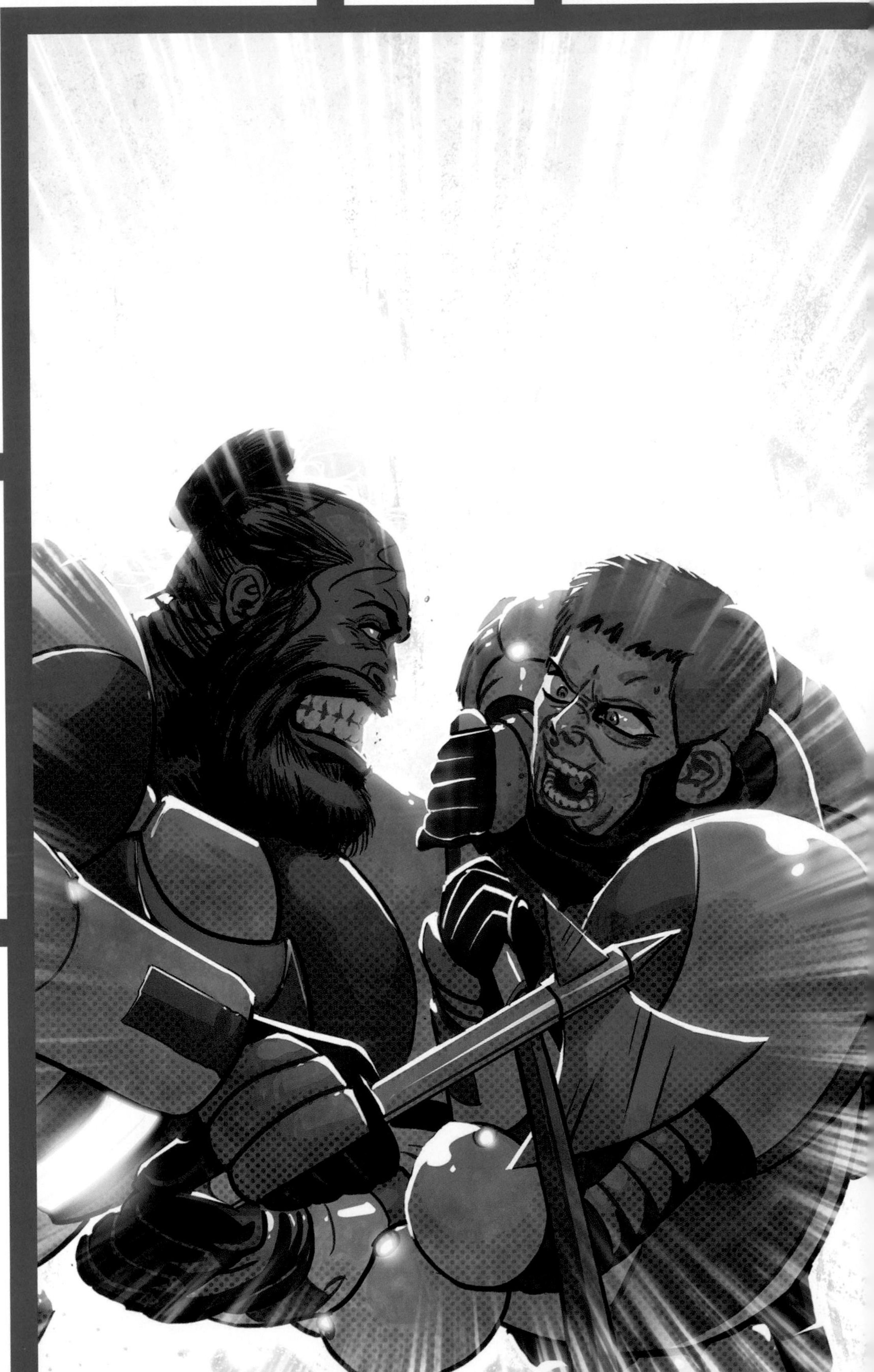
Art by Casey Maloney, Colors by Dusty Yee

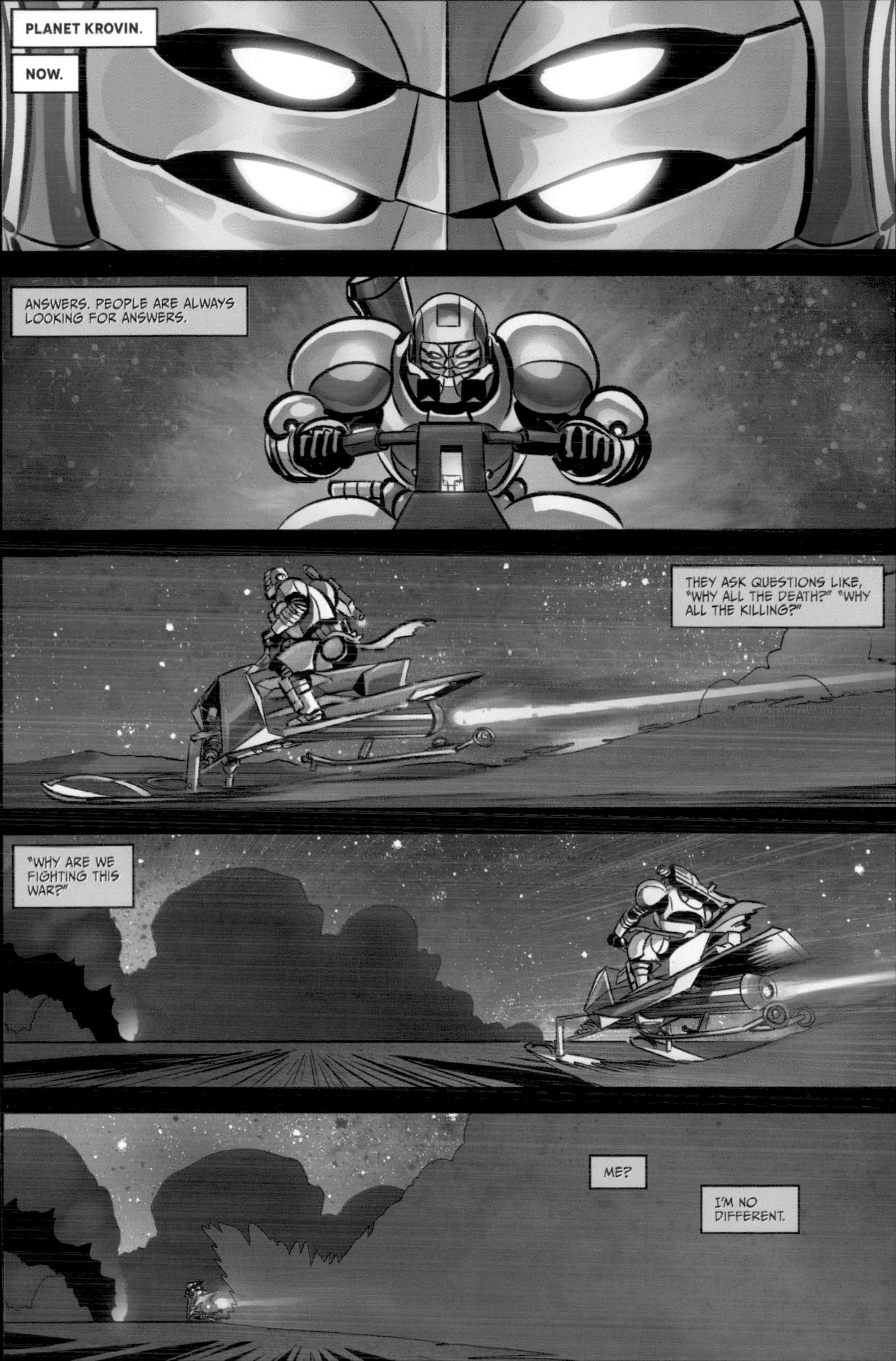
PLANET KROVIN.
NOW.
ANSWERS. PEOPLE ARE ALWAYS LOOKING FOR ANSWERS.
THEY ASK QUESTIONS LIKE, "WHY ALL THE DEATH?" "WHY ALL THE KILLING?"
"WHY ARE WE FIGHTING THIS WAR?"
ME?
I'M NO DIFFERENT.

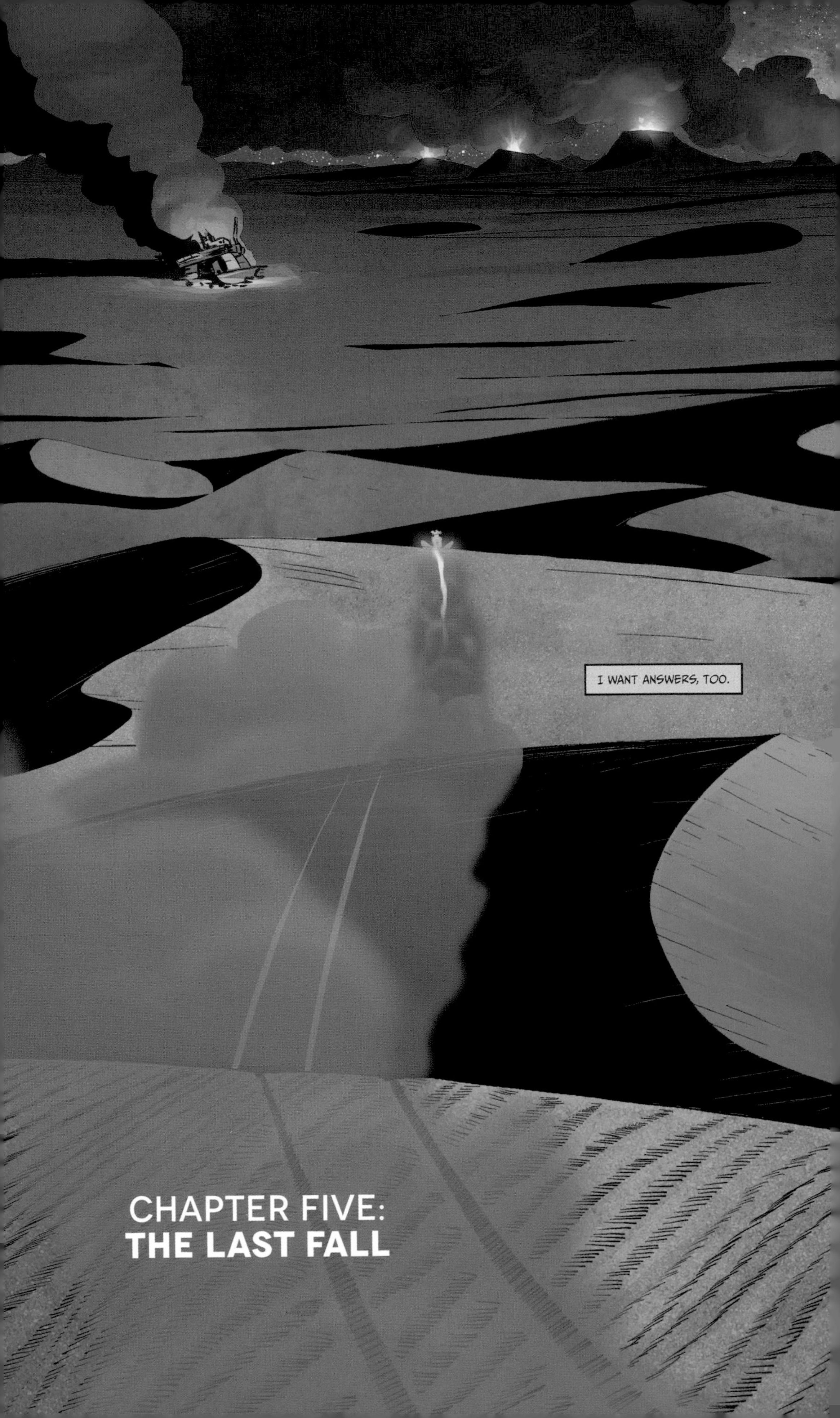
I WANT ANSWERS, TOO.

CHAPTER FIVE:
THE LAST FALL

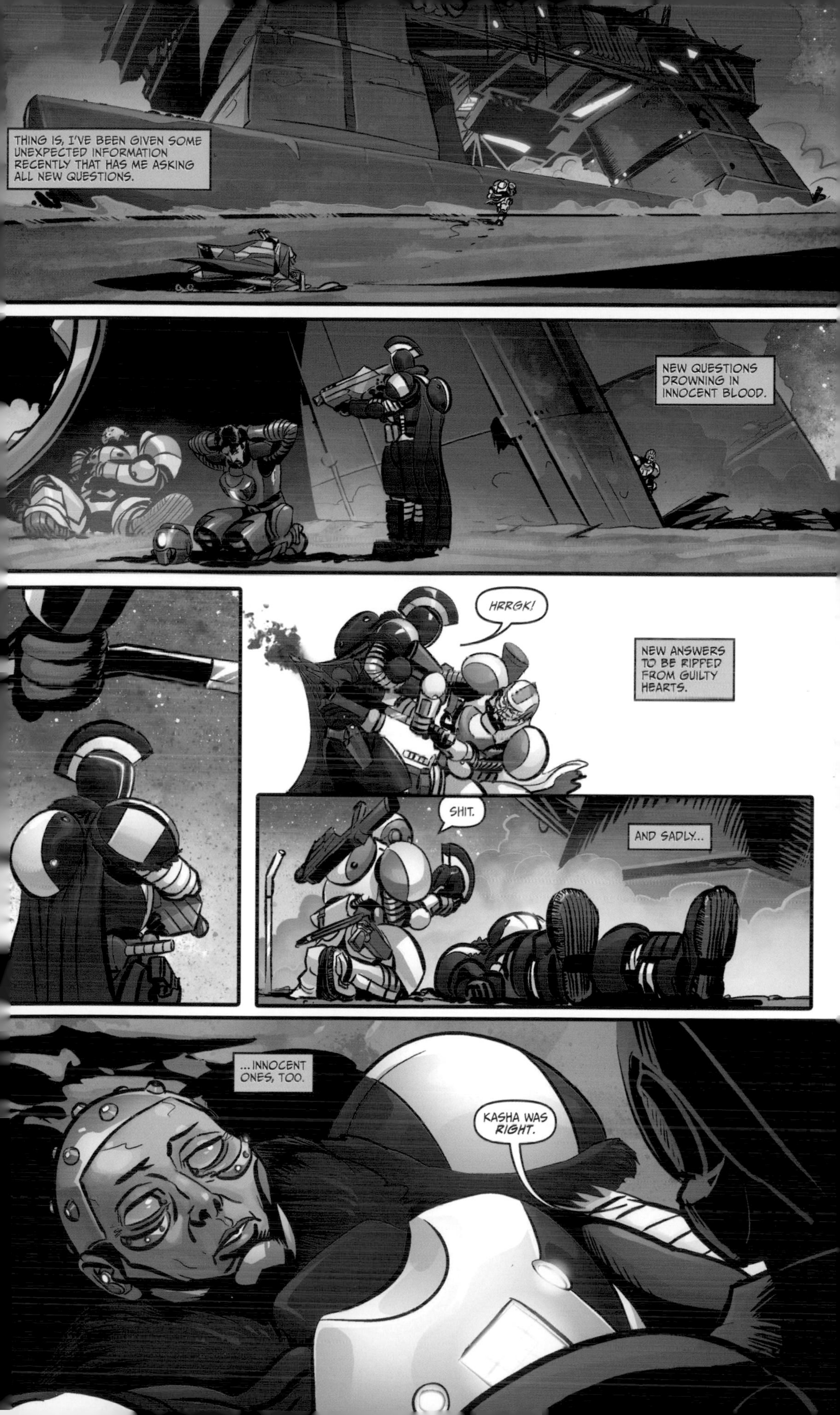
THING IS, I'VE BEEN GIVEN SOME UNEXPECTED INFORMATION RECENTLY THAT HAS ME ASKING ALL NEW QUESTIONS.
NEW QUESTIONS DROWNING IN INNOCENT BLOOD.
HRRGK!
NEW ANSWERS TO BE RIPPED FROM GUILTY HEARTS.
SHIT.
AND SADLY...
...INNOCENT ONES, TOO.
KASHA WAS RIGHT.

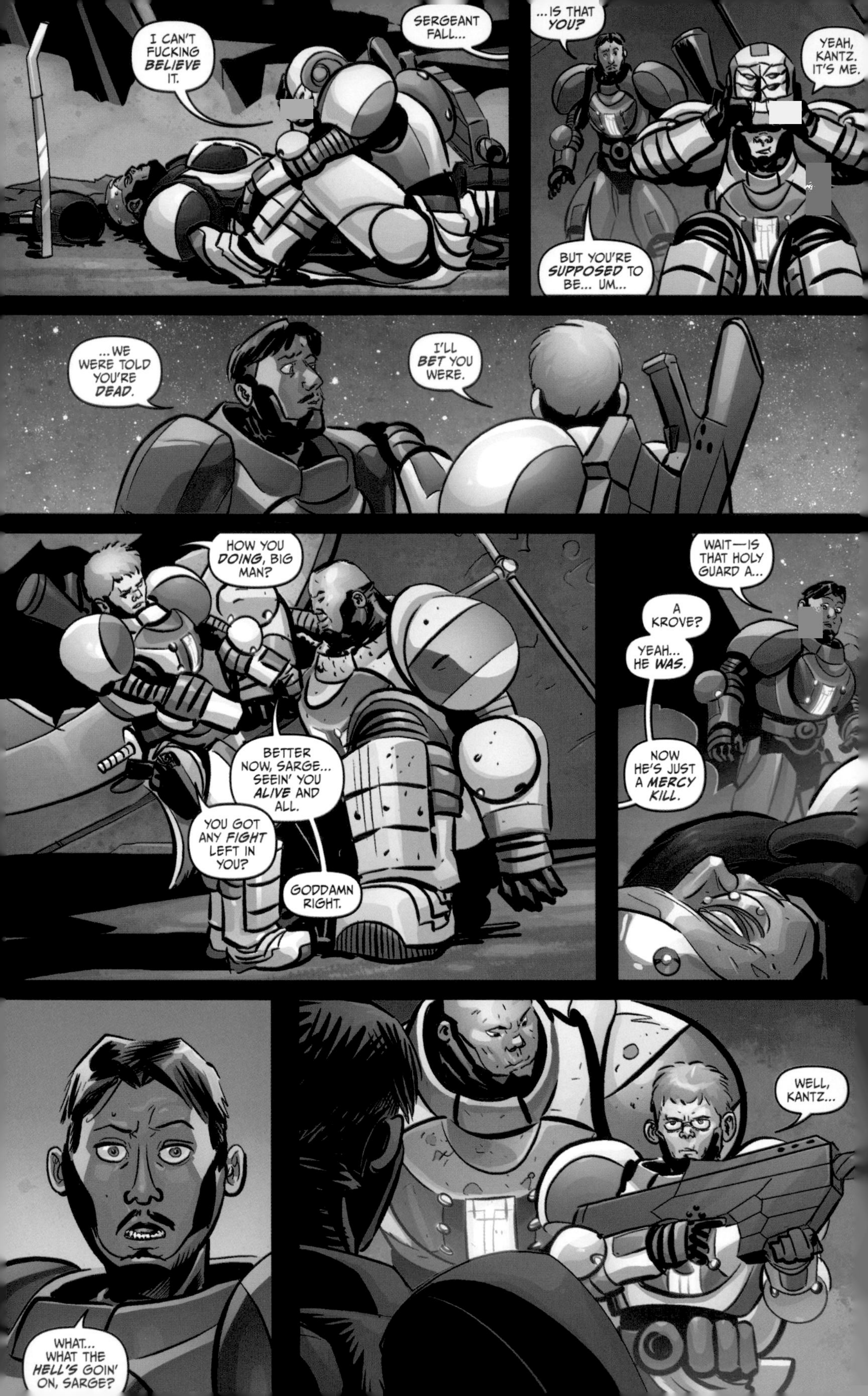
I CAN'T FUCKING *BELIEVE* IT.
SERGEANT FALL...
...IS THAT *YOU?*
YEAH, KANTZ. IT'S ME.
BUT YOU'RE *SUPPOSED* TO BE... UM...
...WE WERE TOLD YOU'RE *DEAD.*
I'LL *BET* YOU WERE.
HOW YOU *DOING*, BIG MAN?
BETTER NOW, SARGE... SEEIN' YOU *ALIVE* AND ALL.
YOU GOT ANY *FIGHT* LEFT IN YOU?
GODDAMN RIGHT.
WAIT—IS THAT HOLY GUARD A...
A KROVE?
YEAH... HE *WAS.*
NOW HE'S JUST A *MERCY KILL.*
WHAT... WHAT THE *HELL'S* GOIN' ON, SARGE?
WELL, KANTZ...

"...WRONG
THE WRONG
ASSHOLES
ALL ALONG."

WHAT DO YOU MEAN THEY'RE *NOT* MERKONIAN, KASHA?

I MEAN WHAT I SAY, MARCUS— YOUR *RED SOLDIERS* ARE NOT OF YOUR *OWN* KIND.

THEY ARE OF *MINE.*

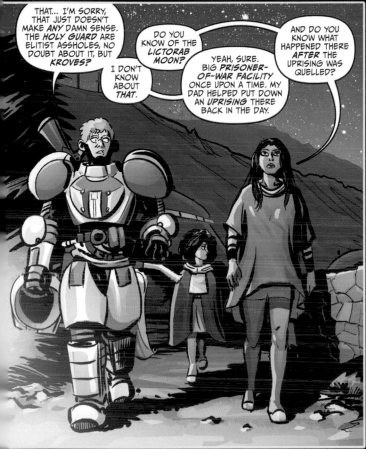

THAT... I'M SORRY, THAT JUST DOESN'T MAKE *ANY* DAMN SENSE. THE *HOLY GUARD* ARE ELITIST ASSHOLES, NO DOUBT ABOUT IT, BUT *KROVES?*

DO YOU KNOW OF THE *LICTORAB MOON?*

I DON'T KNOW ABOUT *THAT.*

YEAH, SURE. BIG *PRISONER-OF-WAR* FACILITY ONCE UPON A TIME. MY DAD HELPED PUT DOWN AN *UPRISING* THERE BACK IN THE DAY.

AND DO YOU KNOW WHAT HAPPENED THERE *AFTER* THE UPRISING WAS QUELLED?

FAR AS I KNOW, THEY *SHUT* THE WHOLE THING DOWN.

IT WAS COSTING THE *GOVERNMENT* AN ARM AND A LEG TO KEEP IT RUNNING, AND THE ARMY *REAL* ARMS AND LEGS TO KEEP IT UNDER CONTROL, SO THE TAXPAYERS GOT FED UP WITH BOTH SITUATIONS AND THE BRASS FINALLY *PULLED* THE PLUG.

AND THE *PRISONERS?*

AMNESTY. THEY SENT THEM ALL BACK *HERE* TO KROVIN.

NO MORE WAR AND NO MORE PRISON, SO REALLY NO POINT IN HAVING PRISONERS OF WAR *ANYMORE,* I GUESS.

'COURSE THAT *BACKFIRED* BIG TIME WHEN THOSE *TERRORIST BASTARDS* STARTED POPPING UP EVERYWHERE ON MERKONIA WITH THEIR GODDAMN SUICIDE BOMBS.

WHICH ULTIMATELY LED *BACK* TO WAR, YES?

YEAH.

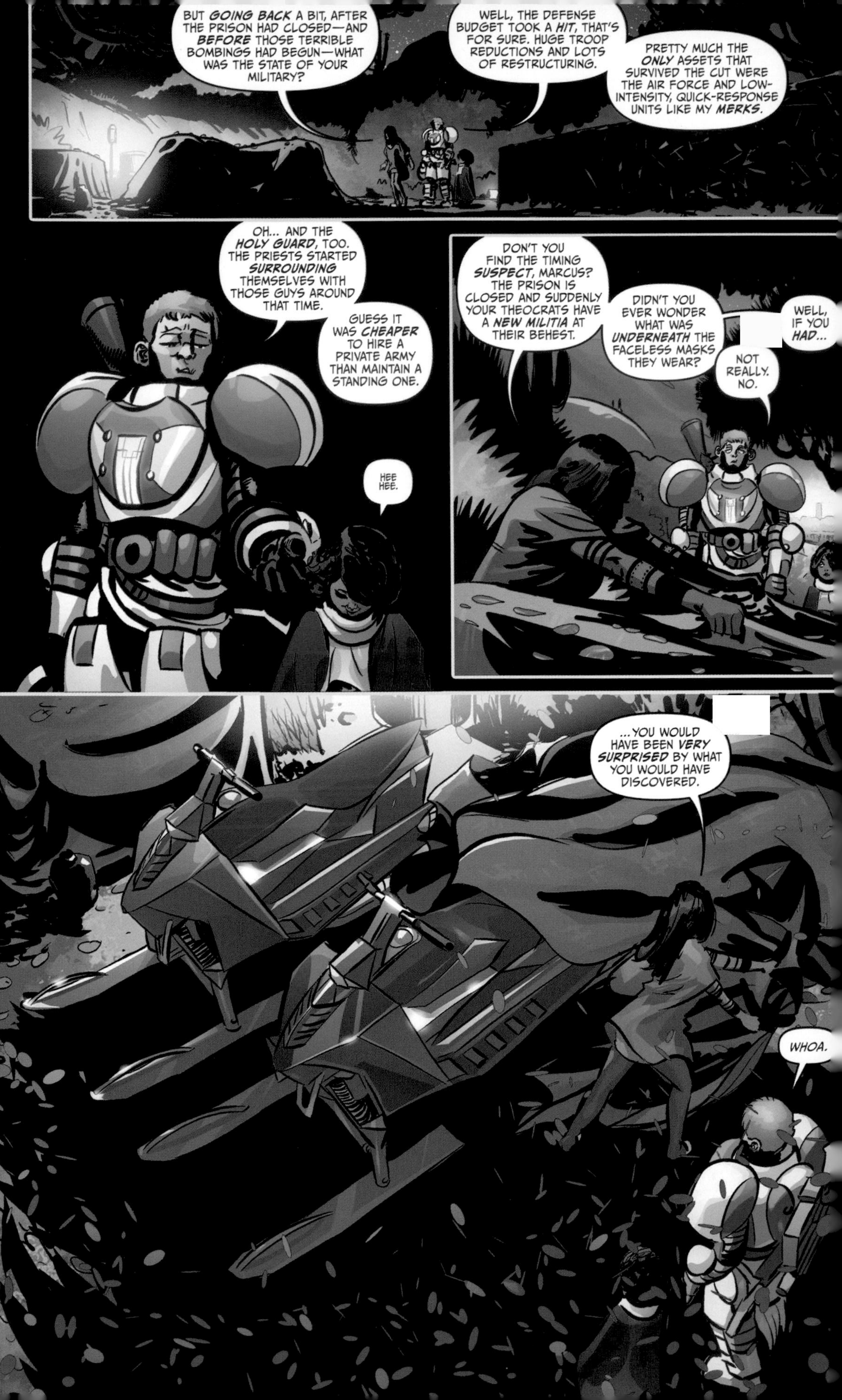
BUT GOING BACK A BIT, AFTER THE PRISON HAD CLOSED—AND BEFORE THOSE TERRIBLE BOMBINGS HAD BEGUN—WHAT WAS THE STATE OF YOUR MILITARY?
WELL, THE DEFENSE BUDGET TOOK A HIT, THAT'S FOR SURE. HUGE TROOP REDUCTIONS AND LOTS OF RESTRUCTURING.
PRETTY MUCH THE ONLY ASSETS THAT SURVIVED THE CUT WERE THE AIR FORCE AND LOW-INTENSITY, QUICK-RESPONSE UNITS LIKE MY MERKS.
OH... AND THE HOLY GUARD, TOO. THE PRIESTS STARTED SURROUNDING THEMSELVES WITH THOSE GUYS AROUND THAT TIME.
GUESS IT WAS CHEAPER TO HIRE A PRIVATE ARMY THAN MAINTAIN A STANDING ONE.
HEE HEE.
DON'T YOU FIND THE TIMING SUSPECT, MARCUS? THE PRISON IS CLOSED AND SUDDENLY YOUR THEOCRATS HAVE A NEW MILITIA AT THEIR BEHEST.
DIDN'T YOU EVER WONDER WHAT WAS UNDERNEATH THE FACELESS MASKS THEY WEAR?
NOT REALLY. NO.
WELL, IF YOU HAD...
...YOU WOULD HAVE BEEN VERY SURPRISED BY WHAT YOU WOULD HAVE DISCOVERED.
WHOA.

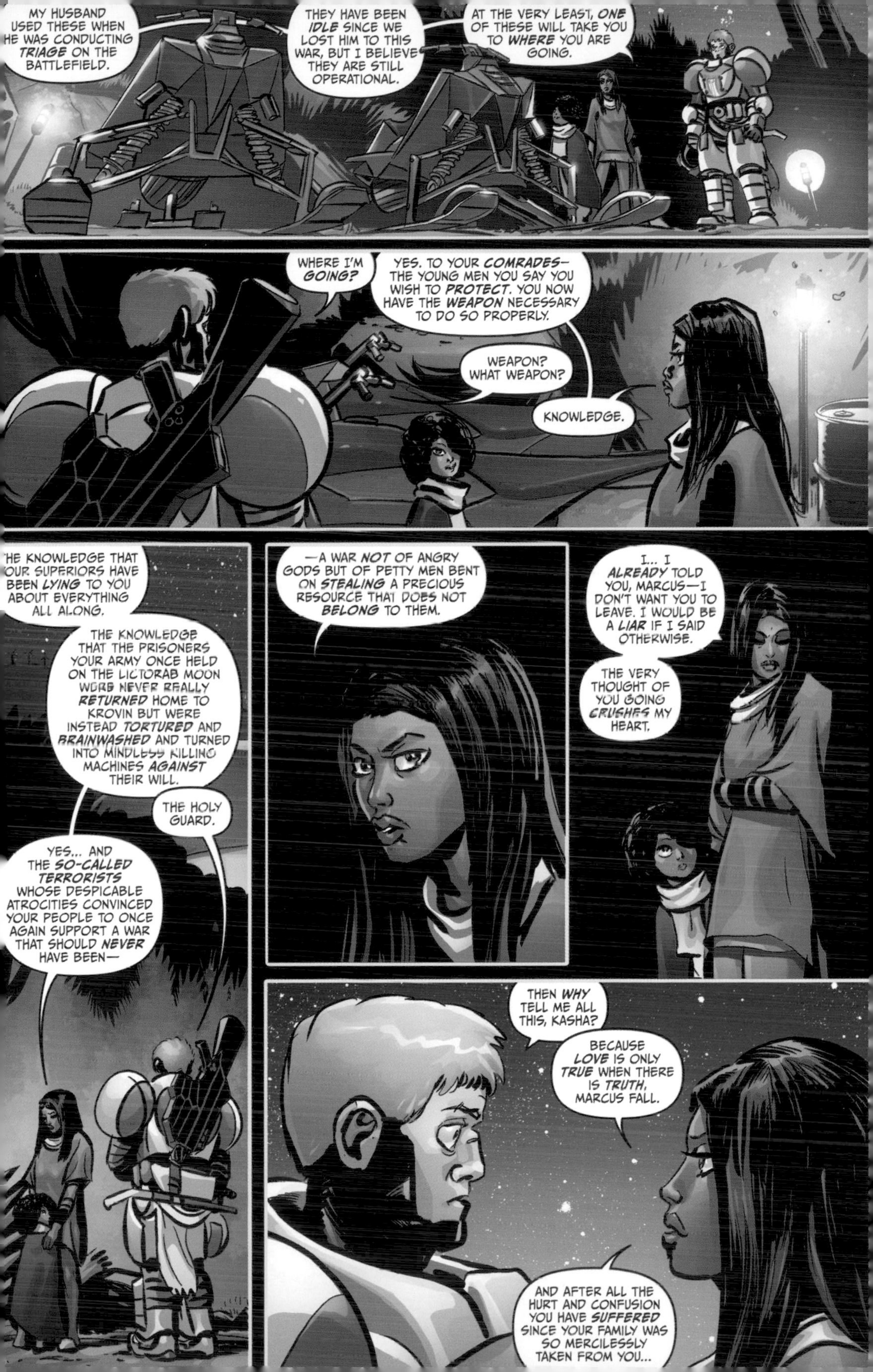
MY HUSBAND USED THESE WHEN HE WAS CONDUCTING TRIAGE ON THE BATTLEFIELD.
THEY HAVE BEEN IDLE SINCE WE LOST HIM TO THIS WAR, BUT I BELIEVE THEY ARE STILL OPERATIONAL.
AT THE VERY LEAST, ONE OF THESE WILL TAKE YOU TO WHERE YOU ARE GOING.
WHERE I'M GOING?
YES. TO YOUR COMRADES—THE YOUNG MEN YOU SAY YOU WISH TO PROTECT. YOU NOW HAVE THE WEAPON NECESSARY TO DO SO PROPERLY.
WEAPON? WHAT WEAPON?
KNOWLEDGE.
THE KNOWLEDGE THAT YOUR SUPERIORS HAVE BEEN LYING TO YOU ABOUT EVERYTHING ALL ALONG.
THE KNOWLEDGE THAT THE PRISONERS YOUR ARMY ONCE HELD ON THE LICTORAB MOON WERE NEVER REALLY RETURNED HOME TO KROVIN BUT WERE INSTEAD TORTURED AND BRAINWASHED AND TURNED INTO MINDLESS KILLING MACHINES AGAINST THEIR WILL.
THE HOLY GUARD.
YES... AND THE SO-CALLED TERRORISTS WHOSE DESPICABLE ATROCITIES CONVINCED YOUR PEOPLE TO ONCE AGAIN SUPPORT A WAR THAT SHOULD NEVER HAVE BEEN—
—A WAR NOT OF ANGRY GODS BUT OF PETTY MEN BENT ON STEALING A PRECIOUS RESOURCE THAT DOES NOT BELONG TO THEM.
I... I ALREADY TOLD YOU, MARCUS—I DON'T WANT YOU TO LEAVE. I WOULD BE A LIAR IF I SAID OTHERWISE.
THE VERY THOUGHT OF YOU GOING CRUSHES MY HEART.
THEN WHY TELL ME ALL THIS, KASHA?
BECAUSE LOVE IS ONLY TRUE WHEN THERE IS TRUTH, MARCUS FALL.
AND AFTER ALL THE HURT AND CONFUSION YOU HAVE SUFFERED SINCE YOUR FAMILY WAS SO MERCILESSLY TAKEN FROM YOU...

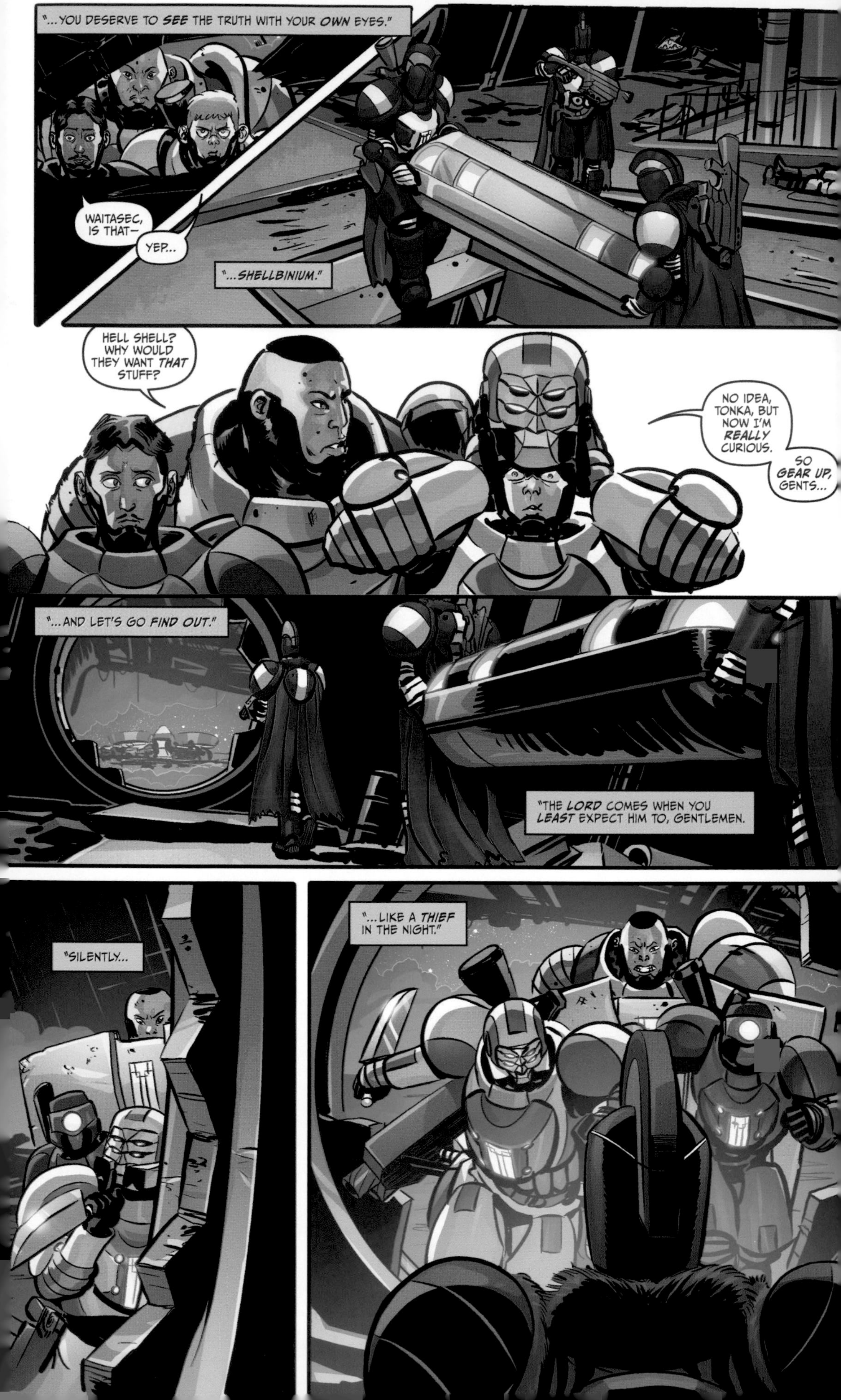
"...YOU DESERVE TO SEE THE TRUTH WITH YOUR OWN EYES."
WAITASEC, IS THAT—
YEP...
"...SHELLBINIUM."
HELL SHELL? WHY WOULD THEY WANT THAT STUFF?
NO IDEA, TONKA, BUT NOW I'M REALLY CURIOUS.
SO GEAR UP, GENTS...
"...AND LET'S GO FIND OUT."
"THE LORD COMES WHEN YOU LEAST EXPECT HIM TO, GENTLEMEN.
"SILENTLY...
"...LIKE A THIEF IN THE NIGHT."

"SWIFTLY...

"DELIBERATELY...

"...HE DELIVERS *TERRIBLE PUNISHMENT* TO THE WICKED.

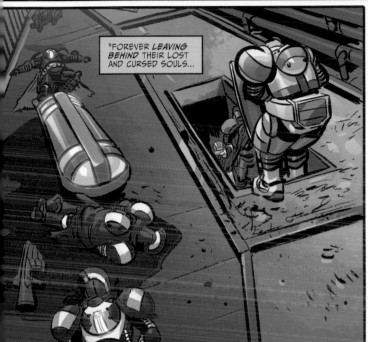

"FOREVER *LEAVING BEHIND* THEIR LOST AND CURSED SOULS...

"...MOVING *ONWARD* TO SEEK OUT HIS CHOSEN FEW.

D UPON *FINDING* THEM, IS UTTER WISDOM AND ACE..."

...DISPENSES HIS *JUST* REWARDS.

WHILE TAKING HIS *RIGHTFUL* SACRIFICE.

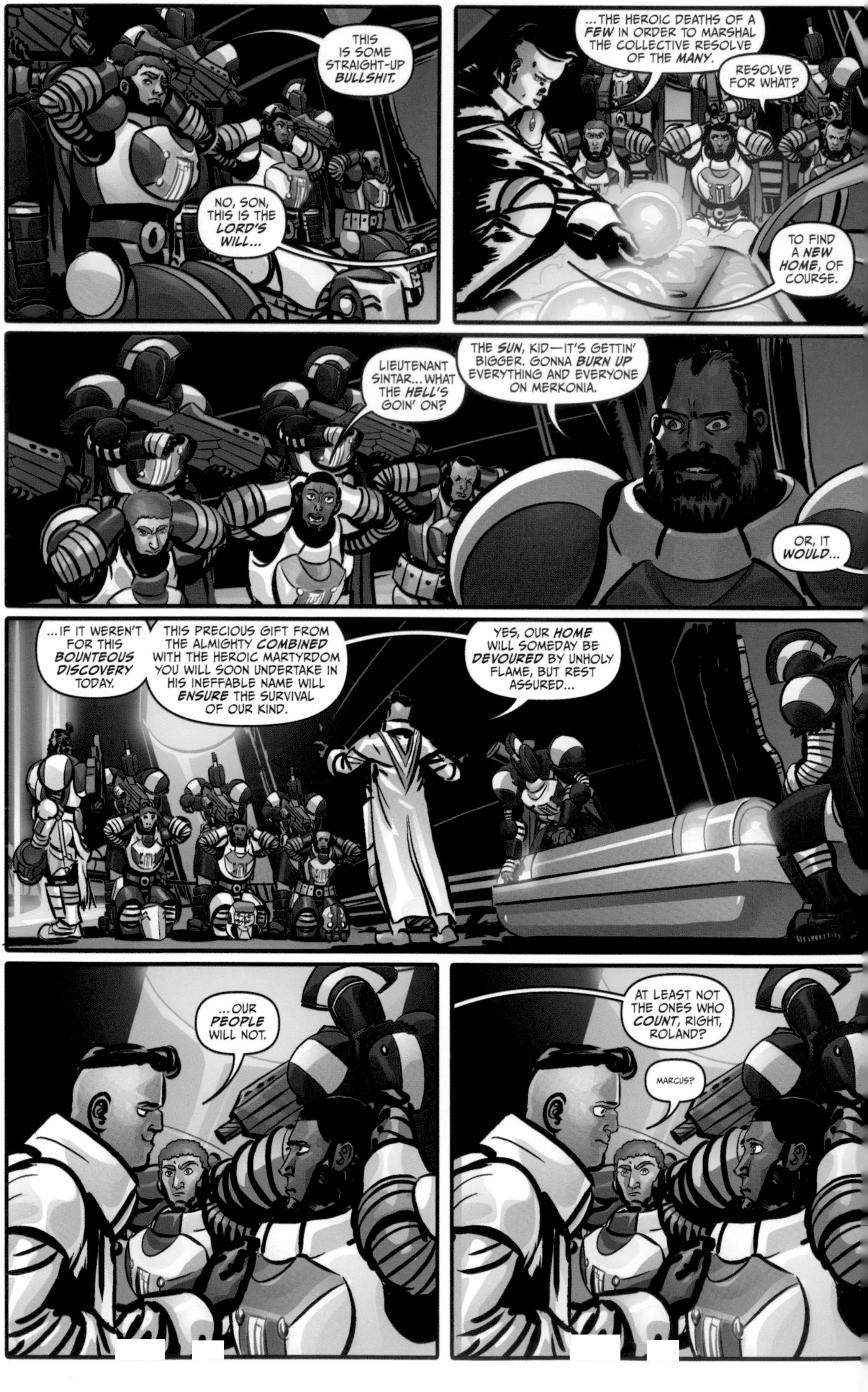
THIS IS SOME STRAIGHT-UP BULLSHIT.
NO, SON, THIS IS THE LORD'S WILL...
...THE HEROIC DEATHS OF A FEW IN ORDER TO MARSHAL THE COLLECTIVE RESOLVE OF THE MANY.
RESOLVE FOR WHAT?
TO FIND A NEW HOME, OF COURSE.
LIEUTENANT SINTAR... WHAT THE HELL'S GOIN' ON?
THE SUN, KID—IT'S GETTIN' BIGGER. GONNA BURN UP EVERYTHING AND EVERYONE ON MERKONIA.
OR, IT WOULD...
...IF IT WEREN'T FOR THIS BOUNTEOUS DISCOVERY TODAY.
THIS PRECIOUS GIFT FROM THE ALMIGHTY COMBINED WITH THE HEROIC MARTYRDOM YOU WILL SOON UNDERTAKE IN HIS INEFFABLE NAME WILL ENSURE THE SURVIVAL OF OUR KIND.
YES, OUR HOME WILL SOMEDAY BE DEVOURED BY UNHOLY FLAME, BUT REST ASSURED...
...OUR PEOPLE WILL NOT.
AT LEAST NOT THE ONES WHO COUNT, RIGHT, ROLAND?
MARCUS?

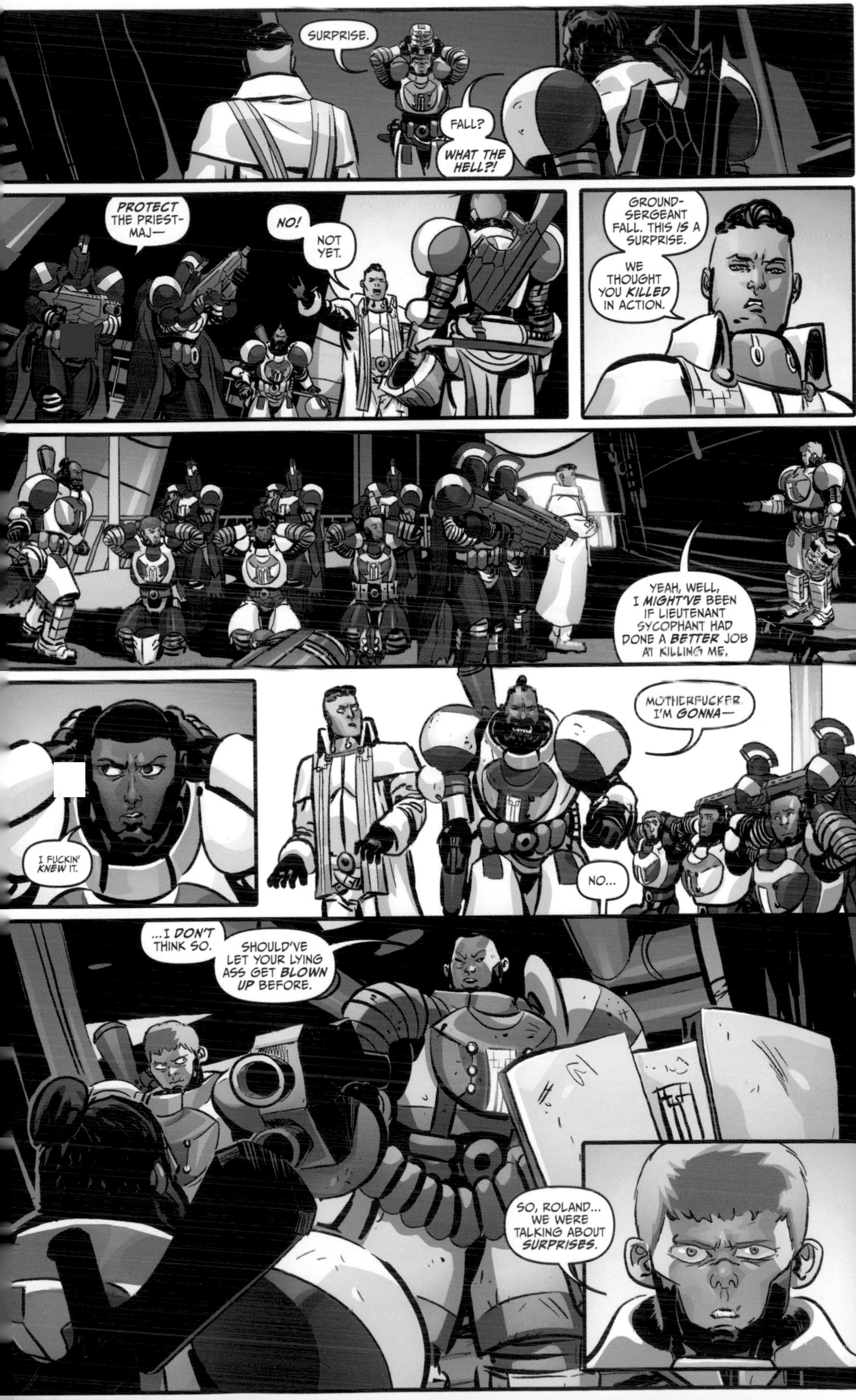

SURPRISE.
FALL?
WHAT THE HELL?!
PROTECT THE PRIEST-MAJ—
NO!
NOT YET.
GROUND-SERGEANT FALL. THIS IS A SURPRISE.
WE THOUGHT YOU KILLED IN ACTION.
YEAH, WELL, I MIGHT'VE BEEN IF LIEUTENANT SYCOPHANT HAD DONE A BETTER JOB AT KILLING ME.
I FUCKIN' KNEW IT.
MOTHERFUCKER, I'M GONNA—
NO...
...I DON'T THINK SO.
SHOULD'VE LET YOUR LYING ASS GET BLOWN UP BEFORE.
SO, ROLAND... WE WERE TALKING ABOUT SURPRISES.

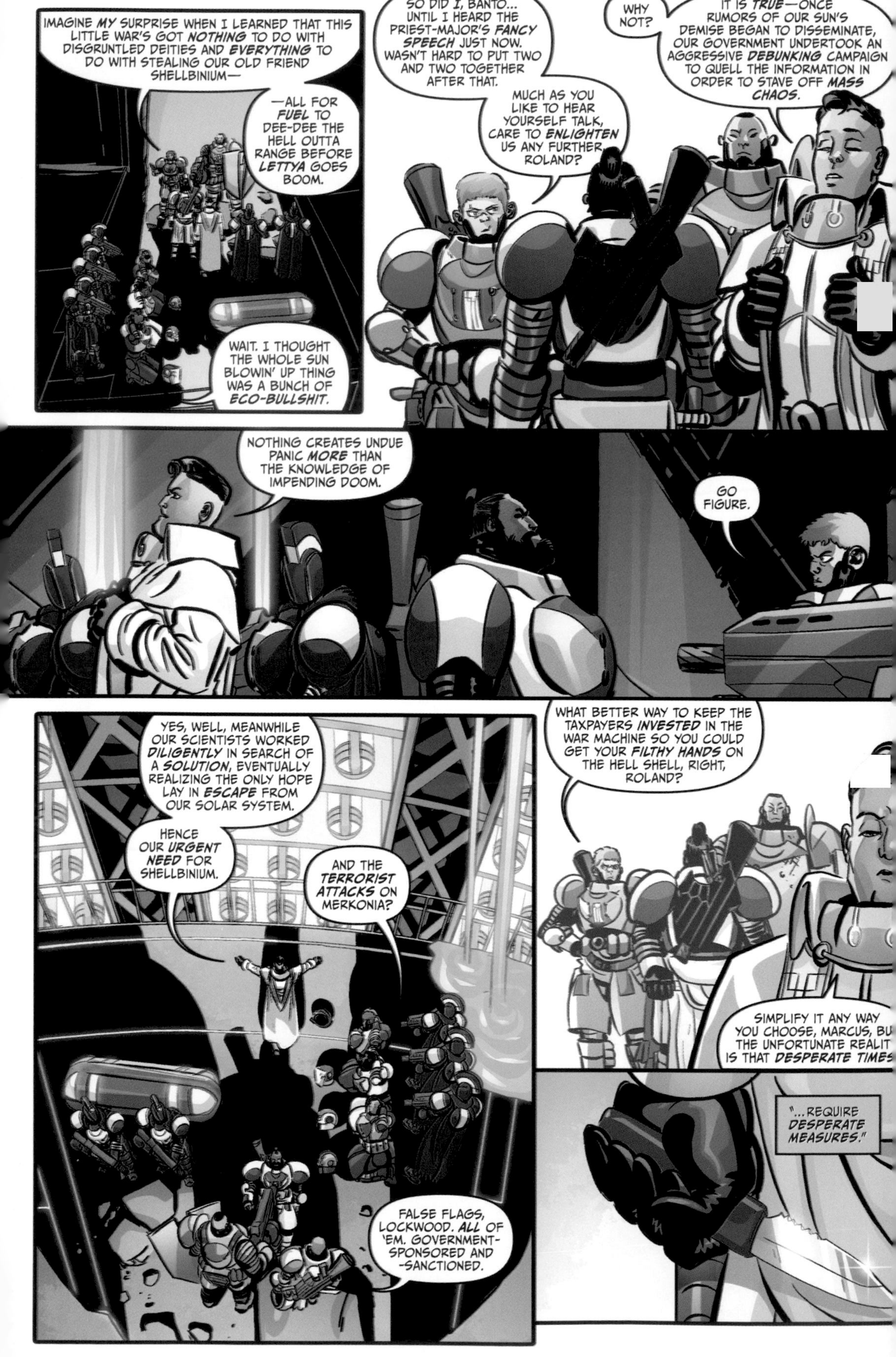
IMAGINE MY SURPRISE WHEN I LEARNED THAT THIS LITTLE WAR'S GOT NOTHING TO DO WITH DISGRUNTLED DEITIES AND EVERYTHING TO DO WITH STEALING OUR OLD FRIEND SHELLBINIUM—
—ALL FOR FUEL TO DEE-DEE THE HELL OUTTA RANGE BEFORE LETTYA GOES BOOM.
WAIT. I THOUGHT THE WHOLE SUN BLOWIN' UP THING WAS A BUNCH OF ECO-BULLSHIT.
SO DID I, BANTO... UNTIL I HEARD THE PRIEST-MAJOR'S FANCY SPEECH JUST NOW. WASN'T HARD TO PUT TWO AND TWO TOGETHER AFTER THAT.
MUCH AS YOU LIKE TO HEAR YOURSELF TALK, CARE TO ENLIGHTEN US ANY FURTHER, ROLAND?
WHY NOT?
IT IS TRUE—ONCE RUMORS OF OUR SUN'S DEMISE BEGAN TO DISSEMINATE, OUR GOVERNMENT UNDERTOOK AN AGGRESSIVE DEBUNKING CAMPAIGN TO QUELL THE INFORMATION IN ORDER TO STAVE OFF MASS CHAOS.
NOTHING CREATES UNDUE PANIC MORE THAN THE KNOWLEDGE OF IMPENDING DOOM.
GO FIGURE.
YES, WELL, MEANWHILE OUR SCIENTISTS WORKED DILIGENTLY IN SEARCH OF A SOLUTION, EVENTUALLY REALIZING THE ONLY HOPE LAY IN ESCAPE FROM OUR SOLAR SYSTEM.
HENCE OUR URGENT NEED FOR SHELLBINIUM.
AND THE TERRORIST ATTACKS ON MERKONIA?
FALSE FLAGS, LOCKWOOD. ALL OF 'EM. GOVERNMENT-SPONSORED AND -SANCTIONED.
WHAT BETTER WAY TO KEEP THE TAXPAYERS INVESTED IN THE WAR MACHINE SO YOU COULD GET YOUR FILTHY HANDS ON THE HELL SHELL, RIGHT, ROLAND?
SIMPLIFY IT ANY WAY YOU CHOOSE, MARCUS, BU THE UNFORTUNATE REALIT IS THAT DESPERATE TIMES
"...REQUIRE DESPERATE MEASURES."

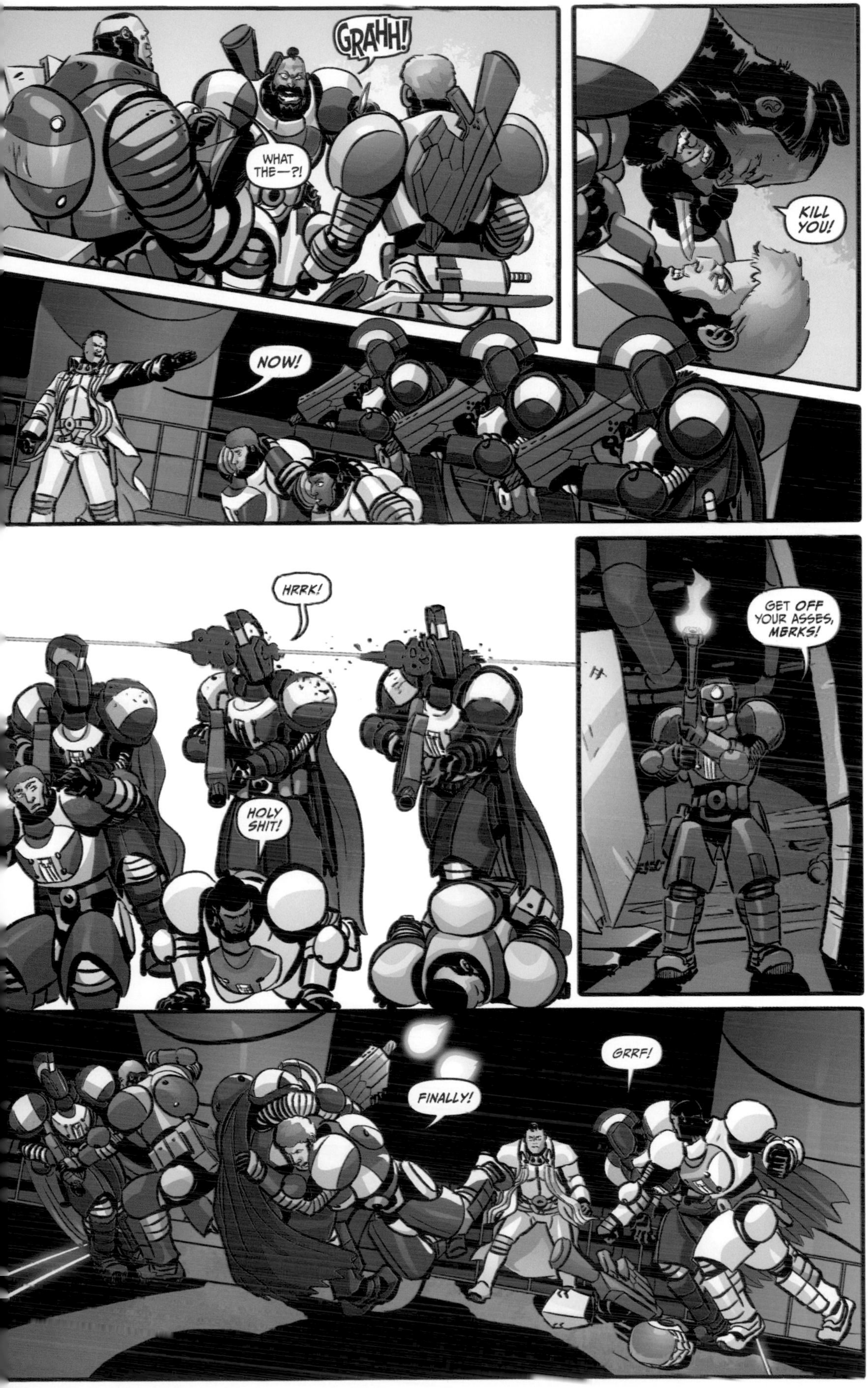
GRAHH!
WHAT THE—?!
KILL YOU!
NOW!
HRRK!
HOLY SHIT!
GET OFF YOUR ASSES, MERKS!
GRRF!
FINALLY!

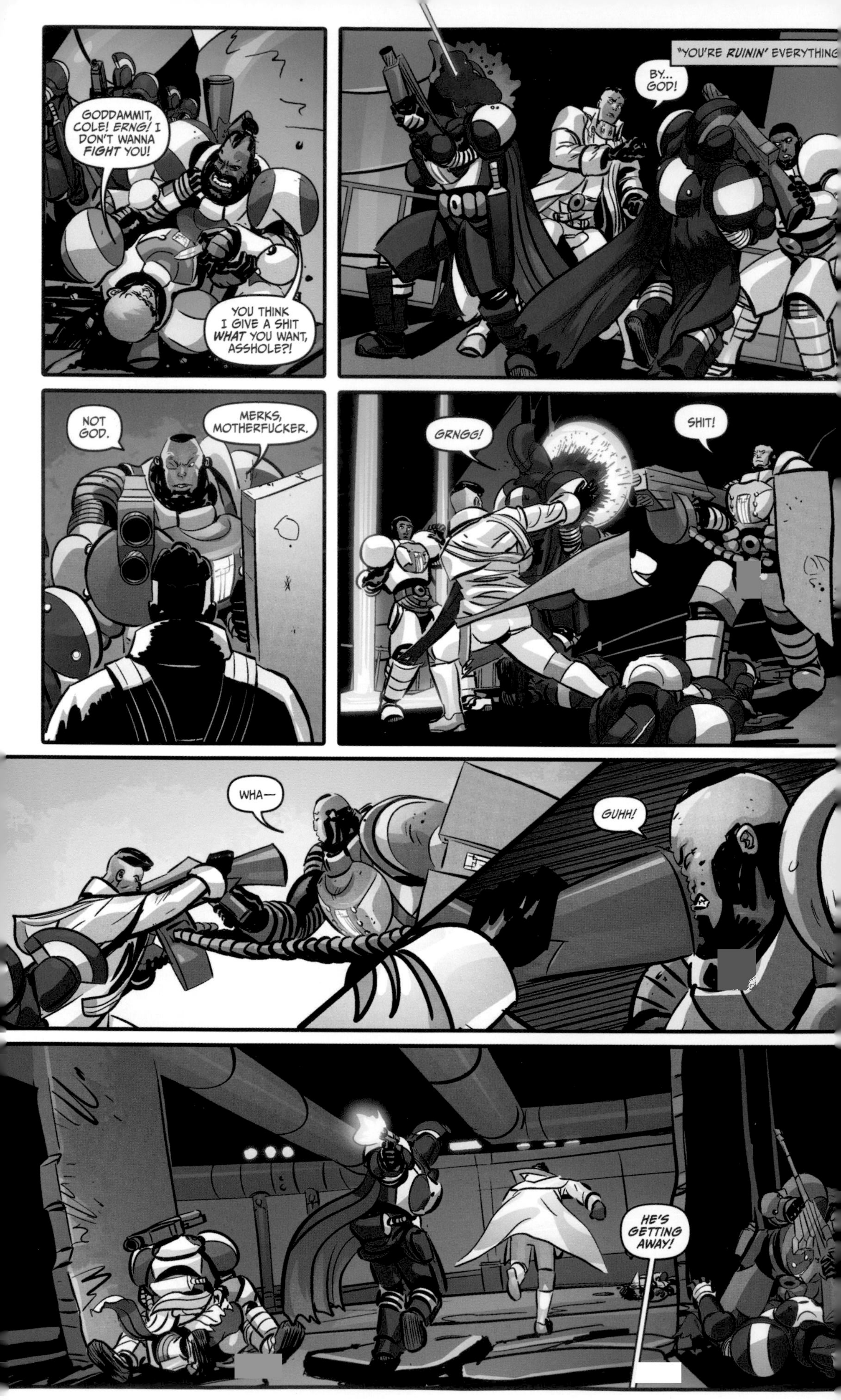
GODDAMMIT, COLE! ERNG! I DON'T WANNA FIGHT YOU!
YOU THINK I GIVE A SHIT WHAT YOU WANT, ASSHOLE?!
"YOU'RE RUININ' EVERYTHING
BY... GOD!
NOT GOD.
MERKS, MOTHERFUCKER.
GRNGG!
SHIT!
WHA—
GUHH!
HE'S GETTING AWAY!

MAN...

"...TODAY FUCKIN' SUCKS."

DAMMIT!

HUKK!

ALMOST...

STOP!

GAHH!

NNFF... DAMNED... GRHH... INFIDELS...

NO!

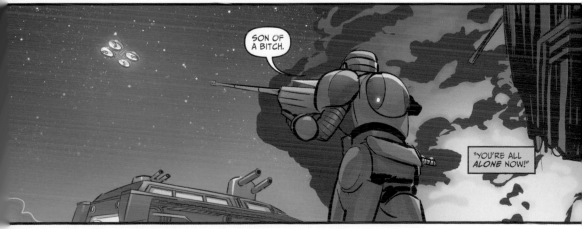

SON OF A BITCH.

"YOU'RE ALL ALONE NOW!"

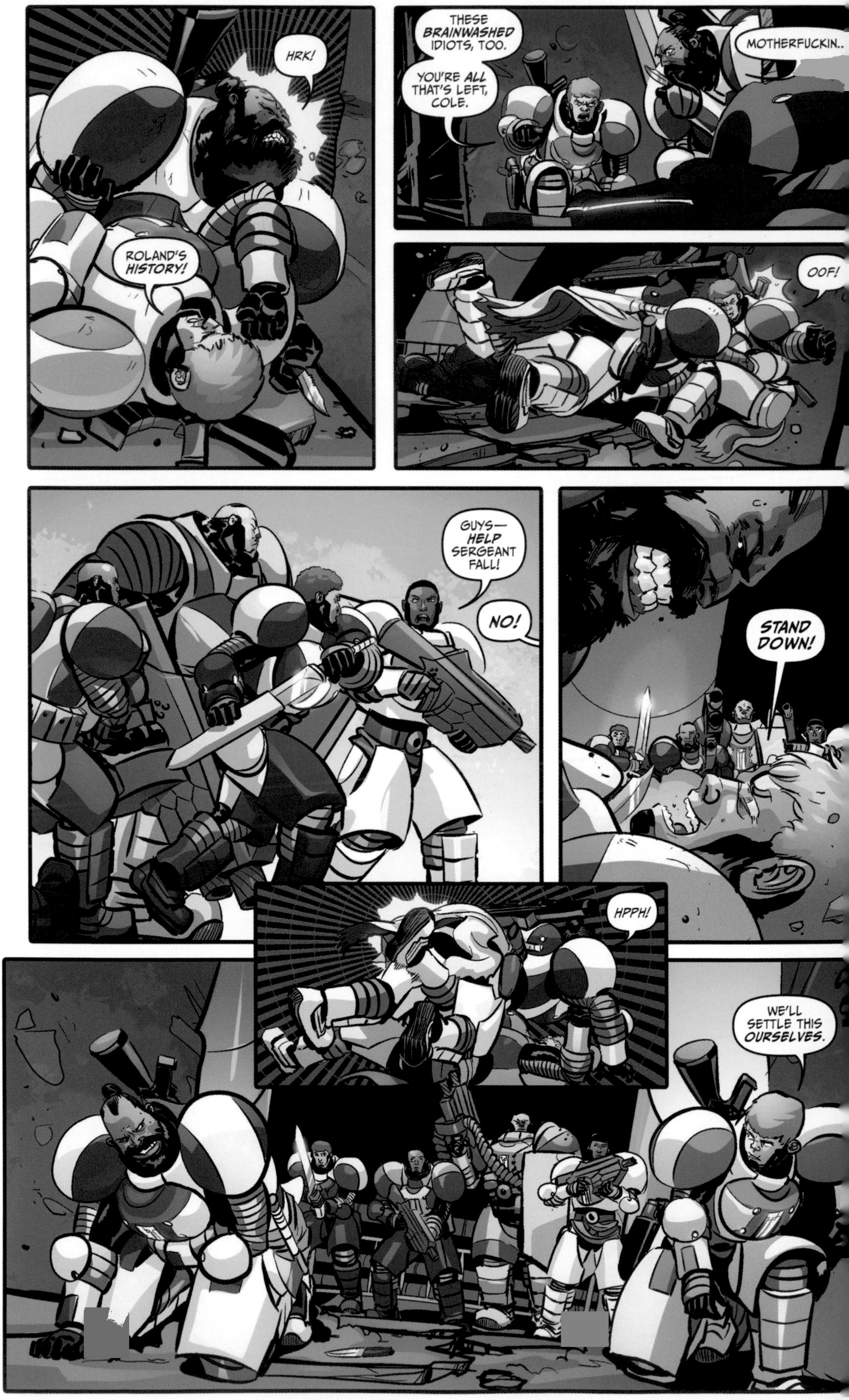
HRK!
ROLAND'S HISTORY!
THESE BRAINWASHED IDIOTS, TOO.
YOU'RE ALL THAT'S LEFT, COLE.
MOTHERFUCKIN..
OOF!
GUYS— HELP SERGEANT FALL!
NO!
STAND DOWN!
HPPH!
WE'LL SETTLE THIS OURSELVES.

YOU READY TO *LISTEN* TO ME?

FUCK YOU... ASSHOLE.

WHATEVER ROLAND PROMISED YOU, I *GUARANTEE* YOU HE AND HIS HOLY ROLLER FRIENDS— AND THOSE RICH *ELITE* ASSHOLES BACK ON MERKONIA—ARE GONNA TAKE THE HELL SHELL WE'VE BEEN BLEEDING FOR AND THEY'RE ALL GONNA *BLAST* THE FUCK AWAY FROM THE SOLAR SYSTEM *FIRST* CHANCE THEY GET.

AND IF YOU THINK THEY'RE GONNA SAVE A SEAT FOR *YOUR* STUPID GRUNT ASS, YOU'RE *CRAZIER* THAN I THOUGHT.

C'MON, MAN—WE'VE BEEN GETTING *LIED* TO ALL ALONG ABOUT THIS WHOLE DEAL. WHAT MAKES *THIS* ANY DIFFERENT?

NO—FUCK YOU. YOU *SHOT* [M]E SO I THINK I'M [O]WED A LITTLE [T]ALKING TIME.

YOU'RE GETTING TAKEN FOR A *RIDE*, COLE—OR, MAYBE I SHOULD SAY, YOU'RE *NOT* GETTING TAKEN. DEEP DOWN, YOU *KNOW* THAT, RIGHT?

THE *WRONG* PEOPLE HAVE BEEN *DYING* FOR YEARS NOW, COLE— *INNOCENT* PEOPLE.

THOSE *COWARDS* IN CHARGE AIN'T ABOUT TO LET YOU LIVE AND RISK THE *TRUTH* GETTING OUT BEFORE THEY MAKE THEIR LITTLE ESCAPE.

THE TRUTH? REALLY?

YOU WANNA KNOW WHAT THE GODDAMN *TRUTH* IS, FALL?

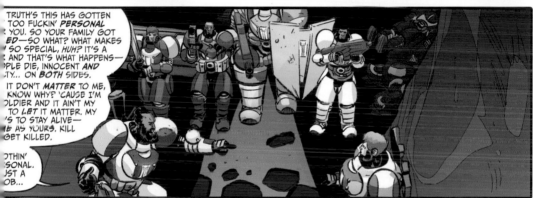

[ ]TRUTH'S THIS HAS GOTTEN [ ] TOO FUCKIN' *PERSONAL* [ ] YOU. SO YOUR FAMILY GOT [KILL]ED—SO WHAT? WHAT MAKES [THEM] SO SPECIAL, *HUH?* IT'S A [WAR] AND THAT'S WHAT HAPPENS— [PEO]PLE DIE, INNOCENT *AND* [GUIL]TY... ON *BOTH* SIDES.

[BUT] IT DON'T *MATTER* TO ME, [YOU] KNOW WHY? 'CAUSE I'M [A S]OLDIER AND IT AIN'T MY [JOB] TO *LET* IT MATTER. MY [JOB]'S TO STAY ALIVE— [SAM]E AS YOURS. KILL [OR] GET KILLED.

[NO]THIN' [PER]SONAL. [JU]ST A [JO]B...

...A JOB I *INTEND* TO FINISH.

IF YOU'RE [HO]PIN' ROLAND'S [GO]NNA *FORGET* [ABO]UT THIS SHIT, THEN [YOU']RE *CRAZIER* THAN [I,] FALL. AND WHEN [HE] COMES BACK...

...HE'LL SEE TRUSTIN' ME WAS THE *RIGHT PLAY* ALL ALONG.

NO! WAIT!

SHIT!

HOLD YOUR FIRE!

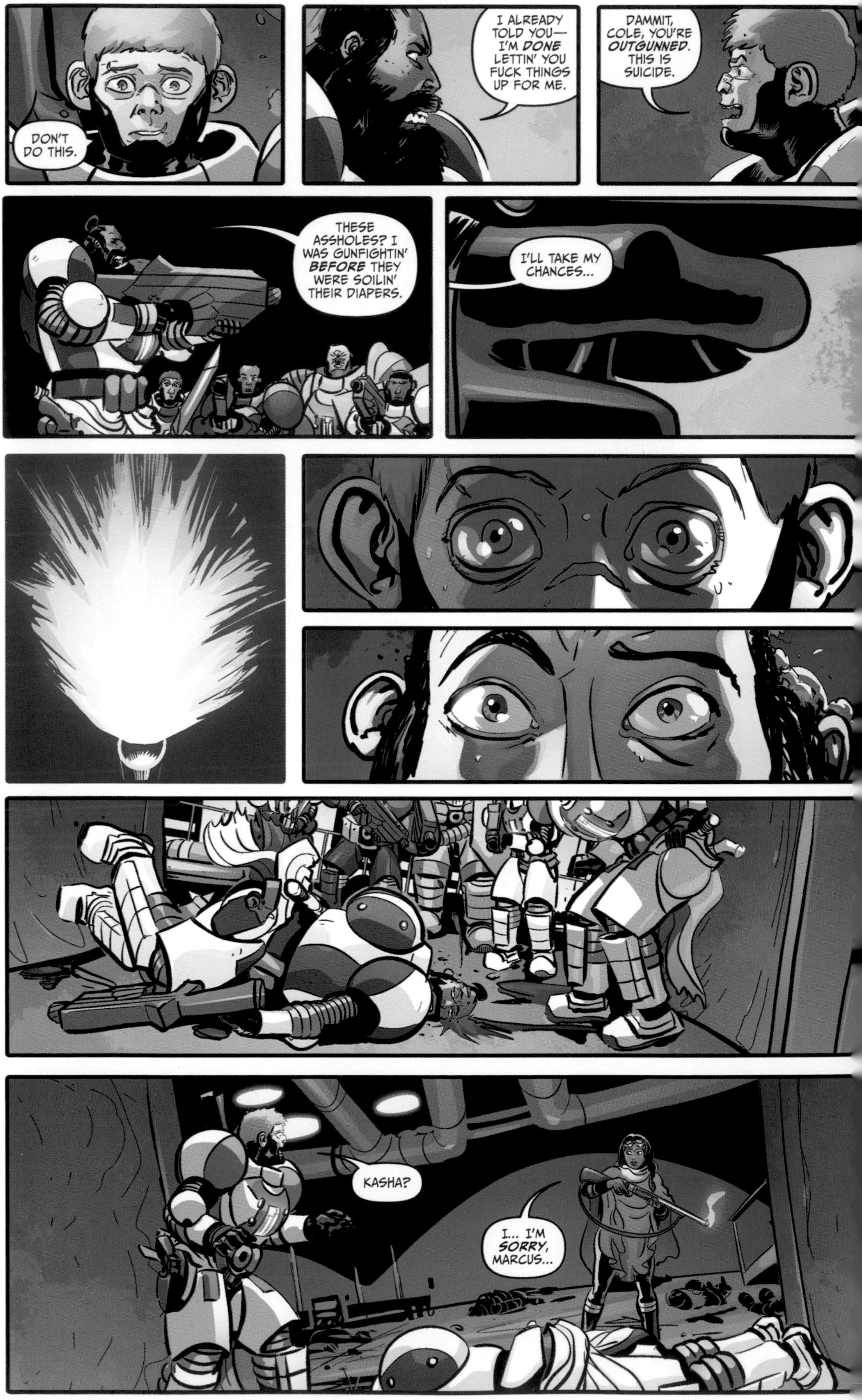
DON'T DO THIS.
I ALREADY TOLD YOU— I'M DONE LETTIN' YOU FUCK THINGS UP FOR ME.
DAMMIT, COLE, YOU'RE OUTGUNNED. THIS IS SUICIDE.
THESE ASSHOLES? I WAS GUNFIGHTIN' BEFORE THEY WERE SOILIN' THEIR DIAPERS.
I'LL TAKE MY CHANCES...
KASHA?
I... I'M SORRY, MARCUS...

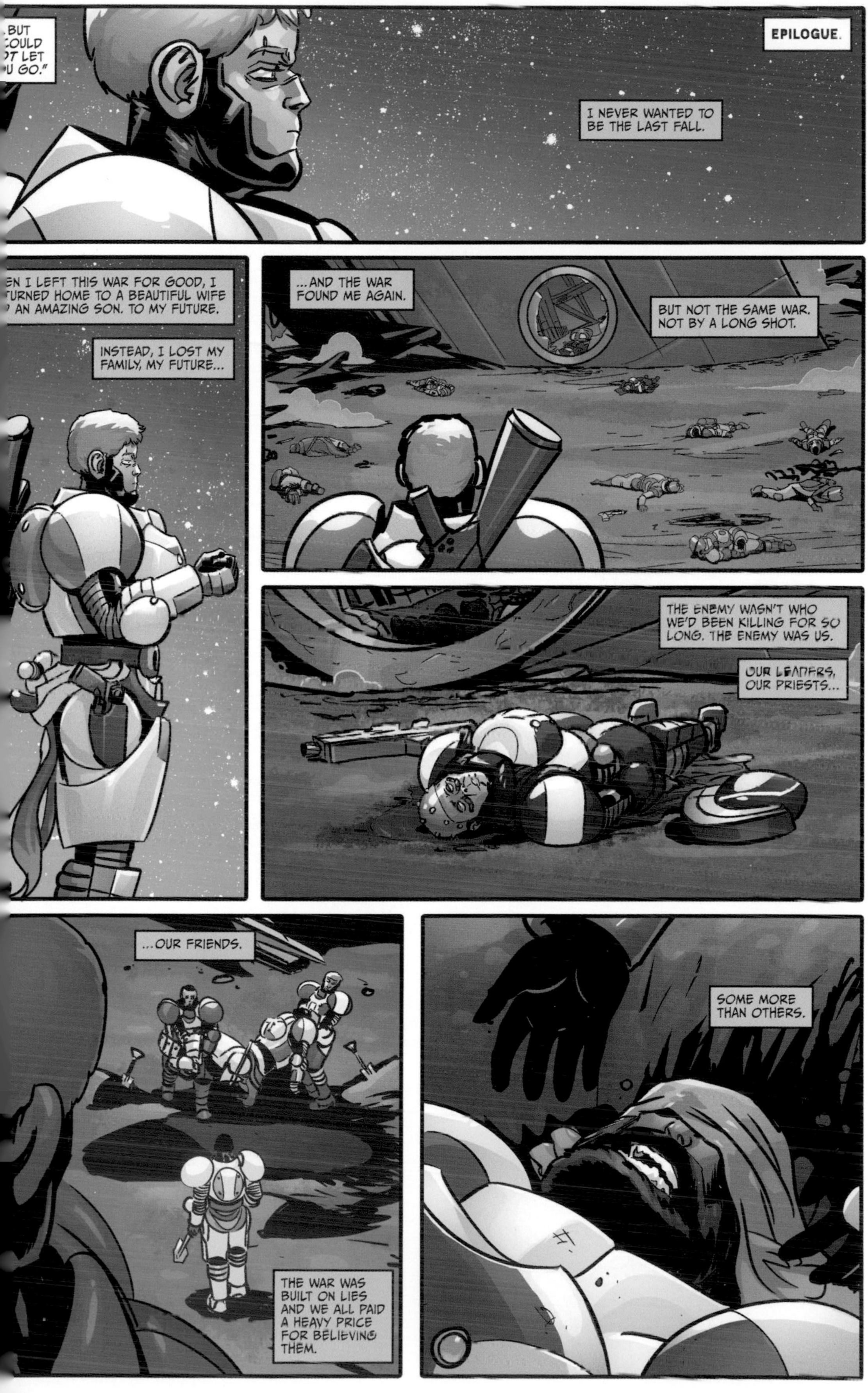
BUT
COULD
OT LET
U GO."
EPILOGUE.
I NEVER WANTED TO BE THE LAST FALL.
EN I LEFT THIS WAR FOR GOOD, I TURNED HOME TO A BEAUTIFUL WIFE AN AMAZING SON. TO MY FUTURE.
INSTEAD, I LOST MY FAMILY, MY FUTURE...
...AND THE WAR FOUND ME AGAIN.
BUT NOT THE SAME WAR. NOT BY A LONG SHOT.
THE ENEMY WASN'T WHO WE'D BEEN KILLING FOR SO LONG. THE ENEMY WAS US.
OUR LEADERS, OUR PRIESTS...
...OUR FRIENDS.
THE WAR WAS BUILT ON LIES AND WE ALL PAID A HEAVY PRICE FOR BELIEVING THEM.
SOME MORE THAN OTHERS.

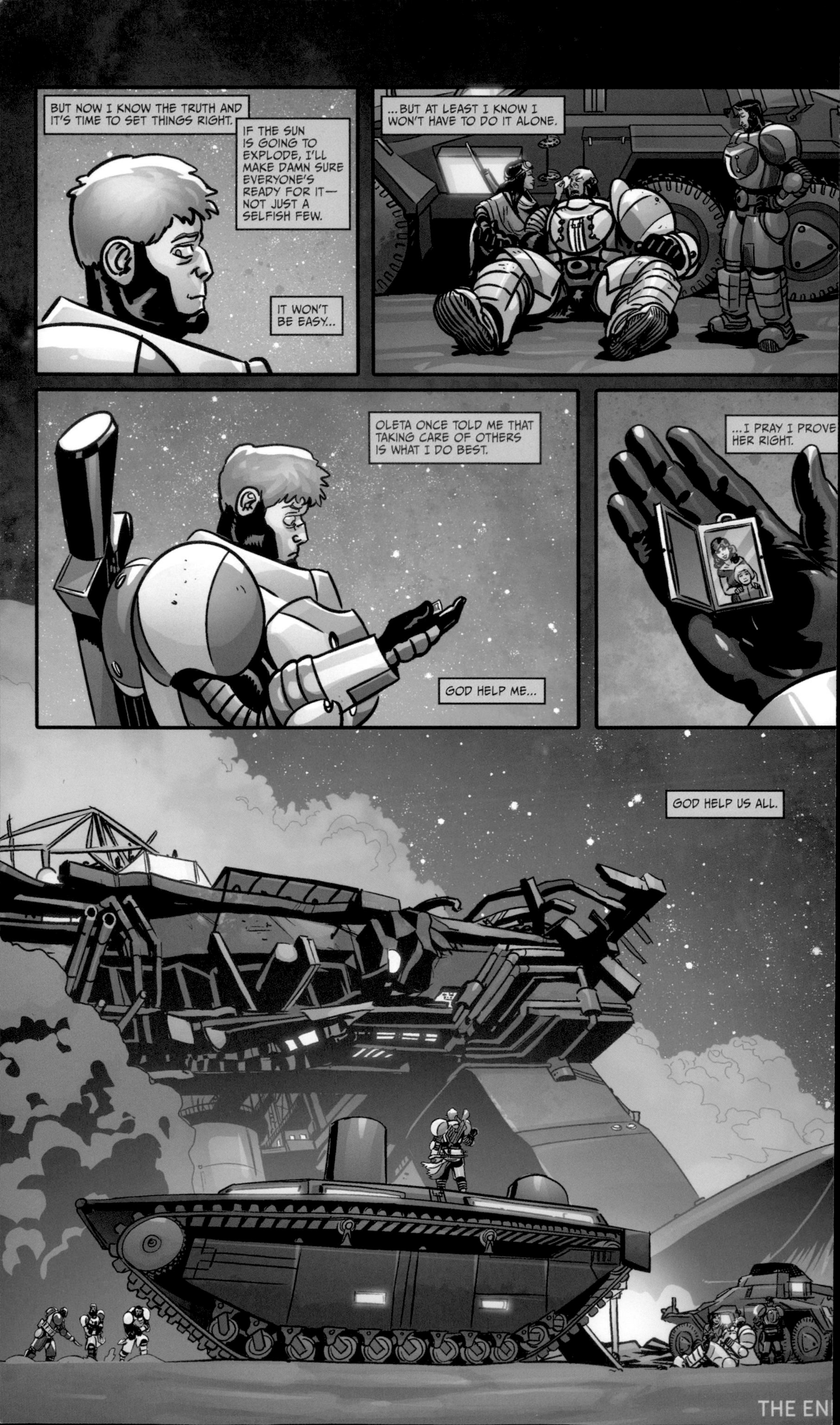
BUT NOW I KNOW THE TRUTH AND IT'S TIME TO SET THINGS RIGHT.
IF THE SUN IS GOING TO EXPLODE, I'LL MAKE DAMN SURE EVERYONE'S READY FOR IT—NOT JUST A SELFISH FEW.
IT WON'T BE EASY...
...BUT AT LEAST I KNOW I WON'T HAVE TO DO IT ALONE.
OLETA ONCE TOLD ME THAT TAKING CARE OF OTHERS IS WHAT I DO BEST.
GOD HELP ME...
...I PRAY I PROVE HER RIGHT.
GOD HELP US ALL.
THE EN

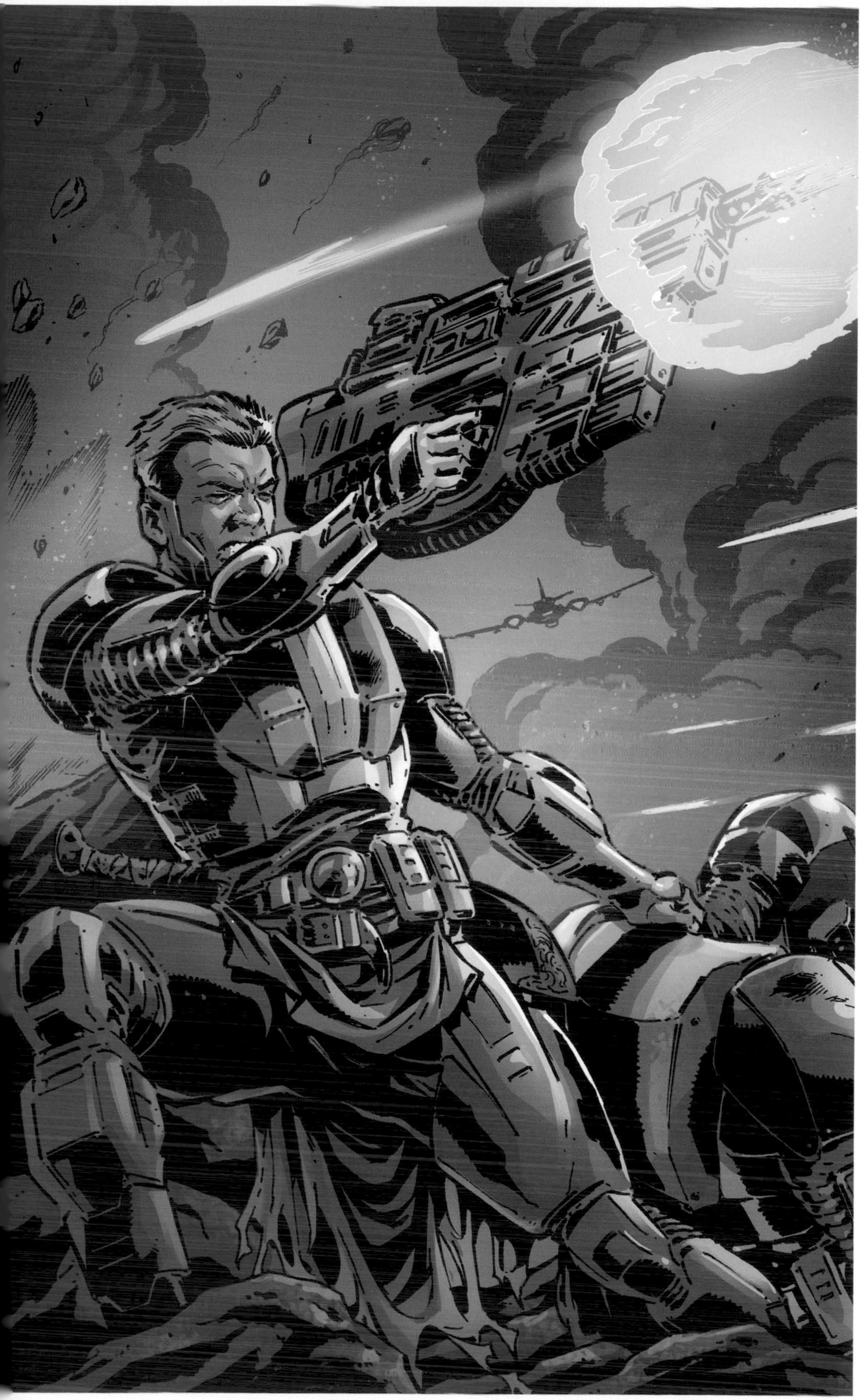

Art by SL Gallant, Colors by Esther Sanz

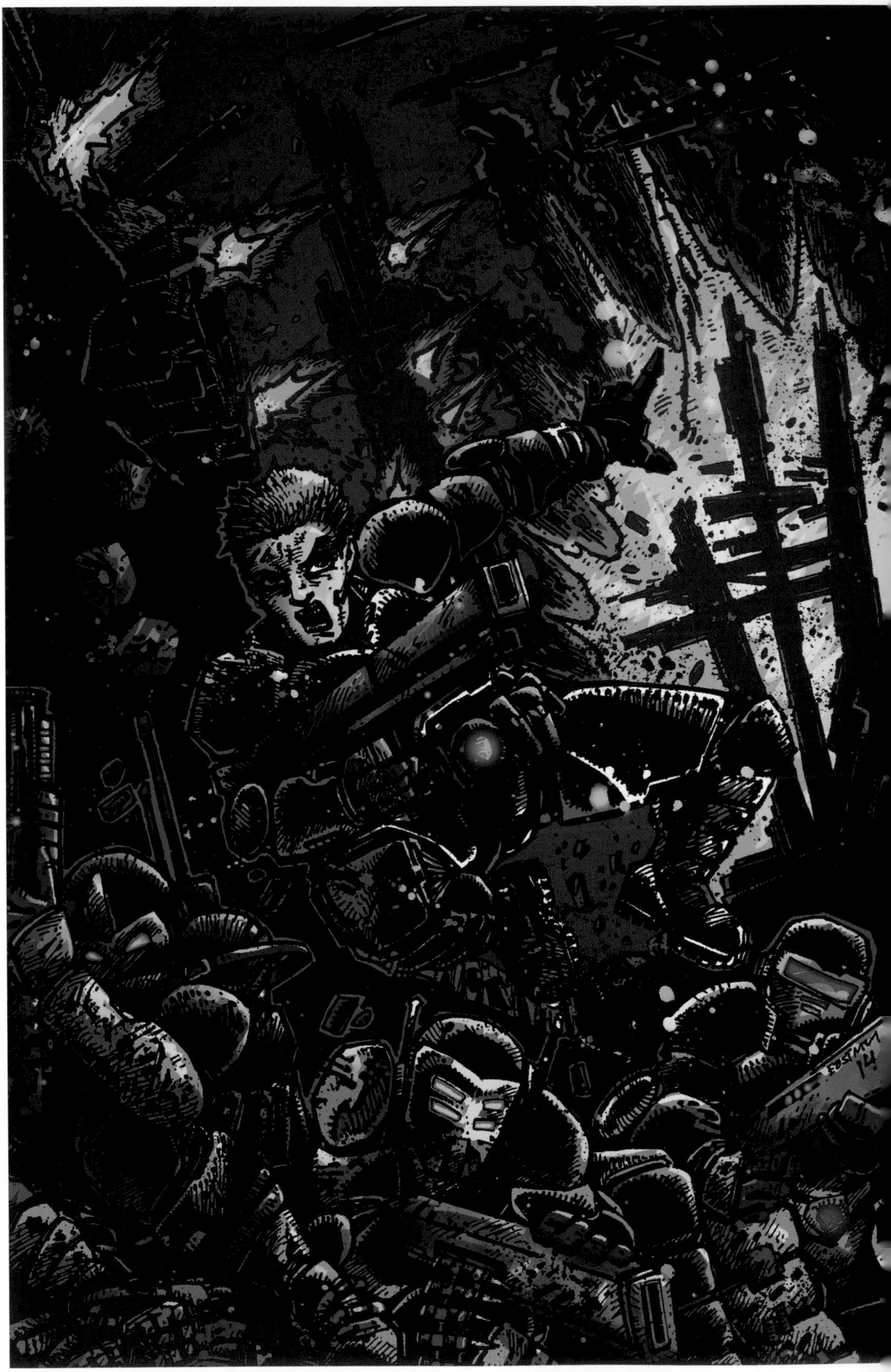

Art by Kevin Eastman, Colors by Adam Guzowski

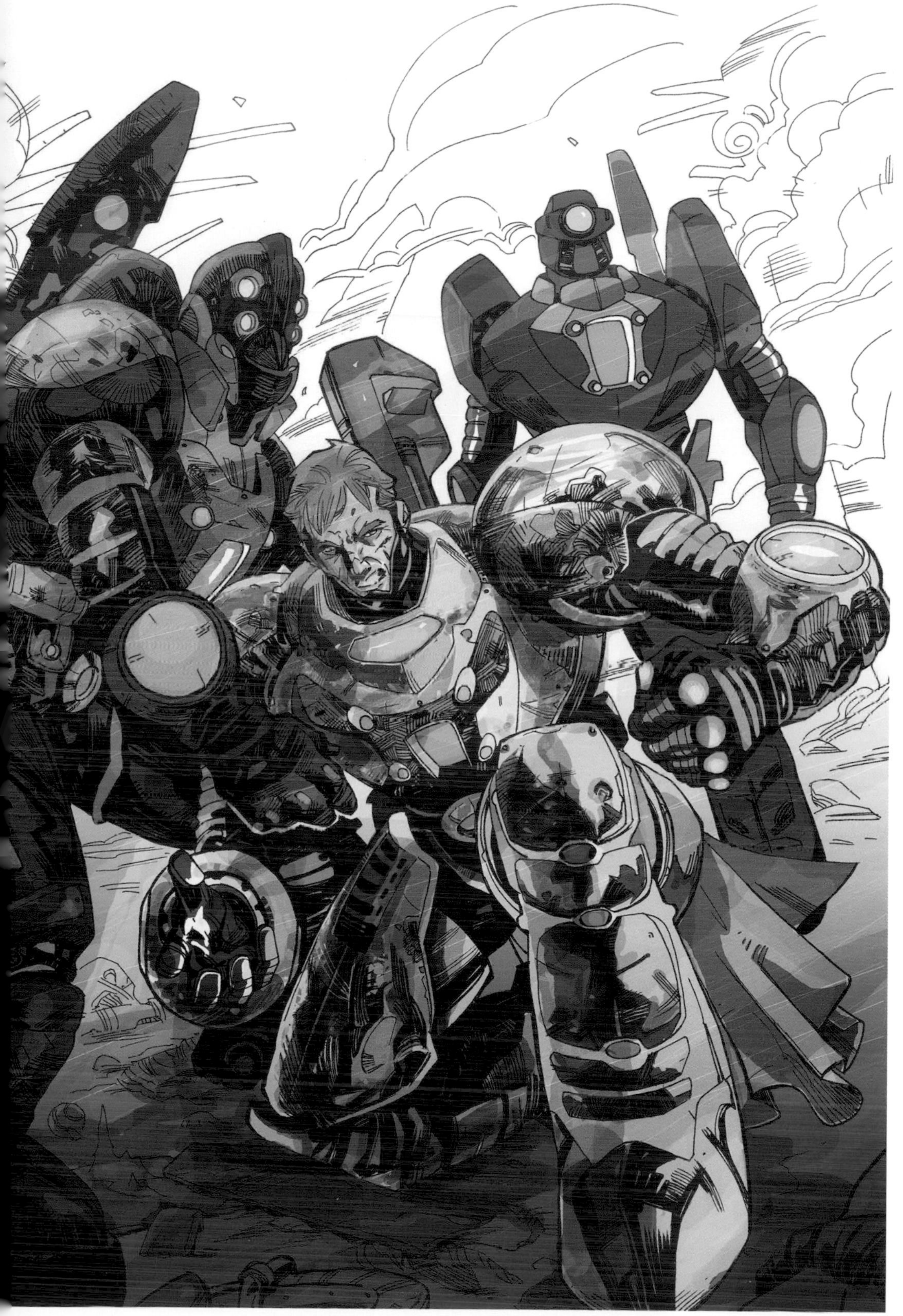

Art by Jose Holder

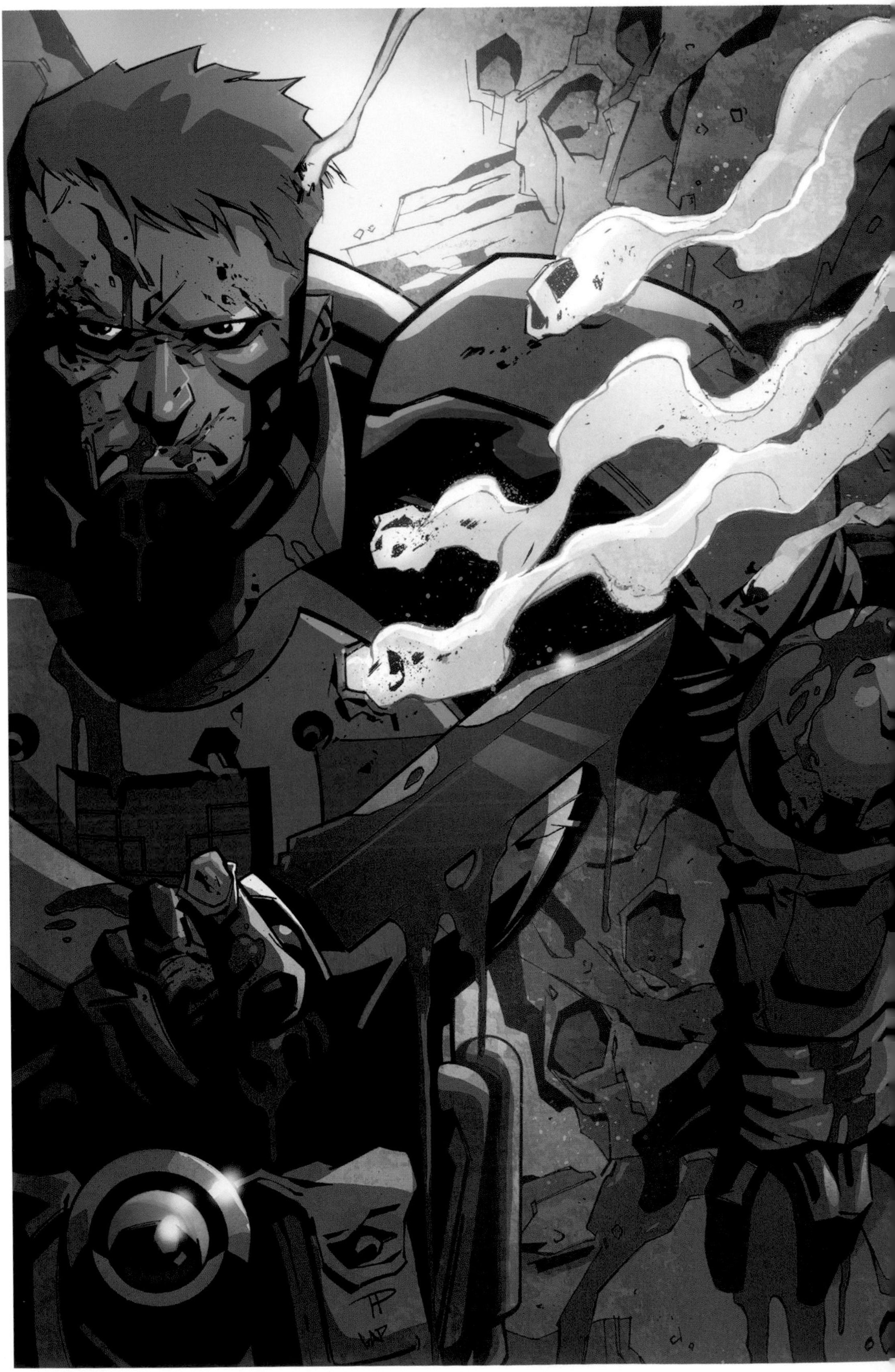

Art by Phil Hester, Colors by Esther Sanz

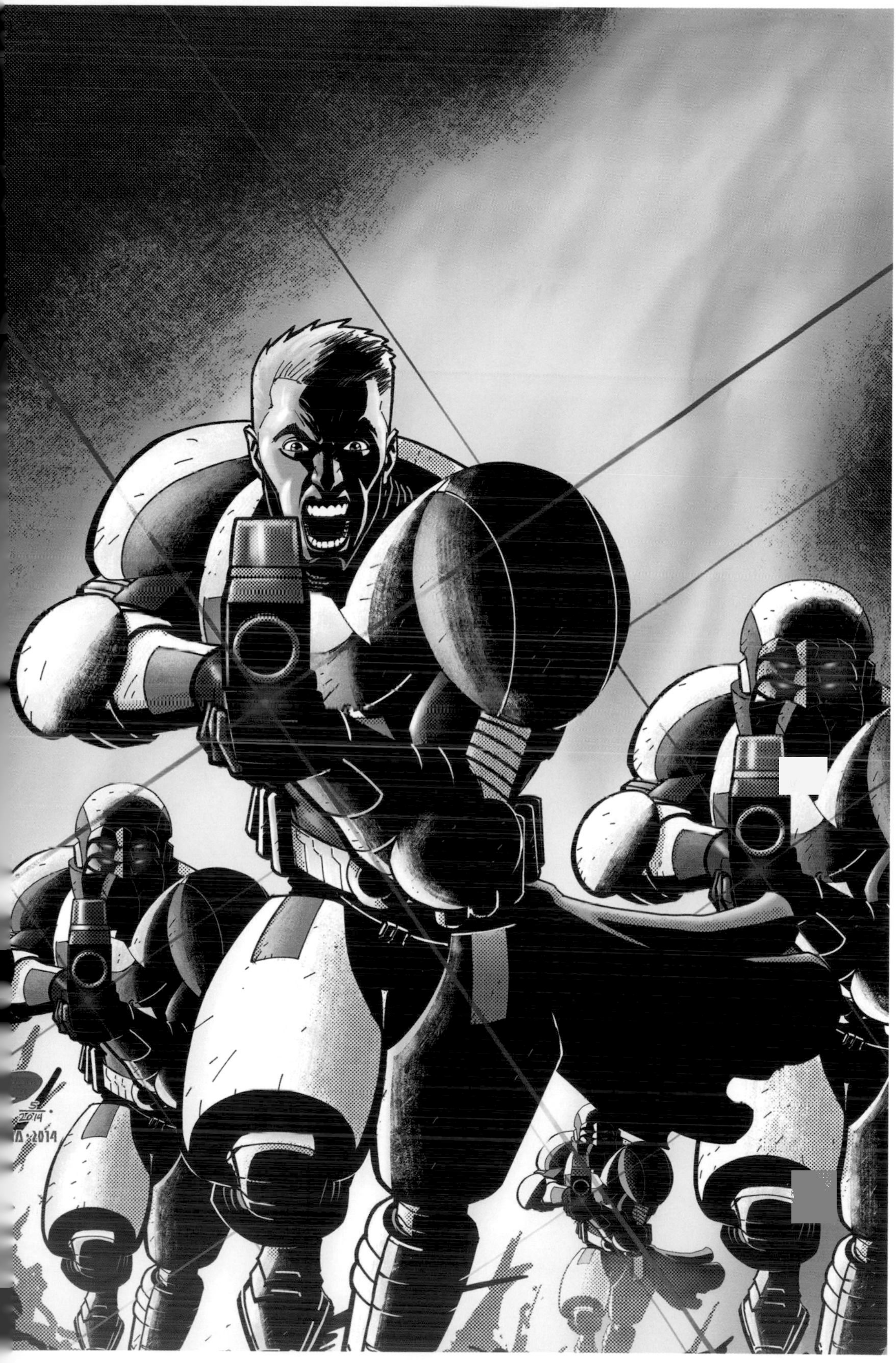
2014
2014
Art by Roger Robinson, Colors by Idalia Robinson

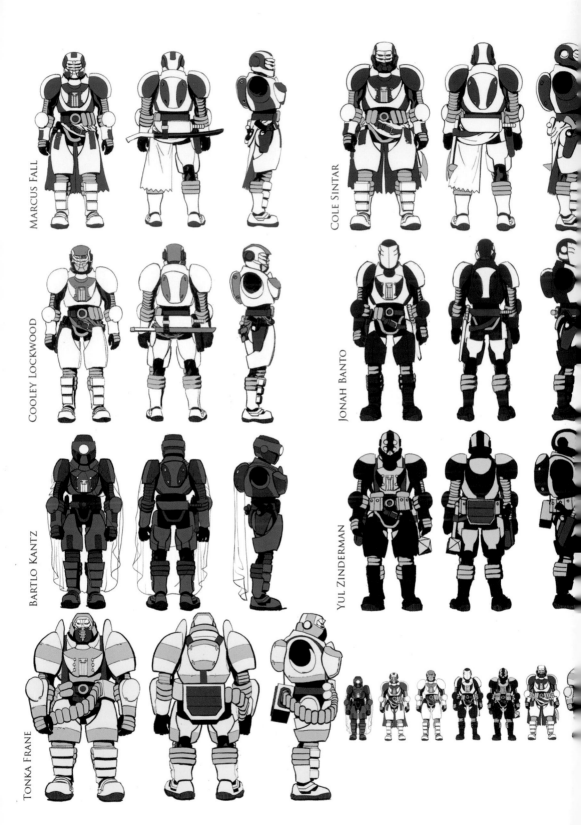

MARCUS FALL

COLE SINTAR

COOLEY LOCKWOOD

JONAH BANTO

BARTLO KANTZ

YUL ZINDERMAN

TONKA FRANE

Character Designs by Casey Maloney

Holy Guard

Character Designs by Casey Maloney

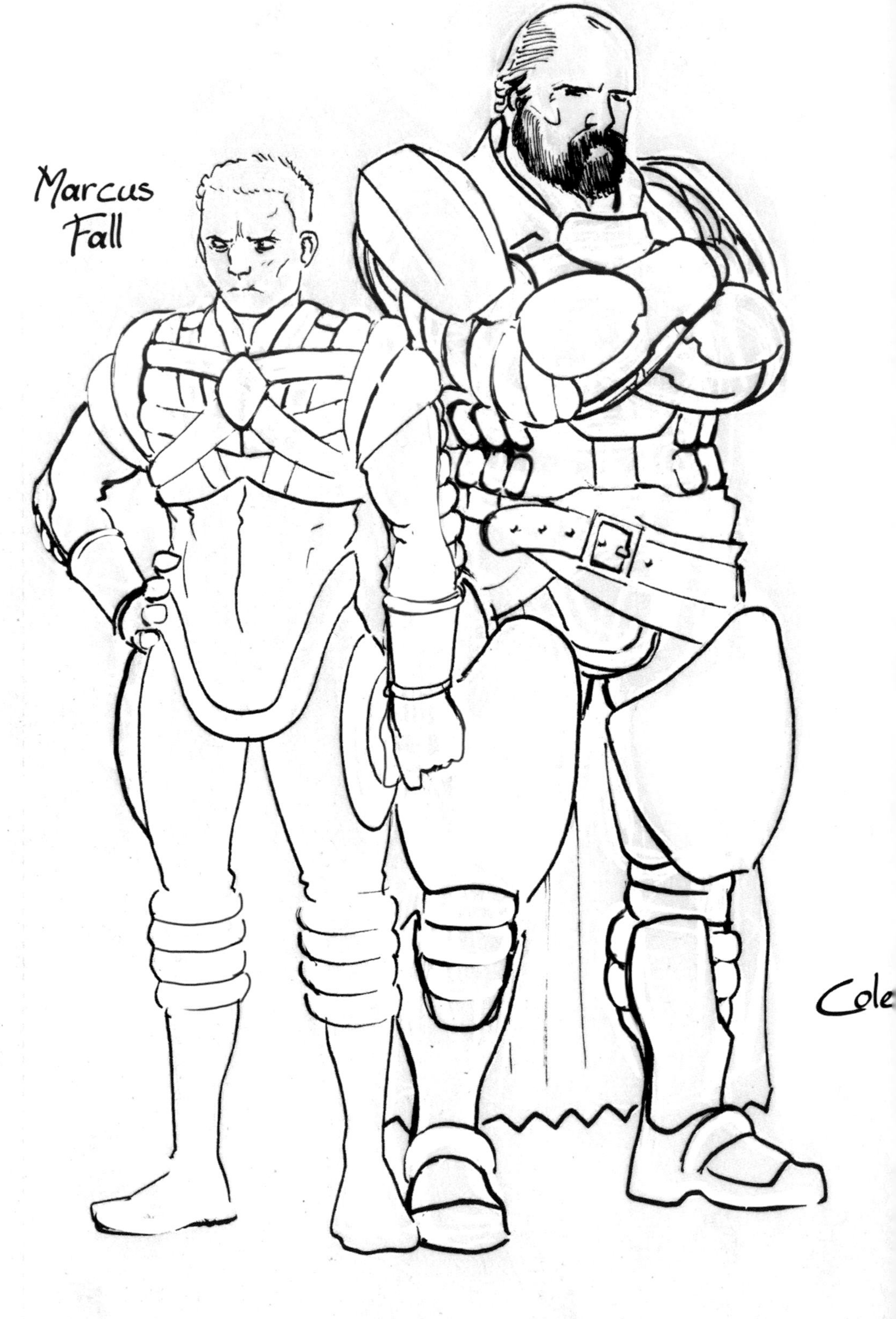
Marcus
Fall
Cole

Character Designs by Casey Maloney

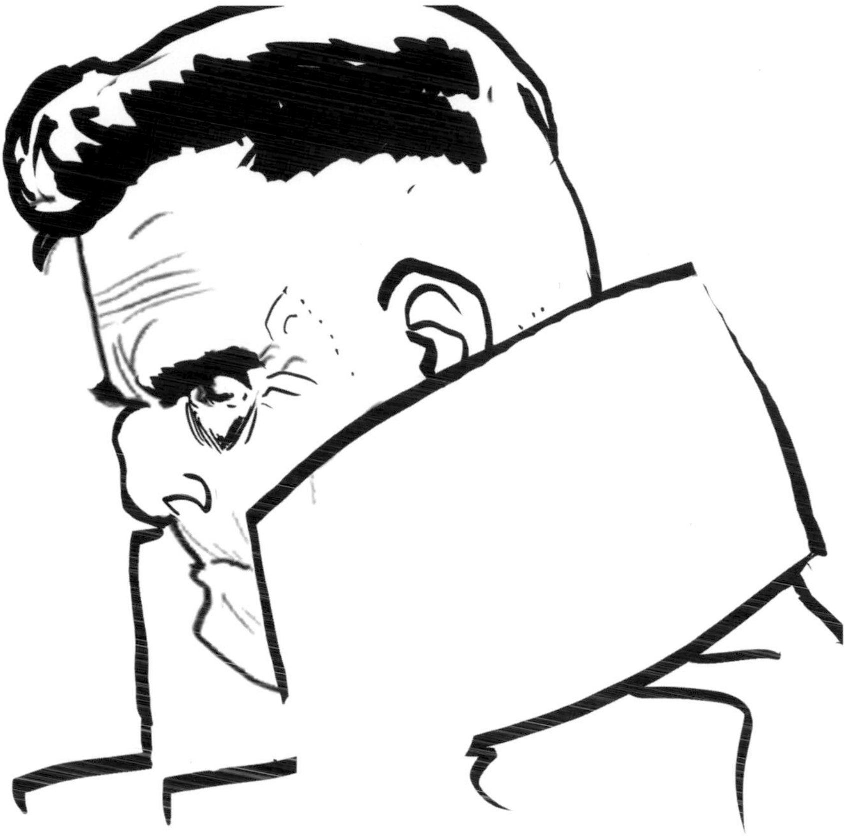

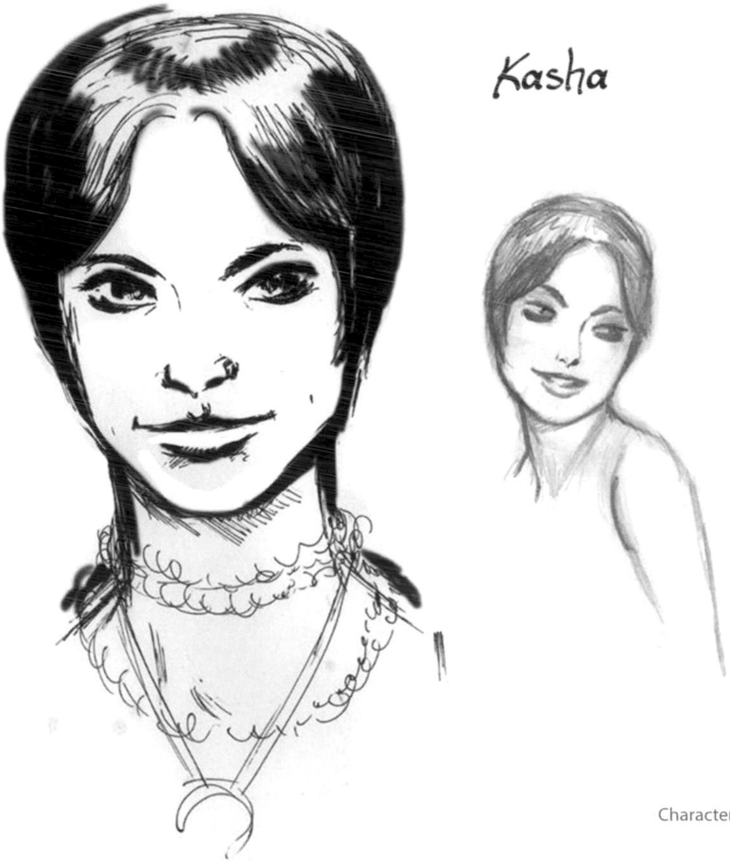
Kasha

Character Designs by Casey Maloney

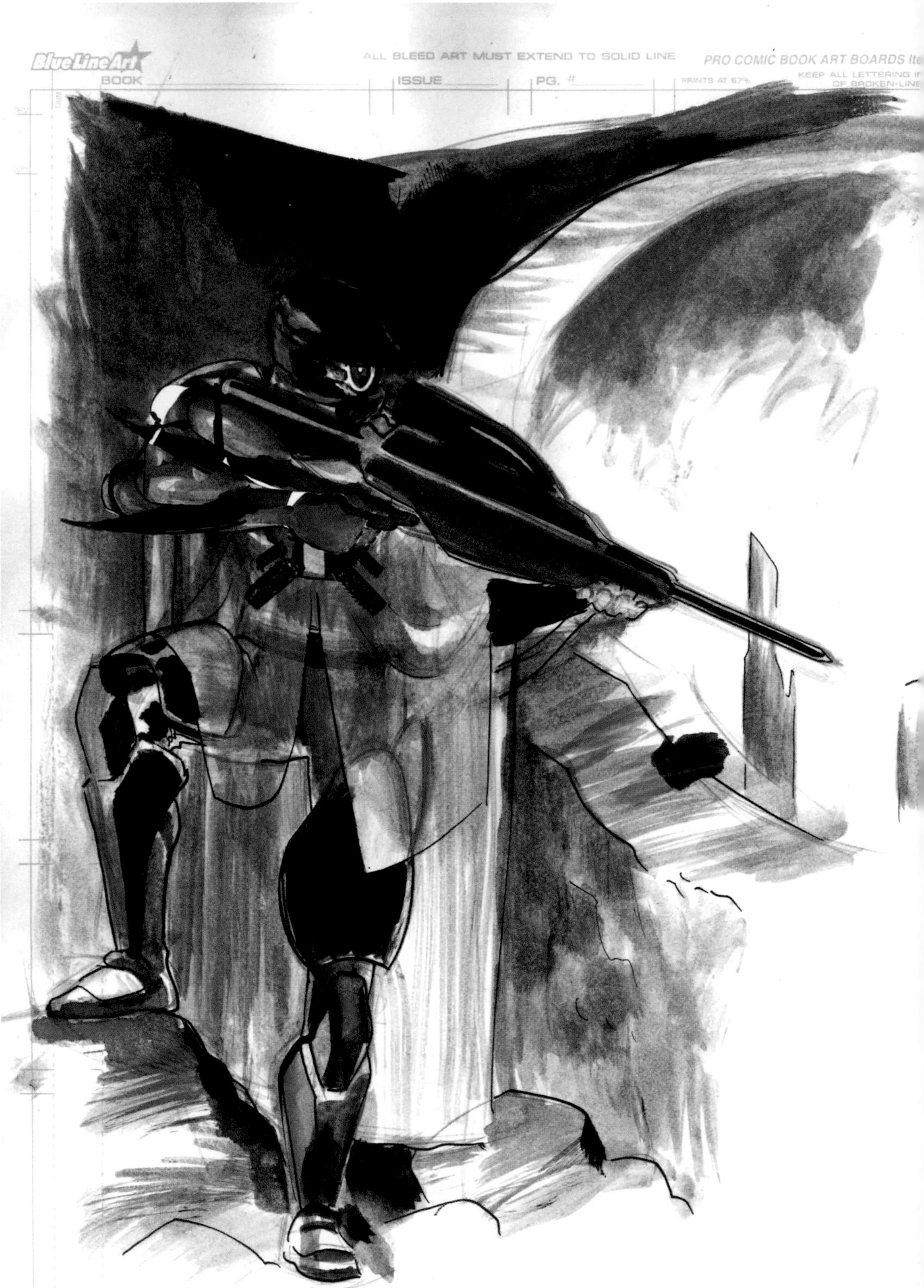
BlueLineArt
ALL BLEED ART MUST EXTEND TO SOLID LINE
PRO COMIC BOOK ART BOARDS
BOOK
ISSUE
PG. #
PRINTS AT 67%
KEEP ALL LETTERING
OF BROKEN-LINE

Art by Casey Maloney

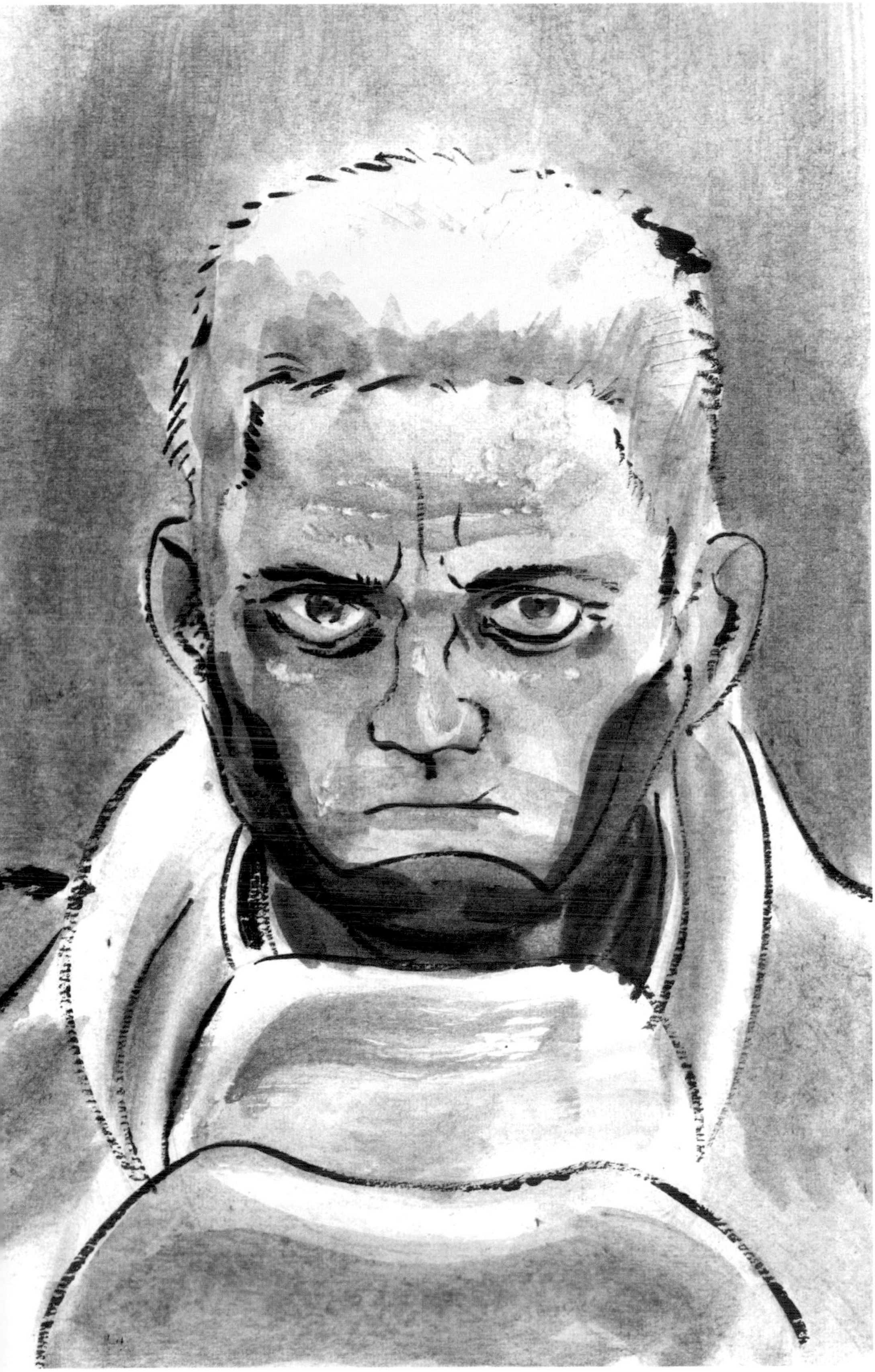

Art by Casey Maloney

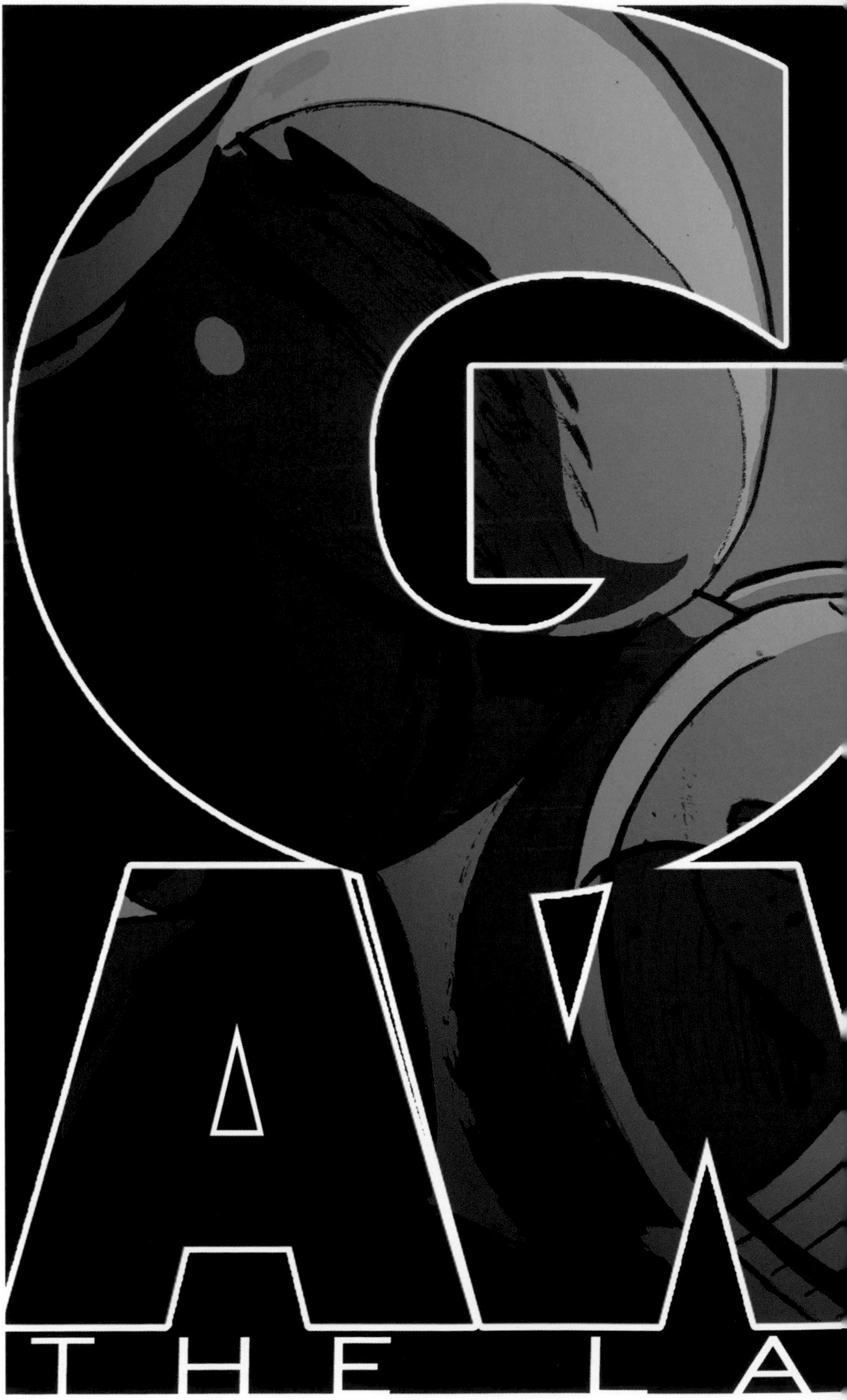
THE LA

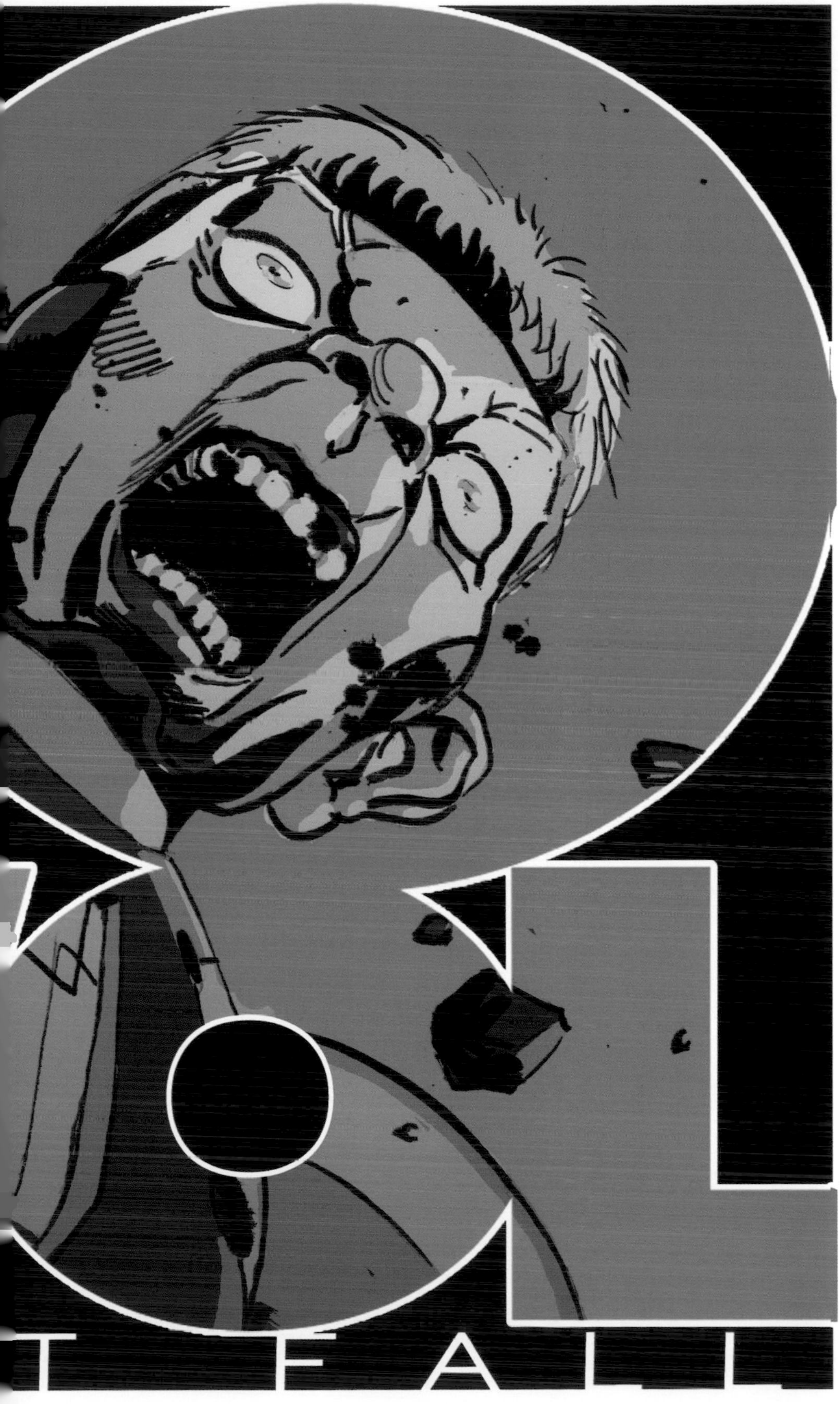
TEALL

Art by Casey Maloney

THE LAST FALL

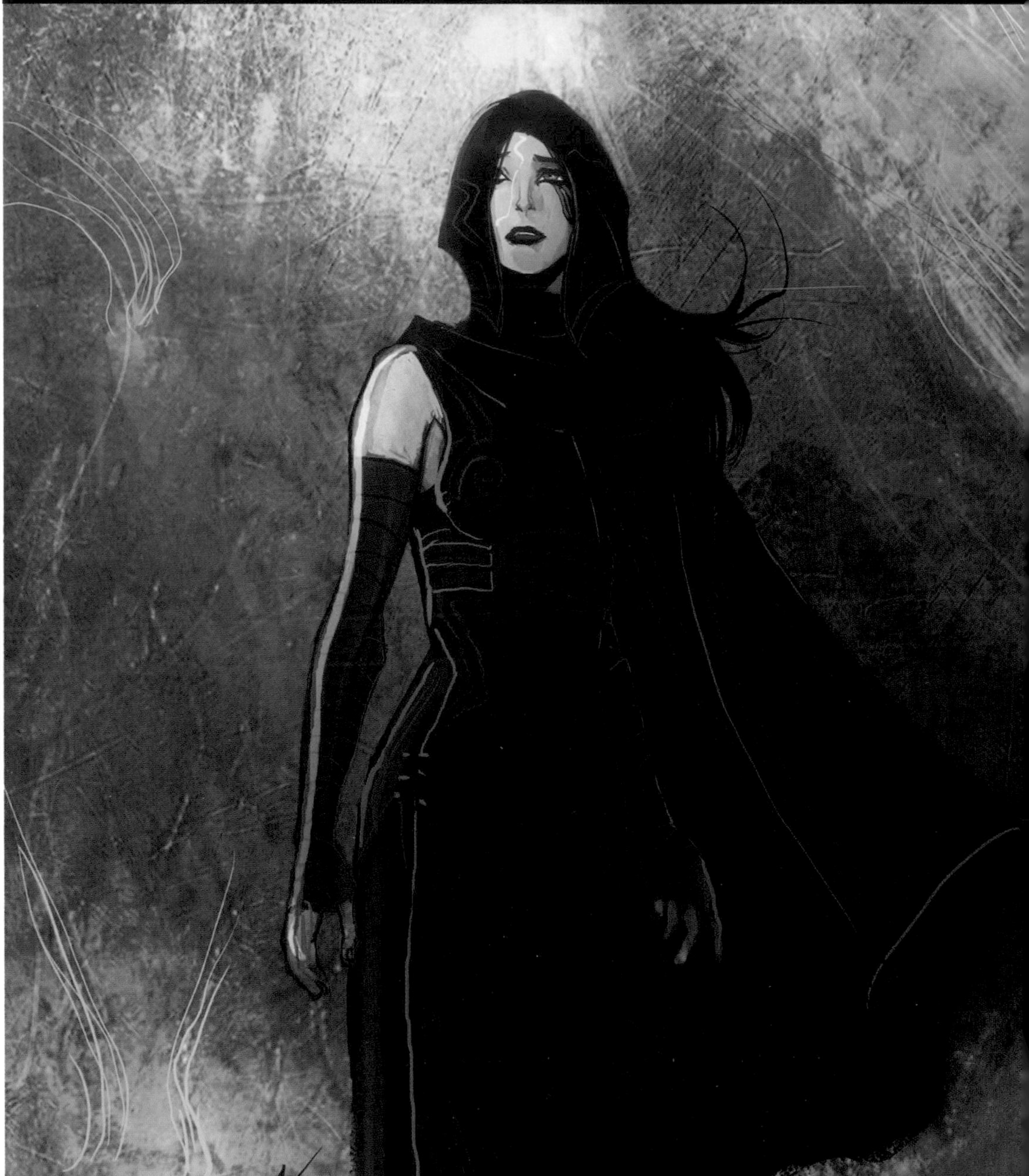

Art by J.F. Bruckner